CLINGING TO THE WRECKAGE

JOHN MORTIMER

CLINGING TO THE WRECKAGE a part of life

WEIDENFELD AND NICOLSON
LONDON

For Penny and Sally, Jeremy and Emily Mortimer, the survivors

First published in Great Britain by
George Weidenfeld and Nicolson Limited
91 Clapham High Street, London sw4

The words from *It's Foolish But It's Fun*
reproduced on page 40 are © United Artists Music;
the words from *St James's Infirmary* on page 119
are © 1930 Mills Music Inc., New York,
reproduced by kind permission of Belwin-Mills
Music Ltd, 250 Purley Way, Croydon, Surrey,
England.

ISBN 0 297 78010 7

Printed and bound by
Butler & Tanner Ltd, Frome and London

ILLUSTRATIONS

My father about to avoid doing anything too heroic
My mother as a young woman
The Sloane Square Wolf Cubs
Duelling with *The Times* music critic
Turville Heath when my father built it
My father, when he could see, ready to do battle in the Divorce Court
Doing battle in the Probate Court
About to be deposed in the prep school production of *Richard II*
One-man band
Leaving Harrow
At Oxford, simulated study of law
Wedding group, 1949
Having caught Arthur Jeffries' gondola
An extended family, 1958 (*photo: Michael McKeown, Daily Express*)
'Into the New Wave as the tube doors were closing' (*Mander & Mitchenson*)
Jeremy as a Roman soldier in discussion with my father
Reading aloud, stories of cruelty, adultery and wilful neglect to maintain
Keeping down the mutiny in the garden
In my 'barrister's set' (*Ron McTrusty cartoon, Evening Standard*)
An encounter with Rumpole (*John Ireland cartoon, The Sunday Times*)
Turville Heath today (*Thames Television*)
Working at Turville Heath today with my daughter Emily (*Daily Mirror*)

'For the absurd man it is not a matter of explaining and solving, but of experiencing and describing. Everything begins with lucid indifference.'

Camus, *The Myth of Sisyphus*,
translated by Justin O'Brien

A man with a bristling grey beard came and sat next to me at lunch. He had very pale blue eyes and an aggressive way of speaking.

'What do you do,' he said, at once and without any preliminary introduction, 'when your boat hits a Force 10 gale in the Channel? What do you do with your female crew?'

'I don't know,' I said, suspecting some kind of joke. 'What do you do with your female crew?'

But he answered seriously, 'Double your fist, hit her on the head and stun her. That way she's far less likely to be swept overboard. I stunned my female crew last Saturday. When she came round she said, "Shall we send up a flare?" "Don't be so bloody stupid," I told her, "make a cup of tea." '

'But isn't it very dangerous, your sport of yachting?'

'Not dangerous at all, provided you don't learn to swim. I made up my mind, when I bought my first boat, never to learn to swim.'

'Why was that?'

'When you're in a spot of trouble, if you can swim you try to strike out for the shore. You invariably drown. As I can't swim I cling to the wreckage and they send a helicopter out for me. That's my tip, if you ever find yourself in trouble, cling to the wreckage!'

It was advice that I thought I'd been taking for most of my life.

1

THE DISTANT PAST, WHEN I WAS ACTING MY SOLO VERSION of *Hamlet* before the blind eyes of my father, duelling with myself and drinking my own poisoned chalice or, further back, when I was starting an English education, with huge balloons of boxing-gloves lashed to the end of white, matchstick arms, grunting, stifled with the sour smell of hot plimsolls which is, to me, always the smell of fear, seems clear as yesterday. What are lost in the mists of a vanishing memory are the events of ten years ago.

The end of the sixties, Flower Power and Children's Lib, the Underground Press and the Alternative Society seem as remote as the Middle Ages; 'Make Love Not War' as dusty an apophthegm as some saying of the Early Fathers of the Church. Childhood requires no effort of memory, but it is hard work to recapture the feeling of 1971, a year when Richard Neville, a young Australian writer, asked some vaguely liberated children to help him produce a 'Schoolkids' number of his magazine *Oz*, thereby promoting an obscenity trial which lasted for six hot weeks of that summer at the Old Bailey. As the trial started the children demonstrated in the street, carrying, as I remember it, banners bearing the legend 'An Orgasm A Day Keeps the Doctor Away'. The front row of the public gallery contained girls whose T-shirts were decorated with a portrait of the Inspector in Charge of the case. He stared up from his position of power in the well of the Court at a repeated view of his own flushed features strained between the small breasts of teenaged girls. The adult editors of *Oz*, Richard Neville, Jim Anderson and Felix Dennis, wore, for their first day in the dock, gym-slips and long blonde wigs, treating the proceedings with an apparent levity far removed from the respectful stance and deferential silence of the more acceptable prisoners at the bar. Among the witnesses called was the comedian Marty Feldman, and I remember him whispering to me, on his way to the witness-box, 'Great to be working with you at last.'

What, I now wonder, did everyone think was going on? A children's revolution, the dawn of a new world when long-haired headmasters would chant Bob Dylan songs at assembly and an adolescent House of Commons would rap away in perfect love enveloped in a pungent smell like slow-burning Turkish carpets; and war, shamed by a poem of Allen Ginsberg's, would vanish from the face of the earth? The dream, whatever it was, has faded more rapidly than most, and the schoolkids of the *Oz* age are no doubt now paying their mortgages and driving their Ford Cortinas with a nodding dog in the back window, and holding down tough jobs as chartered accountants. Even the trial became calmer after its dramatic beginning, and the great majesty of the Criminal Law of England bent itself to a careful consideration of, among other things, Rupert the Bear, an animal long beloved for his docility and innocence, who was unusually portrayed, in *Oz* magazine, with a gigantic erection.

I sat in Court, I can dimly recall, wondering what pre-ordained and inherited paths I had pursued to arrive, forty-eight years old, wearing a horse-hair wig and black tailed coat, to join in the examination of Rupert Bear at his point of high amorous excitement. Up in the public gallery the attendant teenagers played a form of Russian roulette. They passed round a joint together with an innocent cigarette, and when the officer in charge pounced he invariably confiscated the unadulterated roll-up. During the frequent lulls in the proceedings my mind was filled with other anxieties. I had written a play which was about to open; into it I had collected my memories of my father, and written lines for him, so that a man who had filled so much of my life seemed to have left me and become someone for other people to read about and perform. In one way I felt detached from it; but a play is a public exhibition with its own peculiar dangers, another sort of trial. Not for the only time in my life I felt that the theatrical drama in which I was involved was more real than the Old Bailey and the due process of law. Also I was about to tell a wider public a fact which, in our small family, had been the subject of a discreet conspiracy of silence, something, which in our English determination to avoid the slightest embarrassment, we never mentioned. My father had been blind.

My father was a very clean man, who never took less than two baths a day. One day I came home from school and found him wearing a white towelling dressing-gown and sitting on the closed lavatory seat in the bathroom. My mother was squeezing out his toothpaste. She found his hand and put the toothbrush into it. Then she guided his hand towards his mouth. That was the first time I saw that he was totally blind.

We talked about other things, my parents asked me about my school, and, as usual, I found it impossible to tell them; just as they found it impossible to say that my father could no longer see me, that my children would be, to him, only the sounds of laughter and small screams in the dark. Bombs, air raids, bits of food prodded at him, and the edge of the pavement would, from now on, strike him as equally alarming, and for the rest of his life I would look, in his mind's eye, like a scrawny and awkward schoolboy of thirteen.

After he had finished his long process of washing I went for a walk with my father, along the Embankment, past Cleopatra's Needle and the Sphinxes, black beasts which the pigeons had decked with a white crust. He was a tall man, over six foot in height, with fair hair which left the top of his head but never went grey. His legs were long and very thin, his feet and hands small, his stomach grew in swelling isolation. He had a high forehead; but his nose was thick, his chin grew fat and his lower jaw protruded so that he couldn't be called handsome. His eyes were a clear, light blue; and now that he could no longer see he had abandoned his spectacles. As I led him by the river I felt his hand, small, long-fingered, the skin brown and already ill-fitting, like a loose glove, warm on my arm. I wanted to shake him off, to run away. I had an impulse to lose him, to allow him to wander off, hopelessly among the trams.

We passed a procession of British Fascists on the march. The Public Order Act forbade them to wear their black shirts which they carried solemnly on coat-hangers, as if bringing them home from the cleaners. In those days we were all waiting for the war with the concealed impatience with which those saying 'goodbye' on station platforms secretly long for the start of the train removing them from their nearest and dearest. I was trying to decide if I should sign on as a conscientious objector or join the RAF. Embarrassed by the blind man publicly attached to my arm, I decided to say whatever was best calculated to make him leave me in disapproval and rage.

'I think I'll be an objector.'

'A what?'

'I think I'll go into a Quaker Medical Corps or something.'

'Oh, you mean a conchy!' My father dropped the mask of bewilderment. 'I once shared diggings with one of those. In Chiswick. Do you really think you're brave enough for that?'

5

'What do you mean?'

'I think in your case,' my father turned his unblinking eyes to where he thought I might be, 'I should avoid the temptation to do anything heroic.'

Eyesight was a problem for both of us. Up to the age of five I enjoyed the privileges of myopia, seeing the world in a glorious haze like an Impressionist painting. My contemporaries appeared blurred and attractive, grown-ups loomed in vague magnificence. I went daily to school and kept my eyes politely on the blackboard where I could see only chalky confusion. After a year of this my mother noticed that my education was at a standstill and sent me to the oculist: the world sprang at me in hideous reality, full of people with open pores, blackheads and impetigo. A deep-focus moustache appeared on an art mistress whom I had considered beautiful. Flinching from this unusual clarity I went to school and sat in my usual place at the morning assembly, unrecognizable in a nose-pinching pair of wire-framed specs. The headmaster, whose awareness of his pupils was always somewhat vague, thought that this bespectacled intruder was a new boy. As I was too shy to disillusion him, I was put back in the bottom class to restart my unpromising academic career. I suppose I had become a new person, one who looked on life and actually saw it; but when faced with anything I am really reluctant to see, a pornographic film in the course of business, or an animal killed and plastered across the road, I still have the defence of taking off my glasses and returning the world to the safe blur of childhood.

In the years before I could see clearly my father was not yet blind.

Although I now feel I knew him so well he was remote to me then, a hard-working barrister with a flourishing practice in the Probate, Divorce and Admiralty Division of the High Court. There was nothing he enjoyed more than a good old-fashioned battle as to whether or not adultery had taken place. Often he would tell me of his triumphs and I must have been very young when he said, 'Remarkable win today, old boy. Only evidence of adultery we had was a pair of footprints upside down on the dashboard of an Austin Seven parked in Hampstead Garden Suburb.'

But if Divorce was my father's daily bread, Probate was his special treat. Before I was born he had sat up night after night writing in lucid prose what became a standard textbook on the validity of Wills. When respectable relatives, red in tooth and claw, met to prove or disprove the sanity of an aged uncle who had left his entire fortune to the Matron of some doubtful nursing home, when it was a question of due execution, or partial revocation, or lucid intervals, whenever greed or disappointment and old family ill-will led middle-aged children to abuse each other in Court, *Mortimer on Probate* was the Bible by which the Judge regulated their ambitions and decided their disputes. When Wills were written, as Wills so often were, on blown duck eggs or in minute handwriting on the tails of kites, my father was there with an appropriate precedent. When testators were perfectly sensible, as testators often were, on every subject except for their nightly chats with the late Emperor Napoleon the Third, my father was there with his long experience of monomania and the lucid interval. He was good on Divorce, but at Probate he became unbeatable. It was only when the Wills and incriminating hotel bills were put away, when nautical charts were unrolled and old Sea Dogs came clumping into the witness-box, when the Anchor was hung behind the Judge's chair and the Admiralty Court was in session, that my father discreetly withdrew. He knew absolutely nothing about ships.

Busily engaged on his legal practice my father seemed, no doubt understandably, anxious to postpone his complete introduction to me, his only child. It's true that I saw him occasionally, when he got me to rub his tobacco and pretend it was Indian 'pemmican', a game which had an element of mystery as I had no idea what 'pemmican' might be; but in those early days he was a remote figure. His clerk came to drive him to the Law Courts each morning, tucking a rug around his legs and removing him in a large, hearse-like Morris Oxford. My father's clerk was called 'Leonard', which was not his name. It is true that my father had once had a clerk called 'Leonard' who, tragically, had been killed on the Somme, after which my father called all clerks 'Leonard', although the one I remember, who was to be his clerk for many years, was undoubtedly a secret William.

William's wife Elsie was my nurse, governess and friend, and with her I spent my life. Even when we went on holidays, usually to such exotic resorts as Eastbourne or Littlehampton, my father was reluctant to stay with me, and while he and my mother put up at a four-star hotel the nurse and I were billeted in some boarding-house at the far end of the promenade. I have a memory of being taken to see my father in an Eastbourne hotel; it was late in the morning but he was lying in an ornate bed, placed on a sort of dais and covered with a canopy, and he was sucking his handkerchief. I do not remember his being particularly pleased to see me, and the visit was a short one.

Those years seem populated by governesses and filled with the smell of maids' bedrooms, a curious, pungent odour compounded, I suppose, of sweat and face-powder and Woolworth's perfume, the smell of my childhood which I haven't encountered for half a century. The maids were invariably kind and seemed, to my short-sighted eyes, beautiful. One I remember received me in her bedroom and chatted as she squatted on a large, rose-patterned chamber-pot; another made me a Highland costume out of kitchen paper. A new governess escorted me each morning to Sloane Square on the Underground when the time came to begin my formal education. In my fantasies I always hoped that she would kidnap me and take me home to her husband whom I imagined to be a burglar living in Shepherd's Bush, which I had somehow heard of as an area of ill repute. However nothing of the sort occurred and I was delivered safely to the exclusive, no doubt ruinously expensive, Sloane Square school where I was put down to the bottom of the form for wearing glasses.

Unmistakably middle class, I was being educated above my station. Few of the children emerged as I did from the Tube. Many were delivered in Rolls-Royces. Before the school had taught us to write it demanded lengthy written examinations. Accordingly our mothers had to act as our secretaries. On the appointed day languid ladies-about-town, including at least one Maharanee, swathed in mink and Chanel, nervously inserted their silk-stockinged legs below schoolboy desks and took whispered dictation from their inky six-year-olds on the subject of everyday life in Ancient Britain. My own mother came, a tall, shy woman with large dark eyes and a cloth coat with an astrakhan collar. I had a shameful hope that she might be taken for a nanny. I remember all that, but most often I remember a man I knew as 'Mr 'It Me' and the lesson he gave me on the nature of fear.

The school prided itself on teaching boxing and, at the end of the term, took over the gym at Chelsea Barracks for our Lilliputian contests. We had towels flapped at us by Guards Sergeants, we were given a gulp from the water-bottle and then made the journey to the centre of the enormous ring to rain feeble blows on each other's noses. Training for the end-of-term boxing match was in the charge of 'Mr 'It Me', our sole instructor.

I suppose he was a retired pugilist. Certainly he seemed old, and of an immense size. He had a broken nose, cauliflower ears and the far-away look of a man whose brain had been clumsily manhandled from an early age. He had a huge barrel chest and arms like weight-lifters' thighs. His method of teaching was simple. He would sit sprawled in a wooden armchair wearing a singlet, dirty grey flannel trousers held up by an elastic belt, and boxing-gloves. We stood in a queue before him and, as each boy presented himself in turn, he would grunt, ''it me!', his only other instruction being, ''arder!'

We would then step forward and land some puny punch, which must have had all the impact of a butt from a maddened gnat, on the rock formation of his chest. The majority of these attacks produced no reaction from the dozing pugilist but occasionally, perhaps once in ten times, he would strike back, a huge fist would come out of nowhere and a stunned and dizzy child would be sent flying across the room. These lessons, which were like playing Russian roulette with an earthquake, filled me with terror and disgust. Even if I wasn't struck I didn't relish any sort of contact with the sweat-soaked singlet, and my tentative tap was always met with a deep roar of ''arder!' And rather often, as it seemed to me, the blow would fall, the punch would land, and I would be left with stinging, shameful tears and a headache.

This weekly appointment with fear continued until a day came when I persuaded my mother to take me to the movies, a double bill of such undiluted horror that St John's Ambulance nurses were posted round the doors to catch the fainting customers. Children clearly were admitted so it couldn't have been a very advanced study in the macabre but there was, as I recall it, an Egyptian setting and a Mummy who was reluctant to remain quietly entombed. As an antique foot and trailing grave-cloth moved eerily across the screen I found the effect slightly comic; but the row of seats in front of us began to creak and judder and a terrible sobbing was heard. The trembling blob which caused the disturbance and momentarily blotted out the screen seemed to have a familiar flat-topped head and cauliflower ears and, as a lady from the St John's Ambulance rushed to the rescue, I realized that I had been privileged to see 'Mr 'It Me' in a state of pure terror. Many years later I wrote a play about our boxing instructor which caused him to melt, in my memory, into a fictional character, but at the time I found my discovery of the varieties of fear liberating. I lined up cheerfully the next week and hit him as hard as I could.

I can never think of that far-off Sloane Square school, with its pugilism and affluent mothers, without paying a tribute to Miss Boustead. Miss

Boustead was Commander-in-Chief of the Sloane Square Wolf Cubs, an élite corps of which I was a junior member. She was a woman built on generous lines and when she turned out in an immense khaki skirt and wide-brimmed scouting hat, with her whistle on a lanyard and her long-service decorations, she made a formidable figure. Miss Boustead's ideas on Cub training were single-minded and resulted in one activity only. She formed up her platoon at Sloane Square Underground Station and led us, by public transport, to Wimbledon Common. Once out in open country Miss Boustead would choose some suitable clearing or glen and stand in it with her legs akimbo. She would then give the order, 'Cubs, scatter!' Ours was not to reason why, and each loyal Cub rushed into the middle distance and flung himself into the undergrowth. It was then a Cub's task to advance, squirming on his belly, taking advantage of every bit of ground cover, daring a dash in full view whenever the Commander's head was turned, towards the bulky figure in the clearing. The rules were simple. The Cub who got between Miss Boustead's legs before she spotted him was awarded the box of Cadbury's Assorted. I shall always feel grateful to Miss Boustead for organizing the only form of competitive sport I have ever enjoyed.

The past is like a collection of photographs: some are familiar and on constant display, others need searching for in dusty drawers. Some have faded entirely, and some have been taken so amateurishly and on a day so dark that the subjects are seen like ghosts in a high wind and are impossible to identify. Assembled they can be called anything you like: illustrations of the vanished professional, middle-class world of England between the wars; or the snapshots of an only child who had, in those slow-moving days, much time to notice things.

2

MY MOTHER'S FAMILY CAME FROM LEAMINGTON SPA. I HAVE a photograph of my grandfather fishing; surrounded by his three daughters and formidable wife, he's wearing a sort of cricketing cap, a starched collar and a tweed jacket. He was, like my father's blindness, a taboo subject and no one ever said much about him except that he was called Mr Smith and his profession was, as my father said with the sole purpose of irritating my mother, a 'bum-bailiff' or Warwickshire debt-collector. I have no idea why he shot himself, but my mother, at the end of her life, told me that it happened while she had a job as a schoolmistress in South Africa. She learnt of it because her family sent her out a copy of the local paper with the announcement of her father's death carefully marked as a news item which might interest her. From what she told me I understood that they sent no covering letter.

My mother had studied art in Birmingham, to which city she bicycled daily. Later she taught drawing in Manchester, at a Lycée in Versailles, and at a girls' school in Natal, where she rode bareback across the veldt and swam naked under waterfalls. She was a 'New Woman' who read Bernard Shaw and Katherine Mansfield, whom she resembled a little in looks. My grandmother was a High Church Anglican whose bedside table supported a prayer-book and a crucifix, but my mother had no use at all for God, although she was to become revered as a heroine and a saint in her middle age. She earned these titles, of course, for putting up with my father, an almost impossible task.

When, after his blindness, my father insisted on continuing with his legal practice as though nothing had happened, my mother it was who read his briefs to him and who made notes of all his cases. She became a well-known figure in the Law Courts, as well known as the Tipstaff or the Lord Chief Justice, leading my father from Court to Court, smiling patiently as he tapped the paved floors with his clouded malacca cane and shouted abuse either at her or at his instructing solicitor, or at both of them at the same time. From early in the war, when they settled permanently in the country, my mother drove my father fourteen miles a day to Henley Station and took him up in the train. Ensconced in a corner seat, dressed like Winston Churchill, in a black jacket and striped trousers, bow-tie worn with a wing-collar, boots and spats, my father would require her to read in a loud and clear voice the evidence in the divorce case that would be his day's work. As the train ground to a halt around Maidenhead the first-class carriage would fall silent as my mother read out the reports of Private Investigators on adulterous behaviour which they had observed in detail. If she dropped her voice over descriptions of stained bed-linen, male and female clothing found scattered about, or misconduct in motor cars, my father would call out, 'Speak up, Kath!' and their fellow travellers would be treated to another thrilling instalment.

Much of my mother's life went underground when she married my father, although we were visited occasionally by a red-bearded painter who had been her fellow student. He and my mother used to sit up talking after my father, who held strong views about visitors, had gone to bed. Once, when I was about ten years old, I came downstairs and burst into the living-room, ostensibly to search for burglars, but really to stop my mother committing adultery, the thought of which, I am now convinced, had never entered her head.

I always found my mother's attitude to me curiously disconcerting. She seemed to find most of the things I did slightly comic ('killing' was the word she most often used). Long after my father had died I rang her up to tell her that I had been asked to go to some distant town to sit as a Judge, hoping that she might be impressed. '*You*, a Judge?' She started to giggle. '*You*? Whatever do they think they're doing, asking *you* to be a Judge?' and then she laughed so much that she had to put down the telephone receiver. From time to time she seemed to find it hard to remember essential things about me, such as whether I took sugar, or my name. In later years she often looked at me vaguely and called me 'Daisy', which was my aunt's name. Not until she was very old did I find some short stories which she had written, which showed her concern about me and her anxiety, no doubt entirely justified, about what I got up to when out of her sight.

My father's family had been West Country farmers, but his father was a Bristol brewer who, in a moment of Wesleyan zeal, became a teetotaller and signed the Pledge. After that, my grandfather only drank a temperance beverage of his own preparing which produced in him, my father noticed, many of the outward and visible signs of advanced intoxication. Forbidden by his conscience to carry on brewing, my Methodist grandfather emigrated to South Africa when my father was four years old and started up in the less convivial trade of an Estate Agent.

So my father grew up in Natal at the end of the nineteenth century. As a child, he helped unfasten the horses and draw the carriage of the General who relieved Ladysmith, and he was forever sickened by the sight of a negro prisoner being taken into captivity handcuffed to the stirrup of a white policeman's cantering horse. He went to a South African version of an English public school, but in the holidays his parents often sent him up-country to some small and lonely hotel so that he could 'run wild'. He told me that, when he was a boy, he was given a birthday cake in a tin and he kept it under his hotel bed. When his birthday came he took it out and ate it in a solitary celebration. Both his and my mother's family, it seems, were determined to avoid any situation in which they could sniff the danger of an emotional display.

I have a mental picture of my father in a Norfolk jacket and knickerbockers lying on the baked earth, among the yellowing grass, reading the Conan Doyle stories in the *Strand Magazine* sent out from England, lost in the mists of Baker Street. The other author he greatly admired was Rider Haggard, who wrote the myths of the Englishman's Africa, stories of Umslopagas and Allan Quatermain and the monocled Captain Good and the deathless Queen, 'She Who Must Be Obeyed'. My father and I grew to know each other when I was about ten and he had gone to Switzerland for a series of painful and hopeless eye operations. We would go for walks together in the summer and he would tell me the Sherlock Holmes stories, of which he had almost total recall. On other walks he would make my flesh creep with the account of Huck Finn and the negro Jim on their raft on the swollen Mississippi when an entire displaced house floated past them containing a man who had been shot dead at cards. When my father told me the adventures of Jeeves and Bertie Wooster he would stand on the mountain path, dabbing at his streaming eyes and almost choking with laughter. I enjoyed these stories so much that it was my ambition to become a butler when I grew up.

At some time great stretches of Shakespeare's plays had lodged in my father's head, and he used the lines for odd moments of pleasure, intoning, 'Nymph, in thy orisons be all my sins remember'd' when standing in the Law Courts' lavatory, or during breakfast. When I was young he often greeted me with, 'Is execution done on Cawdor?' a question which, at the age of six, I was at a loss to answer. At other moments he would look at me in a threatening manner and say, casting himself as Hubert and me as the youthful Prince Arthur, about to be blinded:

> Heat me these irons hot; and look thou stand
> Within the arras: when I strike my foot
> Upon the bosom of the ground, rush forth,
> And bind the boy . . .

An even earlier memory is of him pointing a trembling finger to a corner of the room, where, he assured me, the blood-bolter'd Banquo had just appeared to push us from our stools and join the family table, much as he materialized at that embarrassing dinner party of the Macbeths.

So the words of Shakespeare's plays became a sort of family code and the subject of our jokes. 'Is execution done on Cawdor?' was a line of hilarious comedy, and 'Rushforth and Bindtheboy' a firm of dubious solicitors.

When he was seventeen my father came back from South Africa to go to Cambridge, where he read law and made few friends. He won a scholarship in his bar exams and went into the army when the war started. My mother, who had met the Mortimer family in South Africa, wrote to him when she came back to England. He bought a cold chicken and took her on the river at Chiswick, where he proposed to her at once. He was then a subaltern about to go to France where the expectation of life was not much more than a month. However some sympathetic senior officer, taking account of my father's short sight and recent marriage, got him a job in the Inland Waterways. It was, fortunately, a post with no heroic temptations. Years later, as we walked down the Embankment past the Fascist procession, and I felt my life expectancy to be similarly abbreviated, he said, 'You know what, old boy? If they give us war again. Get yourself a job in the Inland Waterways.'

My father and mother had views in common. Neither of them was in any sense religious. My father had been totally persuaded by *On the Origin of Species* that the Almighty would have had his work cut out to produce an earthworm in seven days, let alone beat the deadline by constructing a creature as complex as the horse. When he was depressed by his blindness he never turned to God, but either shouted at my mother or sat reading, with an impatient finger, his Braille copy of Shakespeare's sonnets, swollen by the size of its dotted letters to the dimensions of a telephone directory. My mother's views, I suspect, were more 'modern'. When they first met she led him through *The Intelligent Woman's Guide to Socialism*. He followed, brandishing *The Voyage of the Beagle*.

They had opinions in common but in fact their characters were totally different. My mother had a sort of purity of intention and a seriousness which were quite alien to my father. When she devoted her life to writing out adultery petitions and leading him about the Probate, Divorce and Admiralty Division, she did so with the ungrudging devotion, I am sure, of women who join the Resistance or become nursing nuns. Heroism of any kind was something my father did his best to avoid, and his courage in carrying on his legal practice when he was blind came from a determination to avoid the issue and pretend he could still see perfectly well. If my mother advanced an opinion, which she did rarely, she meant what she said, a form of speech which my father found merely boring. He was a natural advocate, and what he said was rarely called on to express his personal feelings or beliefs. His words were like challenges, thrown out into the darkness in the hope that they would start a tournament, or like clay pigeons shot up into the sky for anyone to pot at. 'Love has been greatly overestimated by the poets', he would say, or, 'No one could possibly get the slightest pleasure out of music', or, 'Ninety per cent of all illness is caused by doctors', or (to me going away to school), 'Try not to mix too closely with the schoolmasters, all schoolmasters have second-rate minds'. A simple way to irritate him, as my mother got to know perfectly well, was not to argue with him.

He had what he would call in the charges made in other people's divorce petitions, a 'violent and ungovernable temper', although I can't remember it getting any worse when he lost his sight. He would shout on railway platforms, in restaurants, in the corridors of the Law Courts where he once yelled Macbeth's curse, 'The devil damn thee black, thou cream-faced loon!' at an instructing solicitor who had forgotten a document. Cold plates, soft-boiled eggs, being kept waiting for anything: such irritations rather than the disaster of blindness would make him thunder at my mother, 'Kath! Kath! Are you a complete cretin?' Only sometimes, after long periods of abuse borne patiently, she would walk away from him and my father would be left standing in the middle of the bedroom, a silver-backed hairbrush in his hand and his braces dangling,

15

panic-stricken and yelling, 'Kath! Kath!' into the unresponsive darkness around him.

We were, of course, considerably privileged. Divorce had not become, as it is today, a national pastime, an industry ceaselessly productive for the workers engaged in it and knowing neither strikes nor stoppages. In my father's day the divorce business was in its infancy, with only a few Courts in London servicing the whole country, but of what cruelty, adultery, incurable insanity and wilful refusal to consummate there was going, my father had his share. And when marital infidelity fell off, or during a lull in the throwing of saucepans, or the making of exorbitant and unnatural sexual demands, there were always dotty testators with their wayward Wills. So we had a house in Hampstead which we rented for five pounds a week, and later we had a flat in the Temple and a cottage in the country. The cottage was among the beech woods in the Chilterns, near to where my father built the house in which I am living and writing this. The cottage was one of a pair. Next door to us lived Mr Mullard, a 'bodger' or maker of chair legs.

There were two Mullard boys, Peter and Ronnie. When I first met them Ronnie was too young to play with and he spent his time confined in an outsize 'Gold Flake' cigarette carton which served as a play-pen and became strongly impregnated with urine. I would see him when I reluctantly entered the living-room. There a smouldering wood fire kept a kettle constantly simmering; beside it stood two elaborately carved commodes on which the Mullard family sat at the appropriate time of day. Outside, in a lean-to shed, up to his knees in a mounting pile of shavings, Mr Mullard worked enormously long hours at an old treadle lathe, turning the beech trees, which he felled and sawed up himself, into twisted, curlicued chair legs for several local factories. His price was about threepence-ha'penny a dozen for the hand-finished article. Once they tried to knock off his ha'penny and he put on a bowler-hat and stiff dickey shirt front and set off on a walk of twelve miles to High Wycombe to protest.

Mr Mullard was a small, red-cheeked man with wire-rimmed glasses hooked over his ears. He had been a cook in the war and would tell me blood-curdling stories of stew made in the trenches from candle grease, shot mule and, he hinted, abandoned limbs, from which no one even bothered to remove the puttees. He had a small oil lamp precariously balanced on his lathe and, if I looked out of our window late at night, I could see his light still on as Mr Mullard tirelessly spun egg-cups complete with eggs, or barley sugar chair legs, out of the white, naked wood. He owned an old phonograph with one cylindrical record called 'The Laughing Friar'. On Christmas Day he would bring this contraption out proudly and the Friar would laugh for the benefit of his family. Any other entertainment, he thought, or entertainment at any other time, would corrupt his two sons, give them ideas above their station and sap their vitality. Mrs Mullard was a tiny, violently active woman. Wearing a sacking apron and an old tweed cap, she scrubbed every inch of their cottage and dug the garden with a huge fork. In her spare time she trotted up the road with a bucket full of soapy water and scrubbed out the telephone kiosk.

One Christmas, when Ronnie Mullard had grown large enough to be taken out of the cigarette carton, my father offered to take us all to *Aladdin* in Reading. We never went. Mr Mullard refused permission. Give his boys the sight of one pantomime, he thought, and where might the taste for pleasure end?

We had oil lamps and a shallow tin bath, which was filled with water from the well. Going to the loo meant an icy journey to the end of the garden and sitting on a bench carved by Mr Mullard. Almost before you were finished he would be behind the shed with a spade, ready to dig and spread among his vegetables.

Apart from the Mullards my great friend was Iris Jones, the gardener's daughter from the cottage along the common. She was exactly my age and we would meet very early in the mornings, and I would steal necklaces for her from Woolworth's. All one summer we made houses on the common, enjoying the sharp, musky smell of the bracken, furnishing our homes with chipped Coronation mugs and bottomless, rusty saucepans which we found in the local tip, and doing our best to con Ronnie Mullard into sitting on an ant-heap. One day Iris offered to show me her knickers. I took off my glasses, not knowing exactly what to expect.

I envied Iris and the Mullards because they would be allowed to stay at home. In the summer they would be back in time to play in the bracken during the long, light evenings; and in the winter they could slither down the hill to the village school. I had a recurring dream which was that at the age of nine I should be taken out and hanged. In my dream I protested to my father at this gloomy destiny, but he seemed not to hear. When I spoke to my mother she gave me her usual large-eyed, reasonable smile and told me that it was something that happened to all small boys and it was really nothing to worry about. I now feel sure that what I was looking forward to as the morning of my execution was my being sent away to school.

At no time did my mother ever explain satisfactorily why she was determined to get me out of the house for the best part of the year, to send me off to face the gloom and discomfort of icy dormitories, terrible fish which wore a sort of black mackintosh and was eaten with tinned peas, and shell-shocked masters who either confused us with the Huns or fell embarrassingly in love with us. Perhaps my mother realized that I was greatly over-privileged and wished to give me an experience of suffering, or perhaps she thought I should be trained to face hardship and loneliness so that I might pursue a career in the Colonial Service. More likely she was only doing what she considered best for me. She thought that I was desperately lonely, lying in the bracken and reading P.G. Wodehouse and Bulldog Drummond and getting an occasional hypnotic glimpse of Iris Jones's knickers. There was no persuading her otherwise. I didn't speak to my father about it. I supposed he wouldn't be sorry to see the back of me, and I understood his point of view.

3

'WHY HAVE YOU SUCH A SLOPE-SHOULDERED, BELLY-protuberant, stooping and deformed appearance? Answer me that, oh ye faithless and hunchbacked generation!'

The headmaster of my prep school looked very much like God. He had long, white, slightly curly hair, and was old and beautiful. He wore a dark suit which had shortish trousers showing the tops of his highly-polished black boots. He also spoke in God's prose, a mixture of the Old Testament and Rudyard Kipling's *Just So Stories*.

'Draw nigh and hearken to me, oh litter of runts and weaklings. I say unto you that you are round-shouldered through the wearing of braces! Unbutton your braces and cast them from you. Each boy to acquire a dark-blue elastic belt with a snake buckle, to be slotted neatly into the loops provided at the top of school shorts.'

'Dear Mummy,' I wrote, in the compulsory letter home, 'I don't like it here at all. I know it said braces on the clothes list, but we're not allowed braces any more. In fact we have to cast them from us. Noah told us this in assembly' (we were expected to call the staff by their nicknames; the headmaster's was 'Noah'). 'Could you send me a dark-blue belt with a snake buckle as quickly as you can?'

'What, gasping for breath, ye red-faced and pop-eyed generation?' Noah looked at us with amused contempt at the following week's assembly. 'Why do you show such clear signs of stomach contraction? Why are you an offence to the eye, all tied up like parcels? I say unto you, there will be no more belts or the wearing thereof. Abandon belts! Each boy to equip himself with a decent pair of sturdy elastic braces!'

'Dear Mummy,' I wrote. 'I still don't like it here. Would you please send me a new pair of braces as soon as you can? I cast mine aside and now I can't find them. And now I have to cast aside my belt. . .'

Noah was also tremendously keen on iodine lockets. These were small china bottles, full of iodine, tied to a tape which, if worn round the neck at all times would, he was persuaded, prevent any known disease from

19

bunions to botulism. We were all issued with these charms, which we used to fight with like conkers.

'I have noticed that some boys', Noah looked sadly around him at assembly and sounded puzzled, 'have taken to wearing small pieces of broken china slung about their necks on a ribbon. I take this to be a primitive superstition, and calculated to ward off the evil eye. "Ham" will be giving us a talk with lantern-slides on African tribes who still cling to such irrational beliefs. This school is a Christian community. Cast aside the amulets, resist the mumbo-jumbo, or behold I will strike ye with my rod and terrible will be the striking thereof!'

I can't remember Noah taking a great part in our education. He bought a little carillon of bells which he hung outside the dining-room, and he used to summon us in to Sunday supper by playing tunes on them. He enjoyed this exercise and long after supper was over, indeed long after lights had been turned out, he would stand in the passage in his dark suit and highly-polished boots, delicately picking out tune after tune with a small hammer, smiling benevolently.

For its period the prep school was progressive. As I have said, we knew the staff by their nicknames. 'Shem' was the headmaster's son, 'Ham' taught Latin and Greek to the top class, 'Japhet' played expertly on the banjolele and sang songs such as *Here we sit like birds in the wilderness* and *We left your baby on the shore*. He also taught us ballroom dancing and I spent a good deal of time being pushed steadily backwards by 'Japhet' to the tune of *Smoke Gets in Your Eyes* as he shouted, '*Chassé*, boy! *Chassé*, damn you!' Ham had shrapnel stuck in his head, which caused him to go periodically out of his mind and strafe us with text-books and blackboard rubbers, attacks for which he was profoundly apologetic when he came to himself and the armistice was signed.

We were allowed many liberties: we could bicycle round the town and take boats out on the river. I early developed a pronounced allergy to any sort of organized sport which has been with me ever since. Perhaps it's because I was an only child, but I never have felt any sort of team spirit. Loyalty to the school to which your parents pay to send you seemed to me like feeling loyal to Selfridges: consequently I never cared in the least which team won, but only prayed for the game to be over without the ball ever coming my way. In the cricket season I learned there was a safe and far-away place on the field called 'deep' which I always chose. When 'Over' was called I simply went more and more 'deep' until I was sitting on the steps of the pavilion reading the plays of Noël Coward, whom I had got on to after Bulldog Drummond. All I wanted then was to be a star of musical comedy and come tap-dancing down a huge staircase in white tie and tails. I got a theatrical costumier's catalogue and wrote up for a silver-topped ebony cane and a monocle.

Future experience was to show me that my early distrust of sport was well founded. I was told of a public school where the lascivious butler used to change into games clothes and crouch behind a bush from which he would leap during the muddy confusion of a 'scrum down' and covertly join the game for the purpose of fondling the boys in an intimate manner. Sport, as I have discovered, fosters international hostility and leads the audience, no doubt from boredom, to assault and do grievous bodily harm while watching it. The fact that audiences at the National Theatre rarely break bottles over one another's heads, and that Opera fans seldom knee one another in the groin during the long intervals at Covent Garden, convinces me that the theatre is safer than sport. In my case the masters at my prep school agreed to the extent of sending me to the local repertory theatre with a bar of Fry's Mint Chocolate. In this way I saw most of the plays of Bernard Shaw, which must have been better than playing cricket.

At the beginning, when I was away at school, I was extremely lonely. Loneliness, however, the birthright of the only child, held no particular terrors for me. In the holidays, having built his new house near to our old country cottage, my father devoted almost all his spare time to a large garden, and as his eyes failed and the flowers and vegetables faded from his view, his gardening became more dedicated, until, when he could no longer see the results of his labours, but had to rely on my mother or me to describe the health of a dahlia or the wilt of a clematis, he spent every possible hour pricking out, or potting on, or groping for dead heads and trying to get a correct aim with his secateurs. He never welcomed visitors and would often ask my mother to lead him away into the undergrowth if they appeared at the gate, so a month or so would pass without our seeing anyone at all. My segregated education seemed to have driven some sort of wedge between me and Iris and the Mullard boys, so holidays were a solitary pleasure which I tried to carry on at school.

Being alone was easier, I had long ago discovered, if you became two people, the actor and the observer. The observer was always the same, the actor played many parts: an officer in the Foreign Legion, for instance, or a ruthless private detective with rooms in Half Moon Street, or a Brigadier in Napoleon's army. 'There he goes,' I was able to say about myself, even in the deeply unhappy days when I lolloped about a frozen football field, keeping as far as possible from the ball, 'cantering across the burning sands with his crack platoon of Spahis (ex-murderers, robbers and at least one Duke disappointed in love, but whoever asked questions of a Legionnaire?) in search of the tents of Mahmoud Bey, and a levelling of the score after the disgrace of Sidi Ben Oud.' Later my character became more sophisticated, as I came more under the influence of Noël Coward and Dornford Yates.

'*Sic vos non vobis mellificatis apes.* Translate, Mortimer.'

'Thus you don't make honey for yourselves, you apes, sir.' Mortimer drew a flat gold cigarette-case from the breast pocket of his immaculate grey, double-breasted jacket. He was bubbling with suppressed laughter: the answer had been deliberately misleading. With a tap the heavy case sprang open and he offered it to the bewildered little man at the blackboard. 'Turkish this side', he said, 'and Virginian the other.'

Later still, when I made a friend, we inflicted our lies on each other. Childhood is a great time for lying. Later in life you may be able to boast of some real achievement or some extraordinary adventure, in childhood all must be supplied from the imagination. So I told my friend that I was the son of a Russian aristocrat, smuggled out of Moscow during the revolution, and had been kindly taken in by the simple English lawyer with whom I happened to live. I had a long story, a rare sporting fantasy, about walking along the tow-path at Hammersmith when the cox of the Oxford crew had a heart attack and, being then of the appropriate weight, steering the eight to victory in the Boat Race. More consistently, I pretended that my parents never stopped going to cocktail parties, bickering, throwing 'White Ladies' and 'Manhattans' into each other's faces and would soon be getting a divorce. If I had one clear ambition during those years it was to be the child of a broken home.

My friend was Bill Mann. I can't remember exactly how we met and when we found each other. Recently, standing side by side in the Gents of a London hotel, we at first failed to recognize each other, yet our relationship was very close. We were in business together and our business was the theatre. At first we merely talked about the plays we had seen. My father went to the theatre regularly, usually after consuming a leisurely four-course dinner at the 'Trocadero', which would mean his being led into the entertainment followed by me in a state of acute embarrassment and an Eton suit, somewhere about the middle of the first act. We always occupied seats in the front row of the stalls, so our arrival never passed unnoticed, either from the stage or the audience. Failing vision and a late start made the plots of new plays extremely hard for my father to follow and the show would be punctuated by deafening whispers of, 'What's happening now, Kath? Go on, paint me the picture!' With Shakespeare of course he had no problem and could remember all the quotations and say lines aloud and with great relish seconds before the actors. Once a year we would go to Stratford and see all the productions. We stayed at an hotel in which the bedrooms were called after plays and decorated with ancient engravings of blood-curdling scenes from the major tragedies. One night I was kept awake by a violent quarrel coming from 'Romeo and Juliet' next door. On another I was frozen with fear at a curiously ghoulish engraving of the witches in *Macbeth*. I turned my eyes from the picture to the wardrobe mirror only to be stricken to a more permanent immobility by the sight of a frightful phantom, product, no doubt, of the witches' cauldron, consisting only of two pale spindly legs and white hooded blur. I had been standing for a long while before I realized that I was looking at the reflection of myself taking off my shirt.

So I had a good many theatrical experiences to discuss with Bill Mann. I could tell him much about the plays I had seen and even more about those I hadn't. As a future music critic of *The Times*, he could tell me about concerts and operas which were then, and remained for many years, a subject of total mystery to me, my father's idea of a musical experience being to repeat Shakespearean quotations or sing several verses of *Pretty little Polly Perkins of Paddington Green*.

After long theatrical discussions, during which we drew out the seating plans for most of the London theatres, we decided to put on plays at my home during weekend visits. This excitingly entailed writing off for review sketches and printed paper scenery from Samuel French Limited, but there were several dangers in inviting my friend home. He would inevitably be exposed to certain disgraceful facts about my family which I had been at pains to conceal, such as the immovable solidity of my parents' marriage, the glaring absence of a cocktail-shaker and my father's growing blindess. These things must have been obvious to Bill Mann, but he was too polite to mention any of them. However I noticed him staring at my mother's finger-nails, which I had described to him as very long and painted green, and taking in the fact that they were rather blunt and chipped from a good deal of potting up.

We put on a review we had written called *Champagne Cocktail* and one we bought from Samuel French called *Airy Nothings*. We stood on the dining-room stairs in bedspreads and pink paper shakos and sang selections from Ivor Novello. We did a play I wrote where we acted the ghosts of two young subalterns killed on the Somme. Whenever she heard that we were going to do what my father called 'An entertainment' my mother would give a little cry of horror at the thought of all the clearing up. When we played the two ghostly officers we laughed so much that we felt compelled to run into the kitchen to eat cold roast potatoes smeared with honey, a dish we thought would be disgusting enough to bring us to our senses.

Back at school the theatrical productions were better regulated and very well done. Each year we did a Shakespeare play and a Gilbert and Sullivan opera, and by a process of extreme democracy, of which the left wing of Equity would approve, the plays were cast by popular vote. In our last year Bill Mann was elected to play Bunthorne and I won Richard II. By that time the school had become, for me, a place of glorious excitement. I lay awake at night repeating:

> 'For God's sake, let us sit upon the ground
> And tell sad stories of the death of kings'

and hardly slept. The masters either attacked us savagely or put on concerts for us, evenings when we drank cider-cup and they sang, to the unaccompanied banjolele, *Olga Pulloffski the Beautiful Spy*, *Abdul the Bulbul Ameer* and *Gertie the Girl with the Gong*. I fell violently in love with a tow-haired small boy called Jenks who reminded me of the signed photograph of Annabella I had written up for. He promised to be faithful to me forever, but when I last saw him he was with his wife and four children at London airport. No time in my life was ever as exciting or triumphant as the term I put up for Richard II and won the election.

Through all this excitement Noah moved in a mysterious way. He had to deal with a major problem. A boy called Ramsden, who never said much in class, put a tin chamber-pot on his head and no one could get it off. To avoid public derision Ramsden was moved from the dormitory to the sanatorium. The doctor was sent for and the school carpenter, but no solution was found. In order to subdue public disquiet Noah would issue a bulletin at almost every meal about the progress of the crisis.

'Ramsden may think he has done something extremely clever,' Noah boomed sadly. 'He may think he has drawn attention to himself in some unusual and original manner. Oh ye of little judgement, would you laugh at Ramsden? What he has done is just very silly and dangerous. He is missing lessons, which will put him well behind for the School Cert. He is causing the unhappy couple who gave birth to him needless anxiety. So I say unto you, go about your daily business, work hard and do your best in the class-room and at school sports. Do not pay Ramsden the compliment of whispering about him in corridors. His exploits are best forgotten.'

In fact Ramsden, when we peered at him through a crack in the sanatorium door, presented an unforgettable spectacle. He was sitting bolt upright in bed, wearing striped flannel pyjamas, his ears flattened by a huge chamber-pot of chipped enamel, his face decorated by a grin that was at once sheepish and proud. At a subsequent meal Noah reassured us. 'A man has been sent for,' he announced. 'Expert in these matters. It is to be hoped that in due course Ramsden will be released. Every boy to remember, this is no subject for laughter!' That afternoon a man in dungarees with a bag of tools drove up in a van, and later on an uncrowned Ramsden rejoined the class and resumed his habitual 'low profile'.

4

'MR JUSTICE CUNNINGHAM GAVE CUSTODY OF THE TWO children to the father. It was proved to his satisfaction that the mother went out to tea dances.'

'That's terrible!'

'Well, I was extremely angry at first. You never like to go down in a case, but you'll find this when you're at the bar. You'll have forgotten all about it by the time you slide the tape off your next brief.'

'I mean, it's terrible to lose your children, just for going to tea dances.'

'She went on her own, you see. I suppose the implication was, she danced with gigolos.'

'What's a gigolo?'

'I don't think', my mother said, 'that's very suitable.'

'Mr Justice Cunningham didn't think it was suitable either.' My father shook his head sadly.

'That Judge sounds an absolute swine. He ought to be locked up. Taking away people's children. Just for dancing!'

'Mr Justice Cunningham is a hard man, old boy,' my father agreed. 'But it's just part of the rough and tumble in the Probate, Divorce and Admiralty Division. No real fun in winning if it's all too easy. You'll find that.'

'I'm not sure I want to. Go to the bar, I mean.'

'How is the viburnum fragans, Kath? Paint me the picture.'

How many choices do we make in a lifetime? Even the selection of a wife or a lover is severely limited by the number of people of a vaguely appropriate age, sex and physical appearance you happen to meet at a given moment who may possibly fancy you, a field, as far as most marriages are concerned, of three or four possible candidates. If I had been born into one of those solidly conservative criminal families of London burglars I was later to defend, my career would have been mapped out for me by a father when he was home from the Nick. He would have planned an apprenticeship in Takings and Drivings Away, a little minor Warehouse Breaking and finally the responsibility of Look-out Man for a firm of bank robbers. Was my life decided when I was a child, bathed and put to bed by the wife of a lawyer's clerk, given bedtime stories from the Divorce Court? I could have chosen not to be a barrister, but every time my father changed the subject I remained on my predetermined path. If I'm still an agnostic on the subject of Free Will, it operates, I am sure, within the narrowest of limits. We spend our time punishing criminals or rewarding heroes, not for the great decisions they have taken for good or evil but for proceeding, with more or less dedication, in the direction in which they were pointed. At the time my father told me about the custody case and the *thé dansants* my cards had no doubt been dealt, a mixed hand adding up to a bid as a barrister and a writer. Flat-footed and tone deaf, the choice of becoming a second Jack Buchanan, deftly tip-tapping up to the footlights with a silver-topped cane twirling under my arm and a silk hat on the side of my head, was never mine.

'I think I'd like to be an actor.'

But my father had turned away, to examine the shrubs in my uncle's Sussex garden, a place full of ornamental ponds and stone walls and wrought-iron gates. Past the rhododendron walks stood the acres of woodland my uncle owned. My Uncle Harold, married to my mother's sister Daisy, was a manufacturer of beds. He was considerably richer than my father and his garden was consequently larger, equipped with waterfalls and even rarer shrubs.

'Not got any lilies out, Harold, have you?' my father asked, knowing that my uncle was deeply superstitious and dreaded the sight of a lily as a symbol of death. When he had his sight my father would try and steer my uncle under ladders or lure black cats across his path. In fact my father treated Uncle Harold with some condescension because he was so superstitious and had so much money.

We usually spent Christmas with Harold and Daisy. My mother drove the Morris Oxford away from our hills and clay soil and beech woods down to the flat, sandy, coniferous country with the ground covered with pine-needles and cones, to the bungalows filled with retired military men and the distant prospect of the sea. When I was young I was regularly sick at Guildford. My Uncle Harold's house was furnished with his expensive thirties' artefacts, white walls and a lot of blue and plum-coloured glass, chromium and mahogany. Bullrushes stood about in tall glass jars, and Lalique swans held the chocolates on the polished dinner-table. The house, always referred to by my father as the 'North Pole', was not overheated and my aunt had a sort of tweed overcoat made to match her dress for indoor wear. My Uncle Harold designed all his own clothes as he designed his furniture, with a slide-rule and to his own specifications. He wore wide-brimmed sombreros and had invented a sort of padded flap which hung down at the back of his waistcoat to keep his bottom warm. He was a meticulous man and appreciated conformity. At one breakfast he measured his rasher of bacon with his slide-rule and sent it back to the kitchen when he found it too long.

What I remember most clearly about my Uncle Harold's house was the bath water. By a prodigious feat of engineering and much use of the slide-rule he had harnessed a stream to his will. I remember sitting on the edge of the bath, about to climb into my first dinner-jacket for the entirely grown-up Christmas festivities, and turning on the tap. Nothing whatever happened for the first quarter of an hour. Then, on a clear day with the wind in the right direction, from a distant hillside you could hear mechanical movements as of sluice gates opening. During the next thirty minutes water could be heard approaching and then a dense cloud of steam gushed from the pipe like a triumphant herald announcing the arrival of a thin brownish trickle which dripped disconsolately into a bath-tub which might have been personally designed for Tallulah Bankhead in the heyday of the Savoy Hotel.

On Christmas Day we would go round and deliver biscuit tins, on which were portrayed the unsmiling faces of King George v and Queen Mary, to the gardeners and woodmen in the cottages. On Boxing Day we went into Brighton, a magical place to me, where the trams were decorated with fairy lights and we had seats for the pantomime. My father always joined loudly in the food song, the words of which descended on a song-sheet from the flys, to embarrass the rest of the family.

'When my wife is on a diet
I daren't mention "Fry it",
Wifie would only be mad.'

'I do like a lovely blo-ater
And so do my mater and pater.'

We saw the Crazy Gang whose pale faces, battered hats and sudden cries filled me with unreasoning fear. I remember three black men, in white suits with belted jackets, who tap-danced in a way it was my ambition to achieve.

'What does John think', my Uncle Harold said at dinner, shocked at the fact that I had wanted a checked sports coat and a silk tie for Christmas and not a catapult or a *Boy's Own Annual*, 'about the jackets of those negro dancers? Does he admire the half-belt effect on the back, or was it a little too gigolo-like from a design point of view?'

'John's going to Harrow next term,' my mother told them with considerable amusement. 'He'll have to have a tailed coat there and a boater.'

And a silver-topped cane, I thought, for going to Lord's. I would use it, privately, to dance like Fred Astaire.

'They do roast the fags at Harrow, I suppose?' my father asked innocently. 'I don't know what I'm paying all that money out for unless you get roasted occasionally.'

'A great deal of money!' said my uncle. 'I must say, you don't do things by halves, Clifford.' He had been pained by my father's extravagance ever since he heard about a barrel of oysters his clerk had been sent out to buy in Fleet Street.

'I do like a lovely blo-ater.' My father put down his knife and fork and sang very loudly, 'And so do my mater and pater.'

'Whatever made you choose Harrow?' my Aunt Daisy interrupted him to ask. When it had vaguely occurred to my father that the time had come for me to go on to a public school Noah had immediately said 'Harrow', a choice for which he gave no sort of explanation. Which of the old boys of that school, I wonder, did he think I might grow up to resemble? Lord Byron, Cardinal Manning, Winston Churchill or the Mayfair playboys who had recently been flogged in prison after a robbery with violence? My father had, in fact, no more chosen Harrow for me than he had chosen to spend Christmas with his superstitious brother-in-law or to suffer from glaucoma. These things happened in the mysterious cause of evolution and at the wayward direction of the Life Force, and that was that. Darwin could probably explain it all.

> 'When my wife is on a diet
> I daren't mention "Fry it",
> Wifie would only be mad.'

My father sang loudly, whilst the others peeled their peaches and tried to pretend that he wasn't happening.

5

SEX, LIKE LOVE, MY FATHER THOUGHT, HAD BEEN GREATLY
overestimated by the poets. He would often pause at tea-time, his biscuit
half-way to his mouth, to announce, 'I have never had many mistresses
with thighs like white marble.' And I was at a loss to tell whether he
meant that he had not had lady friends with particularly marmoreal
thighs, or that he had had few mistresses of any sort. Like most children
I found my father's sex life a subject on which it was best to avoid
speculation. He had had, in his past, a fiancée other than my mother,
whom he always referred to as his 'poor girl' and who had died young.
I never discovered her name or the cause of her death.

'Love affairs aren't much of a subject for drama really,' he told me at
an early age. 'Consider this story of a lover, a husband and an unfaithful
wife. The wife confesses all to her husband. He sends for her lover. They
are closeted in the living-room together. The wife stands outside the
door, trembling with fear. She strains her ears to discover what's going
on in the room. Some terrible quarrel? A duel or fight to the death
perhaps? At last she can stand the suspense no longer. She flings open
the door and what does she see? Blood? Broken furniture? One of them
stretched out on the carpet? Not at all. The two men are sitting by the
fire drinking bottled ale and discussing the best method of pruning apple
trees. Naturally the woman's furious. She packs and leaves for her
mother's.'

Was my father any of the characters in that unromantic story? Not
the husband, but was he, perhaps, the lover? I never asked him and now
I have no means of finding out.

However, my father would often recite, and usually at tea-time, poetry
of a sensual nature. Swinburne had been his undergraduate favourite
and he often repeated, with a relish of rolling r's:

> 'Can you hurt me, sweet lips, though I hurt you?
> Men touch them, and change in a trice
> The lilies and languors of virtue
> For the raptures and roses of vice.'

'Poor old Algernon Charles got it wrong as usual,' he would add by way of commentary. 'The roses and raptures of vice are damned uncomfortable as you'll certainly find out. You have to get into such ridiculous positions.' And he would go on with the recital as my mother cut more bread and butter or spooned out the home-made marrow jam:

'We shift and bedeck and bedrape us,
Thou art noble and nude and antique;
Libitina thy mother, Priapus
Thy father, a Tuscan and Greek.
We play with light loves in the portal,
And wince and relent and refrain;
Loves die, and we know thee immortal,
Our Lady of Pain.'

'Sorry stuff, as it so happens,' my father commented, 'but I like the sound of it.'

It follows from all this that my father's advice on the subject of sex was not of much practical value to an eleven-year-old boy. At about that age the whole business hit me like a raging epidemic, causing me to seek constant opportunities to embrace myself passionately among the dead flies and dusty, outdated law books and moth-eaten blankets in our loft, or in houses in the bracken which I now ran as bachelor establishments. At my prep school I fell in love with Jenks, but this love was largely unconsummated, apart from a clumsy hug in the school museum, a place where the air was polluted by the prize exhibit, a large and inadequately cured elephant's foot which had been turned into a waste-paper basket. I loved Annabella and Ginger Rogers when she wore jodhpurs and a hacking jacket, and Deanna Durbin and Greta Garbo when she was dressed as a boy in *Queen Christina*. I was lately talking to an elderly, but still bright-eyed, General who said, 'I first fell in love with Cherubino with his nice white breeches and dear little sword.' It was years before I got to know *Figaro*, but the image for my prep school years was about right.

The truth was that from the time when I stopped keeping house in the bracken with Iris Jones to the end of my time at Harrow, seven or eight years when I might as well have entered a Dominican order for all the female company I enjoyed, I knew absolutely nothing about girls. In one-sex schools and during lonely and isolated holidays I was in a chrysalis of vague, schoolboy homosexuality. Even when I got to Oxford, and did make some expeditions away from the safe dormitory base, the girls I preferred were still boyish. Betty Grable was less my style than Veronica Lake and Katherine Hepburn who, so Frank Hauser assured us, acted in *Philadelphia Story* as the natural bridge into the heterosexual world.

The sight of a woman at my public school was almost as rare as a Cockney accent in class; and if we spotted one it was, as often as not, a fierce and elderly matron. We were waited on at table by footmen in blue tailed coats and settled down for the night by a butler called 'George'. Our homosexuality was therefore dictated by necessity rather than choice. We were like a generation of diners condemned to cold cuts because the steak and kidney was 'off'.

Harrow-on-the-Hill is in the middle of the suburbs: the tomb in the Parish churchyard where Byron once lay and composed poetry as he looked over rolling meadows now commands a fine view of the semis of Hillingdon and Pinner. It was only a few stops from Baker Street on the Metropolitan Line and we used to sit in the smoke-filled carriages to be jeered at as we went up to Lord's, dressed in top hat, pearl-grey waistcoat, morning coat and silver-topped stick with a dark-blue tassel. We weren't allowed to speak to the boys at the bottom of the hill, although a Prefect might occasionally give one of them sixpence to carry up his suitcase at the beginning of term. We were isolated and put in quarantine both on account of sex and class, although once again I found myself educated above my situation, among various 'Honourables' who were called 'Mister' in roll-call. Within our group we were again strictly segregated. There were the 'one yearers' who had to keep all their buttons done up, 'two yearers' who could undo one jacket button, 'three yearers' who could undo two and 'four yearers' who could wear fancy waistcoats and put their hands in their pockets. 'Five yearers' were said to be allowed to grow moustaches or even marry a wife if such a thing were available. If 'four yearers' mixed with 'one yearers' the worst was suspected and very often turned out to be true.

I cannot say I found Harrow brutal or my time particularly unhappy, but life there never approached the Elizabethan splendours and miseries of my prep school. Harrow's great advantage was that we had rooms of our own, although in the first year these had to be shared with one other boy, and these did provide a sort of oasis of privacy. Each room had a coal fire and a wooden bed which let down from the wall on which various political slogans were burned in poker-work, such as, 'Death to the Boers' and 'No Home Rule for Ireland'. You could bring your own furniture and set out your own books on the shelves and enjoy some of the privileges of a long-term, good conduct prisoner (it's rightly said that the great advantage of an English public school education is that no subsequent form of captivity can hold any particular terror for you. A friend who was put to work on the Burma railway once told me that he was greeted, on arrival, by a fellow prisoner-of-war who said, 'Cheer up. It's not half as bad as Marlborough.')

The first boy I shared a room with was called Weaver. He had smooth dark hair which he slicked down with 'Anzora' ('Anzora masters the hair', I had heard about it on Radio Luxembourg). His parents, he told me, were extremely wealthy and had a large house in the New Forest. I was impressed with Weaver until I met a boy called Marsh who told me,

'Weaver's really extremely common. His parents have side-plates at dinner.'

'Side-plates?'

'Yes. Side-plates. To put your bread on. Not at luncheon. Everyone has side-plates at luncheon. At *dinner*.' He explained carefully, as though to a backward foreigner, matters which seemed to him perfectly obvious.

'But if you don't have side-plates at dinner what do you put your bread on?'

'You crumble it. On the table.' Marsh looked at me with great pity. 'Don't you know anything?'

'Not very much.'

It was clear that I didn't.

'Properly shined shoes are the mark of a good regiment and a decent Classical Shell. It gives me little pleasure to listen to Virgil being construed by a boy with shoes the colour of elephant's hide. Look down, and when you can see your faces in your toe-caps you shall inherit the earth. You shall wear shined shoes at Speech Day and enjoy the delights of strawberries and cream and salmon may-on-naise! You shall wear your shined shoes in the Classical Fifth and in the Classical Sixth also shall you wear them. And if your boots are shined and your puttees neat on parade you shall pass out of the school Corps into the Brigade of Guards.'

It was strange that so many of my schoolmasters seemed to have been permanently affected by the Old Testament as seen through the prose of

Rudyard Kipling. My first master at Harrow was a charming retired Major of the Brigade of Guards. He inspected our shoes and finger-nails each morning, but otherwise treated us with great gentleness.

My Harrow friends stayed longer in my life than those I had met at earlier schools. We were thrown together in the lower regions of our House, we ate together with our faces to the wall, and Keswick, the Head Boy, would shout at us if we turned round. We loitered in one another's rooms and 'took exercise' by changing into running clothes and sitting gossiping or reading Roger Fry in the lavatories below the Fives courts. My closest friend was Oliver, known to his many enemies as 'Oily', Pensotti, who had about him the vaguely seductive aura of holidays in Bandol and bedrooms in Mayfair. He wore scuffed suede shoes and used a sort of dead white face powder to cover his spots. He used to accompany Radio Luxembourg with the soft musical scrape of a pair of wire brushes played on the top of a suitcase. He came into my life, and indeed left it, shrouded in an aura of mystery. If I asked him any questions about himself he would look vaguely amused and avoid giving anything away.

'Where do you live, Pensotti?'

'Where do I live? Ah. That's what I'm always asking myself. Would you like to help me with a few suggestions?'

Or, 'What does your father do, Pensotti?'

'What does he *do*? You mean what does he do, *exactly*? A lot of people have wanted to know the answer to that, especially my Ma.'

I subsequently met an elderly lady who claimed to be Pensotti's mother. She had bright red hair, carried a poodle and spoke in what she alleged was a South American accent. She lived in a flat in Charles Street with glass-topped tables and a lot of wrought-iron furniture. I never met Pensotti *père*, nor did I learn any more about Oliver's childhood. It seemed to have been spent around the world and he could speak French, Spanish and Italian.

The other friend, who lasted in my life for many years, was Martin Witteridge. He was a large, rather clumsy but extremely kind and good-natured boy. He would always laugh at our jokes, buy us great plates of egg and chips in the school shop and consented to listen as I read out page after page of the novel I was writing about Harrow in the nearest possible approach to the style of Aldous Huxley.

On the fringe of our group, yelling abuse at us or occasionally kicking his way into our midst, was Tainton. Tainton was a phenomenon. I have never since met anyone in the least like Tainton. I had always hoped that his kind died out with cock-fights and bear-baiting.

The first thing to be said about Tainton was that he was extremely small. However, he was as tough and leathery as a jockey. He boasted that his mother had given birth to him on the hunting-field, after which minor intrusion into a day's sport she went on to be up with the kill at Thorne Wood according to Tainton, but then Tainton was, on many matters, a most unreliable witness. His habitual expression was a discontented scowl, after which his face would become bright red and suffused with anger. He had yellow curls which stood up on end, and ears like jug handles. On certain very rare occasions he smiled, and his smile had a sort of shy innocence and even charm.

At all times and in all places Tainton was a source of continual trouble. Before a breathless audience he tried to cross the lake by swinging from a sort of trapeze, made up from his bed-linen, and fell in. He broke windows, used unspeakable language to the matron, set fire to the *Morning Post* as Keswick was reading it, put stray cats into people's beds and, at home and during the course of a hunt ball, shut a Shetland pony in the ladies' lavatory, having first dosed it with castor oil. Tainton was apparently born without a sense of fear and was quite impervious to the consequences of his outrages.

Among his other distinctions Tainton was a prize, you could say a champion, masturbator. No doubt we all did our best in this direction, but with Tainton masturbation reached Olympic standards. There was a story about him which earned him considerable respect; but as it depended on the uncorroborated evidence of Tainton himself, it may not have been true. It seems that the school Chaplain, Mr Percy, called on Tainton in his room, surprised him at his usual exercise and said, deeply shocked, 'Really my boy, you should save that up till you are married.' 'Oh, I'm doing that, sir,' Tainton answered with his rare smile, 'I've already got several jam jars full.'

Our House was presided over by a gentle English liberal called Mr Lamb. This housemaster was given hell at lunch-time by Keswick, who warmly espoused the Fascist cause in Spain, whereas Mr Lamb was of the opinion that the Republicans were really doing their best and behaving quite decently, all things taken into account. Like many English liberals, Mr Lamb had his blind spots, including a wish-fulfilling liking for real bastards, such as Napoleon, about whom he spoke with servile admiration in the history class. However, there was absolutely no harm to Mr Lamb. He believed that all laws were founded on common sense and natural justice and, when I suggested to him that might mean I could undo all my buttons during my second year, he attempted a distinction between social conventions and the law of nature which caused him visible pain. It was this gentle creature, devoted to reason, the Webbs, Gladstone and Macaulay who had thrust upon him the appalling task of educating Tainton.

'John. I know that you and I share certain values. About democracy, for instance. And the Republicans in Spain.'

I didn't know whether to throw my fist in the air, embrace Mr Lamb, kiss him on both cheeks and call him 'Camarada'. Instead I said weakly, 'Yes, sir.'

'So I have thought you might be a stabilizing influence if you shared a room with young Tainton. I'm sure', the archetypal English liberal muttered with hopeless optimism, 'that there's much good in the lad.'

I have not read, in my wildest divorce cases, of marriages as violent as my cohabitation with Tainton. As soon as I entered the room a flung chair splintered against the wall; Tainton was in an evil mood and crouched for a spring. His rages were terrible, totally unpredictable and extremely destructive. He would tear up my Van Gogh reproductions, spit in my Virginia Woolf and once he poured a bottle of green ink over the manuscript of my Aldous-Huxley-type novella. At night he would groan, have nightmares, subconsciously re-enact his birth on the hunting-field or, tireless and in solitary fashion, prepare himself for the rigours of married life. At rare moments he would show unexpected charm, when he leafed through his large collection of photographs of Sonja Henie or cultivated mustard and cress on the silken surface of his top hat. My life with Tainton might be described as days of anxiety and nights of fear. I had absolutely no idea what was going to happen next.

We used to be settled down for the night by George the butler, who entered our room in a tailed coat, said, 'Goodnight, Sor!', seized the poker, raked out the fire and departed switching off the light in one fluent gesture. One evening Tainton hit on the expedient of heating the poker's handle until it was just not red hot and put it ready for George to seize and burn off several fingers. Spot on cue George entered, said 'Goodnight, Sor!' and astounded us by seizing Tainton's striped Sunday trousers as a poker-holder, thus burning a large and smouldering hole in the seat. He left us in the darkness and Tainton lay awake until the small hours, grinding his teeth and swearing a hideous revenge.

In fifteen years you canter through evolution, dash through history, covering the development of man from anthropoid ape to medieval monk in the course of a few birthdays. The child has no sooner finished its bikkipeg and had its nappy changed a couple of times before it seems to be standing up in the school debating society, proposing that, 'This House Sees No Alternative to the Economics of the Market Place', or writing essays on 'The Politics of Feminism'. We are all like insecure Third World Republics, granted Constitutions and Bills of Rights before we have banished tribalism, given up eating our enemies or produced Budgets planned on the signs of the zodiac. Ideas are clapped on us as top hats were once set on the grizzled heads of African chieftains; they make us all look more or less ridiculous.

I read to find new characters to adopt on lonely runs round the periphery of football pitches. I read aloud to entertain my father and when we had got through Shakespeare's sonnets, Browning and *The Shropshire Lad*, we went on to *Fragments of an Agon* and *Sweeney Among the Nightingales*. I added *Murder in the Cathedral* (the truncated version) to Ivor Novello's *Glamorous Nights* as another play suitable for solo performance on the dining-room stairs. We went, after a prolonged dinner at the Trocadero, to see an Auden and Isherwood verse drama, it must have been *The Ascent of F.6*, at the Mercury Theatre, and what entertained my father most about the evening was the presence among the incidental musicians of a lady drummer called 'Eve Kish'. Eve Kish became a subject of his sudden gusts of uncontrollable laughter; he would imagine her patrolling the country lanes with her kettledrum, and he would look in the programmes of all other plays to see if he could find the longed-for announcement 'Percussion: Eve Kish'. I remember him sitting down a quarter of an hour late at *The Seagull*, calling out loudly, 'What? No Eve Kish on the drum?'

In spite of this unpromising beginning it would be hard to overestimate the effect Auden had on me and my generation of middle-class schoolboys. He wrote about what we understood: juvenile jokes about housemasters, homosexual longings, the Clever Boy, the Form Entertainer and the Show Off. And yet his poems brought extraordinary news of a world outside the stuffy common-room and the headmaster's study; the vague but heroic struggle to do great things which were also stylized and in capital letters, like Building the Just City. We had been so near a war: I was born less than five years after the Great War ended, and we had grown up with Flanders poppies and pictures of tin hats on innumerable war graves and I knew a boy whose father promised to tell him about the horrors of Passchendaele if he went straight to bed. Now another war was coming so that we too, I sometimes thought with acute depression, would end as being remembered only by an embarrassed silence on a soggy school playing-field on Poppy Day.

All the same, the idea of the new war was a different and clear one. The gloomy ex-jockey who drove my father's car in the country had told me about Italian Fascists dropping their Abyssinian prisoners-of-war out of aeroplanes. At my prep school I turned over pages of *The Illustrated London News* and saw photographs of Spanish villages shattered by German bombs. There were pictures of young Republican militiamen, going up to the front grinning and sucking cigarette-stubs ready to fight a new and unmistakably evil military machine. They had, moreover, the poets on their side, whereas the Fascists were supported by people like Keswick. I knew almost nothing about life, but I knew perfectly clearly that I couldn't stand people like Keswick. So a whole political attitude can grow from a handful of books and a strong loathing for the Head of the House. Naïve as these beliefs were, trivial as their origins may have been, I cannot say they are attitudes I have ever lived to regret, and it seems to me that those who now write their best sellers denouncing the treacherous iniquities of the Cambridge Communists, show little understanding of the emotions of the thirties, when good and evil seemed so unusually easy to distinguish and the Russians appeared simply as allies in the war against Fascism.

I don't know how the invitation to join the Communist Party came. I know that Esmond Romilly is supposed to have started a network of public school cells, but I can't imagine who can have recommended me as a likely candidate. When I joined I formed, so far as I could see, a one-boy communist cell in a sea of Harrovian capitalist enterprise. For a while I received puzzling and contradictory instructions from the Party Headquarters in King Street. When the Stalin–Hitler pact was signed, the Russians lost their enthusiasm for the coming struggle and I was urged to go down on to the factory floor and persuade the workers to go slow. I couldn't, I thought, do much about it except put the word around the classroom that Virgil should be translated as lethargically as possible, a 'go-slow' which needed no particular encouragement. Later, when

Hitler attacked Russia, we were urged to go down on the factory floor and step up production. Again, all I could suggest was the stepping up of the translation of Virgil. After these contradictory commands from King Street I stopped taking the Party's literature and told my friends that the only political views worth having were those of Prince Peter Kropotkin who believed in anarchism, Mutual Aid and the essential goodness of human nature, opinions which were not easy to hold when you were sharing a room with Tainton.

In the flight from Tainton I spent more and more time alone in the high, marmoreal, Victorian library, chasing books in dark corners and up step-ladders, finding in unexpected places like dictionaries, medieval histories or collections of obscure eighteenth-century poetry, ideas which filled me with hilarity, gloom or almost unbearable lust. I found Lord Byron's Turkish slippers in a glass case, and set myself to follow his uneasy pilgrimage round the school, from the tomb of John Peachey where he lay to write poetry, to the grave where his daughter is buried outside Harrow Church to teach her a sharp lesson for being illegitimate.

Then, as now, I found Lord Byron deeply sympathetic. His potent mixture of revolutionary fervour and crusty conservatism, his life of a Puritan voluptuary, of a romantic with common sense, was intoxicating to me. I spent afternoons in the library drinking imaginary Hock and Seltzer, swimming the Hellespont or limping round Newstead Abbey with a harem of housemaids. I stayed up late gambling with Dallas, and awoke to find the chamber-pot overflowing with banknotes. Then I read of Byron's Harrow friendships, especially that with Lord Clare. Years after he'd left school, Byron met Clare by chance on the road to Bologna and was deeply moved, feeling, apparently, his heart beat at his fingers' ends. I tried to imagine a chance encounter with Tainton on Western Avenue in twenty years' time and decided that my fingers' ends would remain unexcited. Life in the intervening years for Lord Byron had not, perhaps, been all that it was cracked up to be.

When war was declared, when we waited, in that far-off and hazy autumn, for the first attack, Oliver Pensotti and I spent a good deal of our time wondering if we would be slaughtered before we had actually been to bed with any sort of lady. This understandable concern was combined, in Oliver's case, with a deep anxiety as to whether he would ever be able to 'take breasts', those additions which he found hugely embarrassing and which distinguished Deanna Durbin from Ryecroft

Minor, the school tart, who was readily available for a box of chocolate biscuits.

Meanwhile the whole nation was in readiness for the shock of invasion. Oliver's mother left her flat in Charles Street and went to live in The Dorchester, which was built of concrete and believed to be impregnable to air raids. As humble privates in the Harrow Officers' Training Corps, Oliver and I were sent to Aldershot on manœuvres organized by the Brigade of Guards. We had chosen a peaceful spot, far away from the action where Tainton, having got hold of a box of flares, was staging his own display of pyrotechnics and setting fire to the undergrowth.

'I suppose we'll be really doing this in a year or two.'

'You may be doing it. I'll have a different sort of job, I imagine. Not that I shall be able to tell you much about it.'

'That'll make a change. I suppose you mean you'll be in the Secret Service, because of the languages they know you speak.'

'And because of the languages they don't know I speak. And because of the languages they know I don't speak.'

I was getting bored with the constant problem of decoding Pensotti. I went back to reading *The Doll's House*, which I had brought with me on manœuvres.

'My Ma's leaving The Dorchester,' Oliver surprisingly volunteered some information. 'She's going to America. It's the end of civilization as we know it. Chap in the Government told her that.'

Civilization as I knew it consisted of Keswick and keeping all your buttons done up for three years and being put to bed by a butler and the slow, meaningless translation of Latin poetry. I said that I couldn't wait for its destruction. Oliver got out his wire brushes and, swishing them against the top of his cap, crooned our favourite Deanna Durbin number:

> 'I love to climb
> An apple tree,
> Those apples green
> Are bad for me,
> They make me sick as sick can be,
> It's foolish but it's fun!'

A tall Guards officer wearing a white armband rode up to us on a huge horse. 'Bang, bang, you fellows!' he said. 'You're dead!'

'I know that's going to happen,' Oliver grumbled as we went back to the riding-school to get a mug of sweet tea, 'I shall be dead before I get a real chance to find out about breasts.'

The rumblings from Europe grew louder. Sandy Wilson joined our form and took to knitting long khaki objects, socks, mufflers and Balaclava helmets, comforts for the troops. When our form master protested at this click of needles, which recalled, in a somewhat sinister way, the foot of the guillotine, Sandy Wilson rightly said that it was the patriotic duty of all of us to do our bit for the boys at the front. The future composer of *The Boy Friend* also organized trips to London to see a play called *The Women* by Clare Boothe Luce which had not a man in the cast. Oliver and I saw it several times. He hired opera-glasses and took a careful view of the cleavages of the cast, but seemed to come no nearer reassurance.

We practised for air raids, going down to the cellars and wearing our gas masks while Gracie Fields sang *Wish me luck as you wave me goodbye* on Mr Lamb's wireless. Our housemaster took a gloomy view of the situation. 'War is hell,' he said. 'I remember the Somme and we never thought we should have to go through that again. Of course we could have nipped this one in the bud, if we'd only fought in Spain. Or even Czechoslovakia.'

'You mean, sir,' I asked, intolerably, 'that war is hell except in Spain or Czechoslovakia?' As a matter of fact I agreed with Mr Lamb entirely, but I had inherited what my father would call the art of the advocate, or the irritating habit of looking for the flaw in any argument.

'School songs' were a great and proud feature of Harrow life. We would assemble in the Speech Room and sing the compositions of long-dead housemasters and music masters, songs redolent of vanished boys playing cricket in knickerbockers, enjoying romantic friendships on summer evenings and going out to die in Afghanistan or on Majuba Hill: *Forty Years On*; *Jerry a Poor Little Fag*; *Byron lay, lazily lay, Hid from lesson and game away, Dreaming poetry all alone, Up on the top of Peachey stone.* That was the repertoire and then a new boy with a childish treble would pipe,

> 'Five hundred faces and all so strange
> Life in front of me, home behind. . . .'

And the gravelly-voiced, hairy-chinned, spotty seniors would trumpet in chorus,

> 'But the time will come when your heart will thrill
> And you'll think with joy of your time on the Hill!'

Winston Churchill, then First Lord of the Admiralty, came down to this strange ceremony which he apparently enjoyed. After the songs were over Mr Churchill climbed with difficulty on to the stage. He cannot have been more than sixty-five years old, but his ancient head emerged from the carapace of his dinner-jacket like the hairless pate of a tortoise, his old hand trembled on the handle of the walking-stick which supported him and his voice, when he spoke, was heavily slurred with brandy and old age. He seemed to us to be about a hundred and three.

'If they ever put *him* in charge of the war,' I whispered to Oliver, 'God help us all!'

'Oh, they won't do that,' he assured me. 'They'll never do that. Chap in the Government told my Ma.'

There were some excellent masters at Harrow and I shall be ever grateful to a large and rather unctuous cleric who taught us English. He read poetry in a fruity voice and used to congratulate himself on his sensitivity.

'You know, boys,' he used to say after reading us Blake's poem about heaven's wrath at caged birds, 'I once took out a gun. It was a fine, dewy morning and I saw a little hare sunning itself on a grassy knoll. I lifted my gun and took a careful aim and do you know what I did then?'

'Yes, sir,' we chorused, having heard the story from him fairly often. 'You *spared its life*.'

'That is right,' the Reverend Gentleman would smile complacently. 'It was, like me, one of God's humble creatures and I *spared* it.'

However, he introduced me to the Romantic poets who didn't figure in my father's anthology, and above all to Wordsworth. I think the Reverend Arthur Chalfont and I were the only people in the class who got any pleasure out of the old Sheep of the Lake District and we used to read each other long passages from *The Prelude* and *Tintern Abbey* to the fury of Tainton who said we sounded like a couple of expiring goats, and read *Titbits* under the desk with his hands in his pockets. I could see why Wordsworth was unpopular. He was clearly short on humour and capable of writing some of the silliest lines in the English language. I also knew that my great friend and ally, Lord Byron, couldn't stand Wordsworth for many years and objected to his frequently ham-fisted way with a stanza and his distinct lack of breeding and panache. All the same, in those endless afternoons when the Reverend Arthur Chalfont and I read to each other I came, slowly and reluctantly, to the conclusion that as between Wordsworth and Lord B., the old fumbler from the Lake District was by far the better poet.

Brought up in a strictly agnostic household I was not only unmusical but without a religious sense. When we had been forced to kneel by our beds at my prep school I had found it embarrassing to pretend to talk to God, to whom, if he existed, I felt I should have nothing very polite to say, and so I counted up to twenty-five and then climbed between the sheets. On Sunday, singing the hymn,

> 'Only believe and you shall see
> That Christ is all in all to thee'

I thought I would try it. I dug my nails into the palms of my hands, stood quite alone in the playground and forced myself to believe for at least ten minutes. Even so I couldn't see it. Our house in the country was all in all to me; my strange father, my friends, my theatrical ambitions and my chances of being chosen to act Richard II. Christ, however hard I made myself believe, I could only see as a remote and historical figure, far from my immediate concerns. And yet there is, I am sure, a religion in everyone which struggles for its own mystical satisfaction. I began to feel that my own came nearest to expression in whatever it was that Wordsworth felt he believed in:

> I have learned
> To look on nature, not as in the hour
> Of thoughtless youth; but hearing often-times
> The still, sad music of humanity,
> Nor harsh nor grating, though of ample power
> To chasten and subdue. And I felt
> A presence that disturbs me with the joy
> Of elevated thoughts; a sense sublime
> Of something far more deeply interfused,
> Whose dwelling is the light of setting suns,
> And the round ocean and the living air,
> And the blue sky, and in the mind of man.

I read that then as I do now, feeling close to tears, and with a sense of wonder which I'm sure must be known to those who are accustomed to religious contemplation and gain pleasure from Evensong on summer evenings in country churches. I shall always be intensely grateful to Mr Chalfont for teaching me about Wordsworth and can even forgive him for sparing the hare.

There were other good things about Harrow. Martin Witteridge and I joined the Art Society and we used to go off on bicycles to make water-colour sketches of Ruislip reservoir under the guidance of Mr Nares, the wanly good-looking Art Master who used to ask us if we could 'see anything that gave us joy'. On the way home Witteridge and I would drink gin and lime in suburban pubs and he would tell me about his mother who had, he claimed, a truly wonderful sense of humour, his beautiful cousins and his uncle who had been an equerry to the King.

Witteridge asked me to stay with his family. His father was a red-haired ramrod of a man, dressed in the uniform of the Irish Guards, who went off to the War Office each morning with a briefcase which Witteridge and I inspected for secret documents. We found it contained nothing but a small bottle of milk and a tomato sandwich. Witteridge had told me that his mother loved practical jokes and she would be first deceived and then endlessly amused if I came to stay wearing a false moustache and talking in a thick Hungarian accent. Although I was nervous during my first stay I did this, fortified by a good many gin and limes, but Lady Witteridge did nothing but ask me polite questions about my family and life at Harrow, and the beautiful cousins, who were uniformly dressed in twinsets and pearls, didn't speak to me at all. After lunch I abandoned the moustache and we went out for another lengthy pub-crawl on our bicycles. We took with us Witteridge's younger brother Tom, who went to Stowe, was extremely good-looking, drew with real talent and irritated us greatly by saying that he liked to sleep next to 'young warm flesh' and *never found it at all hard to come by*.

By the end of a year Mr Churchill had taken over the Government and began to look much younger. Oliver Pensotti and I met in London one winter evening during the holidays. We went for a drink in the bar of the Normandy Hotel where Oliver got into conversation with an ATS named Jeannie, as the bombs started to fall. The sound of breaking glass, the sweet taste of gin and lime, the peril of arbitrary thuds and the silent presence of the rather chunky Jeannie, who smiled but hardly spoke, added to the excitement of the evening. Months before, a fire-bomb had destroyed the kitchen of my father's flat in the Temple and he now lived all the time in the country, potting up, pricking out, trying to get enough petrol to keep the grass cut and getting up early in the black-out to travel to London to deal with the rising tide of divorce. So we went back to the empty flat and sat among the dust-sheets and the ruins of the kitchen. I

found several bottles of port which we drank; descending on a founda-
tion of gin and lime they made the room lurch like a ship at sea. I started
to tell Jeannie about Lord Byron and his fatal love for his half-sister, but
she was looking at Oliver in a strangely fixed sort of way and whispered
words I found extremely enigmatic, 'Have you got a rubber?'

Almost at once they moved into the bedroom. I was left alone with
my memories of his fatal Lordship's love life and pulled down, from my
father's dusty shelves, a book of his poems:

> So, we'll go no more a roving
> So late into the night,
> Though the heart be still as loving,
> And the moon be still as bright.
> For the sword outwears its sheath,
> And the soul wears out the breast.
> And the heart must pause to breathe,
> And love itself have rest.

The crashes were coming nearer. I had a momentary fear of my roving
being put a stop to before it had even begun, my sword being laid to rest
before it had worn out anything at all.

In due course the happy couple re-emerged and the ATS went off to
rejoin her regiment.

'Well,' I said to Oliver. 'How on earth did you manage?'

'Manage?'

'About the breasts, of course.'

'Perfectly all right.' Oliver gave a smile of satisfied achievement. 'You
hardly notice them at all.'

6

'YOU WANT TO BE A WRITER?' MY FATHER SAID, AFTER I HAD told him that I had sold my first short story to the *Harrovian* for ten bob. 'My dear boy, have some sort of consideration for your unfortunate wife. You'll be sitting around the house all day wearing a dressing-gown, brewing tea and stumped for words. You'll be far better off in the law. That's the great thing about the law, it gets you out of the house.'

The war, which had removed most of the young barristers, had done wonders for my father's practice. He rose, most days, in Court, fixed witnesses with his clear blue, sightless eyes and lured them into confessions of adultery, cruelty or wilful refusal to consummate their marriages. As soon as he could he caught the train back from London (no after Court conference with him was ever known to last more than twenty minutes) to the wonders of his garden. I don't know if I can describe it or whether is has become, during the years I have lived here, over-familiar, like faces you see every day.

In his twenty acres of chalky fields there were two inexplicable dells, great holes in the ground which long ago may have been burial-places, or gravel pits, and are now filled with beech trees. Near to them my father built a small thirties' house with white walls and green tiles, a building in the sort of Spanish musical-comedy tradition, handed down through the garages on the Great West Road, which pleased the architect he employed. It still has light-fittings which might have come from the Savoy Hotel. Away from the house he planned huge herbaceous borders to stretch away to a field of magnolias and rarer ornamental trees. In the spring the copses are full of daffodils and narcissi. Tall, pale green and white Japanese flowering cherries, which he planted, tremble in the twilight like enormous ghosts. He planned the large kitchen garden with fruit cages in which loganberries and white raspberries, gooseberries and melons and strawberries grew, usually in the company of some panic-stricken and imprisoned bird. It is a great feeding-place for marauders from the beech woods. Pheasants, jays and pigeons ravish the vegetables.

Deer, which have gone back to nature after escaping from a nearby park, glide across the lawn in the misty mornings and eat the rose-buds. At night there is a great noise of owls, and in my father's day we often used to see glow-worms, although they seem rarer now.

As my father could see none of these splendours he got my mother to describe them to him and in the evenings he would dictate to her a log, a diary of the garden's activities which also contained glimpses, cursorily noted, of human endeavour. Turning the thick volumes, written out in my mother's clear art-school handwriting, I can find out exactly what went wrong with the peas in 1942 and how they coped with greenfly on the roses. It is harder to discover when I was married, had children, got divorced or called to the bar, although most of the facts are there somewhere, stuck at the far end of the herbaceous border. 'A most miserable cold and wet May,' a typical entry reads. 'Laburnums are now at their best. Mrs Anthony Waterer and Lady Waterlow are the only roses in flower. All liquidambars appear to be dead, but remaining newly planted trees and shrubs are doing well. John left for Paris after taking his Real Property exam, which he failed.' or, 'The cats have brought up two litters by stealth. Smith has planted out the wallflowers, staked the borders and started to clean the strawberry beds. The green woodpecker flew through the French windows while we were sitting here. Now the divorce is over John is to be married in August.'

The work in the garden, which had grown so out of proportion to the house it surrounded, was never-ending. My father sat on a wooden stool wearing a straw hat, groping for weeds and dead-heads, with my mother beside him keeping up a running commentary. We had a gardener called Mr Smith, who looked very much like the late King George VI, and a gardener's boy who got blamed for everything and sat behind the potting-shed reading *Titbits* and wrote 'The Garden of Eden' on all the plant labels.

I cannot discover that I did much gardening in those days. Not long after I met my first wife there is an entry which reads, 'On Christmas Eve John and I amused ourselves by digging a hole and planting the Eucryphia in it', but I think I must have been waiting anxiously for a letter or a telephone call, and turned to the entertaining hole for relief. There was one duty my father and I always shared, whenever I was available, and that was drowning the earwigs.

The ceremony of the earwigs, which became, in my father's garden, a cross between Trooping the Colour and a public execution, had its origins in my most distant childhood. My father was fond of big, highly-coloured and feathery dahlias, large as side-plates or ladies' hats, and these blooms were a prey to earwigs. I have no idea where my father learnt to fight these pests in the way he did, or in the macabre imagination of what tweedy gardening expert the plan was born. It suffices to say that is was a scheme of devilish cunning. Stakes were planted in the ground near the dahlias and on top of each stake hung an inverted flowerpot lined with straw. The gorged earwig, having feasted on the dahlia, would climb into the flowerpot for a peaceful nap in the straw, from which it was rudely awakened by my father and myself on our evening rounds. We would empty the flowerpots into a bucket of water. On a good foray we might drown up to a hundred earwigs, which my father would pronounce, with relish, to be a 'moderately satisfactory bag'.

The times I most clearly remember with my father were the long walks we took together when I would guide him through the dark, insect-buzzing woods, steering him past the tentacles of bramble, keeping him away from branches where the gamekeepers had gibbeted magpies and squirrels as a warning to others. We used to sit by the fire at night, he in the wing-chair I still use, massaging his sightless eyes, and I read him what I had begun to write, another novel about Henley, the town below us in the valley, the Brewery and the Regatta. Sometimes he would laugh at the jokes. Sometimes he said, 'Sorry stuff', or, 'Rather poor fooling', and I knew, furiously, that he was right.

In the summer after the war started I began to take a less active part in the earwig hunts and I even missed the walks. I had made friends. This was not an easy thing to do while living with my father due to his extremely hostile attitude to 'visitors' whom he dreaded even more than leaf curl on the peach trees or earwigs at the dahlias.

I had met 'Daphne' (Mrs Cox) when she opened a bookshop in the town. She was small and seemed to me extraordinarily glamorous, like a pocket-sized Garbo or Marlene Dietrich. She moved around her shop in a haze of Chanel perfume which she must have 'laid down' before the shortages of war began. She wore a white skirt and shoes and seemed always, in that inappropriate setting, dressed for a stroll before lunch along the Croisette or the Promenade des Anglais. When I asked if she had a book I wanted, I think it was a novel by Rex Warner, she asked me up to her cottage, which turned out to be almost next door to my father's house, and offered to lend me her own copy. There I met her great friend Betty (known as 'Bill') Baker, a tall, handsome woman who always dressed in men's clothing (not just a more masculine version of female attire, but real men's clothes, tweed jackets and corduroy trousers bought from a Gent's Outfitters in Reading). From a photograph which stood on their window-sill it appeared that Daphne and 'Bill', at a formal dinner party before the war, had worn white mess-jackets with boiled shirts, wing-collars, black bow-ties and evening trousers.

Looking back on it I can't think why they had the kindness to bother with me; but they invited me to teas and dinners and parties with other pairs of 'girls' who lived, refugees from Bloomsbury and Cap Ferrat, in little nests dotted round our part of the Chilterns. They talked about characters who existed for me only in the world of myth: Cocteau and Lord Berners, Lytton Strachey and Colette. I borrowed books from them and bought none, filling the gaps in my entirely English education with *Les Parents Terribles* and *Le Grand Meaulnes* and *Claudine à l'Ecole* and encountering a now forgotten novelist called Julien Green, whose Kafkaesque stories of strange French country houses helped raise my own standards of realism a few inches above the ground. Sometimes I would meet Mrs Cox in London; she would take me to dinner at her bridge club and I sat beside her while the bombs thudded outside and she played cards with a gold-and-tortoiseshell cigarette-holder between scarlet lips and said things to me like, 'You know who I mean by Lady Abdy?' and I nodded deceitfully, vainly trying to give the impression that I knew exactly who she meant.

So my life at home became split between my father's house, where he sat at dinner with the wireless set beside him, his fingers itching to turn on ITMA or *Garrison Theatre* if the arguments became tedious; and Mrs Cox's cottage, where the domesticated doves fluttered in at the window and rested on the statue of a Negro page-boy and Mrs Cox's daughter brought home *her* girl-friend who was called 'Bobby' and who worked in Bourne and Hollingsworth, and where we turned the pages of *The New Statesman and Nation* and *Horizon* and listened to Charles Trenet on the gramophone.

'How do you get on with those women who live next door. The ones you're always visiting?' my father asked.

'They're very interesting. They knew Jean Cocteau,' and I added, in the hope of shocking him at last, 'Cocteau smoked opium.'

'Oh, never smoke opium,' my father warned me. 'Gives you constipation. Terrible binding effect.' And he added one of his best lines, 'Have you ever seen the pictures of the wretched poet Coleridge? He smoked opium. Take a look at Coleridge, he was green about the gills and a stranger to the lavatory.'

So my father's house and Mrs Cox's became the two poles of my existence. And it was in Mrs Cox's ornate and rural Sapphic retreat that I had my first heterosexual experience, no doubt with consequences to my psyche so traumatic that I haven't fully recovered from them. At the time it seemed like a piece of amazing good luck.

There was a party one evening at Mrs Cox's to which many of the neighbouring couples of 'girls' were invited, together with some other Bloomsbury refugees from the cottages along the edge of the common. Among them was Sarah, who was staying with her mother, a stalwart of the Charlotte Street pubs and Gordon Square parties. Sarah had a small, heart-shaped face, and eyes of unexpectedly different colours. She wore a beret on the side of her head as though she were acting in a film with Jean Gabin, and I had totally mistaken her, in the early part of the evening, for one of the 'girls'.

Mrs Cox, or was it 'Bill', suggested a game, a party-stopper which I never played before or since. We took turns to sit blindfold on a stool and were kissed by the other players. The game was to guess who kissed you. To my astonishment I found myself being kissed with some thoroughness and, on removing the blindfold, found that it was by Sarah. We both lingered when the party was over and Mrs Cox, who had always showed me much kindness, lent us her spare bedroom.

For the first ten minutes I cursed the liberated novelists I had been reading at school. Why the hell couldn't they be more explicit? Aldous Huxley never talked about anything but a thousand butterfly caresses (for which there scarcely seemed the time or the demand) and then went into a row of dots. D.H. Lawrence rambled on about harebells and dark forces stirring the loins, without any clear indication of how the thing was actually done. In the course of time, however, I began to feel that the evening was not only like an astonishing and undeserved win at roulette, a jackpot which I had done nothing to deserve, not only the end of childhood, the start of life, a day-trip to a country I only knew imperfectly from reading the guidebooks and hardly hoped to visit, but something which, without great difficulty, I might come to enjoy. I was not in that state very long, however, before the door was flung open and there stood Mrs Cox and 'Bill' both wearing dressing-gowns and smoking furiously.

50

'I can't imagine what you think you're doing,' Mrs Cox said. 'This isn't a brothel!'

I thought that what we were doing was perfectly obvious and she had invited us to stay; but 'Bill' was looking at us as though we were a nasty case of slug damage among the cabbage plants. 'What on earth would your father say?' she asked.

Again there was an answer: my father had never spoken to 'Bill' Baker and no doubt never would. If she approached him to report on my doings he would have vanished, as fast as my mother could lead him, into the shrubbery. That was the answer but it wasn't worth giving. Sarah probably hit on the truth of the matter when she said, 'You don't like us because we're not queer.'

'I think', said Mrs Cox in the husky, unanswerable tones of Greta Garbo as Queen Christina, dismissing a couple of hundred unwanted guests, 'you'd better put on your clothes and leave now.'

So it was that my first experience of love-making was concluded out on the common, among the sharp, musky bracken where I had taken off my glasses to avoid a view of Iris's knickers, and played houses with the Mullard children. As we walked home I was keeping up an unconvincing performance of someone who made love and was thrown out by Lesbians most evenings, and we said we would meet again soon, probably tomorrow.

'What's that?' said my father when I got home. 'Is that the boy?'

'Yes, dear,' said my mother, who was reading out the crossword puzzle clues to him. 'He's back. He went to a party at Mrs Cox's.'

'A party, eh? That can't have been much fun. Well, now you're back, how about a settler?'

So I sat down by the dying fire and read a poem to settle my father down for the night. I chose one of his favourite sonnets:

> The expense of spirit in a waste of shame
> Is lust in action; and, till action, lust
> Is perjur'd, murderous, bloody, full of blame,
> Savage, extreme, rude, cruel, not to trust;
> Enjoyed no sooner but despised straight;
> Past reason hunted. . . .

I read it in a world-weary voice, I thought. I knew all there was to know on the subject.

The next day I went to her mother's cottage to find Sarah, but she had gone back to Cambridge. Eventually she parted from her husband, and we shared a room for a while in Hampstead. I now realize that there is something I haven't written about Sarah, suppressing it with that embarrassment which prevented our mentioning my father's blindness. She was lame. One of her heels wouldn't touch the ground and, while walking, she appeared to run. It was the result of some childhood disability which it became too late to correct. She was eccentric, funny and she never complained. I think of her often, and always with gratitude.

7

I AM AN ADVOCATE, MY FATHER WAS BOTH A FINE ADVOCATE and a good lawyer. He understood the law and loved it and when it was at its most obscure, as in the doctrine of the 'renvoi' in the cases on domicile, or of 'dependent relative revocation' in Probate, he found it as enjoyable as budding roses or doing *The Times* crossword. To the courtroom advocate, who only needs a basic instinct about the rules of evidence and the ability to look things up, law is an unwelcome mystery which only appeals to academics or those who practise in the Chancery Division. To me the law seems like a sort of maze through which a client must be led to safety, a collection of reefs, rocks and underwater hazards through which he or she must be piloted. The basic morality on which law is founded has always seemed to me crudely inferior to those moral values which everyone must work out for themselves; and the results of even the best laws, when consistently applied, are bound to be intolerable in many individual cases. Moreover the law exists when it is being lived through people's lives and in Courts. Looked at in a book, or belted out as a lecture, it can have only a theoretical interest and hold a tenuous grasp on the attention.

'I think we might run to Oxford,' my father had said, 'provided you fall in and read the law.' I still felt that my time was likely to be short and my future, as the news of the war grew more depressing, uncertain. In the meanwhile I fell in and read law with no real faith in ever surviving to practise it. Again I wondered about my father's choice. Why Oxford? He'd been at Cambridge and Brasenose was a college he'd only heard mentioned, in an apparently disparaging way, by someone in his Chambers many years before. But as he offered me Oxford like the sausages and scrambled eggs of the condemned man's breakfast, I felt it churlish to refuse.

Whenever I hear now of the appalling efforts, suffering and anxiety of those who are trying to get their children into the older universities, I think of my entrance examination with a pang of guilt. I went to

Brasenose and was led up some stairs by a college servant. After a long, solitary wait, a bald-headed man wearing carpet slippers and carrying an encyclopaedia of gastronomy came in. He handed me a passage from Lucretius, told me to translate it and shuffled away. I sat for a while puzzled by the complicated stanzas describing the nature of atoms, and then another door opened and I found myself staring at a pair of familiar scuffed suede shoes. Looking higher I saw knife-edged grey flannels, white teeth and well-brilliantined dark curls.

'Good God. Oliver! What're you doing here?'

'The same as you, but rather more efficiently.'

'I'm doing a sort of entrance test. It's not very easy.'

'Is it a test of our knowledge of Latin or our ingenuity? I have chosen to look at it as a test of ingenuity.'

'Look, there isn't time for all that. What do you mean?'

'The question isn't what I mean. It's what I did.' And, bubbling with mysterious laughter, Pensotti held up a small Latin dictionary he had been out to buy at Blackwells. With its aid we wrote out a translation and went to find our examiner. He was having lunch, reading a recipe from the book propped up on a stand in front of him whilst he feasted on – what was it, dried egg or spam salad? He took our work without a word and later we discovered that we had passed into Oxford. I never saw the bald gastronome again, or indeed very much of Brasenose College. It was taken over by the War Office and they sent us to Christ Church.

Oxford, after the Fall of France, as the black-out was pinned up in the Buttery, as Frank Pakenham, not yet Lord Longford and then history tutor at Christ Church, was shot in the foot by a cook whilst drilling with the Home Guard in the Meadows, was at the end of an era and I was at the end of my extraordinary middle-class, thirties' education. I can't say that I came out of this bizarre hot-house and met the 'real world' at Oxford. That encounter, intoxicating, painful, invigorating, hilarious and tragic, was held from me until, in the company of GIS, camera-men, electricians, aircraft workers with their Veronica Lake hairdos tied up in head-scarves, continuity girls and prop-men, I stopped being educated and came, belatedly, to life. Meanwhile I lay becalmed at Oxford.

The Oxford of the twenties and thirties was still there, like college claret, but it was rationed, on coupons, and there was not very much of it left. The famous characters still behaved as though they lingered in the pages of *Decline and Fall*. They were famous for being nothing except

Oxford characters; once they left their natural habitat in Magdalen or The House they grew faint and dim and ended up down back corridors in Bush House, or as announcers on Radio Monte Carlo. They had double-barrelled names like Edward Faith-Peterson and Tommy Motte-Smith. By day they lay naked in their rooms, listening to Puccini or to Verdi's *Requiem*. By night they would issue into the black-out, camel-hair coats slung across their shoulders, bow-ties from Hall Bros settled under their lightly-powdered chins, to take the exotic dinner (maximum spending allowed under the Ministry of Food regulations five bob) at the smartest restaurants. What did it matter if the omelette were of dried egg or the drink rationed Algerian or even black-market Communion wine topped up with spirits (Gin and Altars)? They still talked about Firbank and Beardsley and how, sometime in the long vacation, they had met Brian Howard, supposed model for an Evelyn Waugh character, itching in his 'A.C. Plonk's' uniform in the downstairs bar at the Ritz.

So at Oxford after Dunkirk the fashion was to be homosexual. It seems that it was only after the war, with the return of the military, that heterosexuality came to be completely tolerated. As it was, my sporadic adventures with WAAFS and girls from St Hilda's, my grandly titled engagement to a student of book illustration at the Slade, were subjects I preferred not to discuss with Tommy Motte-Smith when he invited me and my friend Oliver for a five-shilling blow-out at The George.

The high life of Oxford was something I never encountered when I first moved into my rooms in Meadow Buildings. To my dismay I found I was sharing them with Parsons, a tall man with bicycle-clips and a pronounced Adam's apple, who tried to lure me into the Bible Society. One night Oliver and I boiled up Algerian wine, college sherry and a bottle of Bols he had stolen from his mother's flat, in Parsons' electric kettle. When I recovered from the draught I found Parsons wearing cycle-clips and kneeling over me in prayer. I also heard, coming from down the corridor, the sound of Brahms's Fourth Symphony like music from some remote paradise.

In fact my memory of Oxford seems, looking back over a vast distance, to consist almost entirely of Brahms's Fourth Symphony, a piece of music of which I have become decreasingly fond, as I have lost the taste for bow-ties, Balkan Sobranie cigarettes and sherry and Bols boiled up in an electric kettle. But that music came from someone who did affect my view of the world, and of whom I still think with gratitude and bewilderment when I remember his serene life and extraordinary death.

My father, to whom I owe so much, never told me the difference between right and wrong: now, I think that's why I remain so greatly in his debt. But Henry Winter, who slowly and with enormous care sharpened a thorn needle to play Brahms on his huge gramophone, became a kind of yardstick, not of taste, but of moral behaviour. He had no doubts whatever about war, he knew that killing people was wrong. He looked forward with amused calm to the call-up, the refusal to put on uniform, the arguments before the tribunals and the final consignment to Pentonville or the Fire Service. He read Classics, and read them in the way I read Isherwood or Julien Green. He would sit in a squeaking basket chair, smoking a pipe and giving me his version of chunks of Homer and Euripides which, up to then, I had been trained to regard as almost insoluble crossword puzzles or grammarians' equations with no recognizable human content. I was born of tone-deaf parents, and in the school songs had been instructed to open my mouth soundlessly so that no emergent discord might mar the occasion. Yet Winter slowly, painstakingly introduced me to music, and the pleasure I take in it now is due entirely to him.

Winter's rejection of violence, and what seemed to me the extraordinarily gentle firmness of his moral stance, was the result of no religious conviction. He was courageously sceptical, fearlessly agnostic, open and reasonable with none of the tormented Christianity of my ex-roommate. Parsons had applied for a transfer after the desecration of his electric kettle and left me in solitary possession of a huge Gothic sitting-room and a bedroom almost the size of the waiting-room at St Pancras Station, with a chipped wash-basin in which I kept a smoked salmon, caught by my Aunt Daisy in Devon in defiance of rationing.

I suppose Oxford's greatest gift is friendship, for which there is all the time in the world. After Oxford there are love affairs, marriages, working relationships, manipulations, lifelong enemies, but even then, in rationed, blacked-out Oxford, there were limitless hours for talking, drinking, staying up all night, going for walks with a friend. Winter and I were emerging from the chrysalis of schoolboy homosexuality. At first the girls we loved were tennis-playing virgins posed, like Proust's androgynous heroine, forever unobtainable against a background of trees in the park, and carrying rackets and string bags full of Slazengers. There is nothing like sexual frustration to give warmth to friendship, which flourishes in prisons, armies, on Arctic expeditions and did well in wartime Oxford. Winter and I became inseparable and when, as time went on, I began to do things without him I felt twinges of guilt about my infidelity.

I had more time for friendship as I found the legal syllabus enormously dull and spent as little time at it as possible. To fulfil the bargain with my father, I acquired a working knowledge of Roman Law and after a year I knew how to manumit a slave, adopt an elderly senator or contract a marriage by the ceremony of 'brass and scales', skills which I have never found of great service in the Uxbridge Magistrates Court. Roman Law was taught us by a mountainous old man who drank a bottle of whisky a day and who had, like the Royal Family, changed his German name for an old English one. He peered at me through glasses thick as ginger-beer bottles, and was forever veering away from Justinian's views on Riparian ownership to Catullus's celebration of oral sex, a change of subject which I found extremely welcome. Returning to Oxford by train from a legal dinner in London, this ancient Latinist mistook the carriage door for the lavatory and stepped out into the black-out and on to the flying railway lines outside Didcot. After his death I gave up Roman Law.

Other subjects I found encased in a number of slim volumes with titles like *Tort in a Nutshell*, *Potted Real Property* and *All You Need to Know About Libel and Slander*. I read them listening to Winter's gramophone, or as we punted down the river and the ATS in the long grass whistled *You Are My Sunshine* or sang, 'Keep smiling throo, Just as you, Used to do, Till the good times come again one sunny day'. If these were not good times we were deceived by never having known anything better.

The time came when Winter was about to face the tribunal which was to test the genuineness of his conscience. There was a man called Charles Dimont, a journalist and a character of great eminence in the pacifist world, who was said to be able to give Winter a lesson in how best to put his reluctance to kill people to a bench of sceptical and safely patriotic magistrates. Winter told me that a favourite question was, 'What would you do if you saw a German raping your grandmother?' to which he intended to reply, 'Wait until he'd finished and then bury the dear old lady again.' We went by bus to Boar's Hill, where Charles Dimont lived. When we got to his cottage he had a bad cold and was wearing a dressing-gown. There seemed to be a large number of small children about, one of whom was dropping raspberry jam into *The Bible*

Designed To Be Read As Literature. In the corner was a dark young woman of remarkable beauty who said nothing and looked as if she were heartily sick of the tramp of conchies through her sitting-room. Charles Dimont told Winter that it was very difficult to persuade the tribunal that you really didn't like killing people unless you believed in God. He offered us a cup of tea, but the pot was empty and anyway we had to go.

As we waited for the bus I had no idea that Charles Dimont was about to change his mind and obtain an infantry commission. I had still less idea that in some distant peace I would marry the dark, silent Mrs Dimont and bring up her children. And I had no sort of hint of the extraordinary melodrama of violence in which Winter himself would die. I only knew that I was determined to avoid the heroism of the tribunals. I thought I would probably end up in the RAF ground staff.

The war was a time for poetry. I tried to write modern ballads, heavily influenced by Auden, and was very proud when one or two got into *Cherwell*. Since those days I haven't attacked a poem and I hope poetry is for my old age, like spending every day in the garden. John Heath-Stubbs was a remarkable poet then at Oxford, and Sidney Keyes was a war poet who met a war poet's tragic death. When twilight fell over Peckwater Quad a pale, dark-haired Michael Hamburger, moving past the crumbling columns where he claimed bats flitted, used to come to my rooms with a heavy but always gleeful despair and read me his translations of Rilke and Hölderlin. He was also besotted by the tennis-playing girls and seemed in constant fear that one might surrender to him, thereby breaking the spell of Gothic gloom in which he moved so happily.

Starstruck by poets, Michael Hamburger and I used to travel up to London. Drinking beer in the Swiss Pub in Old Compton Street we might even be spoken to by Dylan Thomas or Roy Campbell, or by the Scots painters Colquhoun and MacBride who wore kilts and were inseparable, or by the surrealist John Banting who was quite bald and used to take his false teeth out and buy them a ham sandwich. Sometimes I met Mrs Cox's daughter there, wearing her warden's uniform and accompanied by her silent girl-friend from Bourne and Hollingsworth, and we would discuss the latest news from the common and I would try, in vain, to discover what had happened to Sarah. We would go to the pubs in Charlotte Street in which sat older women with long memories, like Nina Hamnett whose youthful torso, sculpted by Gaudier-Brzeska, stood in the Tate Gallery, but who then seemed old and rather lost in the Blitz and was sometimes, at the end of the evening, sick into her handbag.

When the pubs were shut we went to a terrible cellar called the 'Coffee Ann' where Lucian Freud always sat with a beautiful girl at a corner table, and a huge Alsatian dog lay on a clapped-out billiard-table, chewing the ivory balls. A verse was pinned up in the lavatory which read, 'It's no use standing on the seat, the bloody crabs can jump ten feet.'

One drunken lunch-time Dylan Thomas, telling us in his breathy, Charles Laughton voice, that he was looking for a girl with an aperture as small as a mouse's ear-hole, led us to the offices of *Horizon* where Stephen Spender and Cyril Connolly, large as life, were sitting drinking tea with a girl wearing wooden-soled, hinged utility shoes. I remember none of the literary conversation. Full of brown ale I was too occupied in trying to stop the room from tipping gradually on to its side.

Oliver Pensotti left to become, thanks to his knowledge of languages, a subaltern in the Intelligence Corps. He bought a sickly-looking poison ring from an antique shop in Broad Street and wore it with his uniform, dark glasses and scuffed suede shoes. He looked less like a spy catcher than some minor member of an unsuccessful South American military junta.

Henry Winter's sincerity was obvious to the tribunal which tried his case and he was sent to a Pacifist Service Unit near Paddington Station. There he helped to dig bodies out of the rubble after air raids and carry the injured to hospital.

I was examined on a number of occasions by a puzzled doctor in North Oxford. Not only could I not see distant, or not so distant, objects with any clarity, but I was painfully thin, had doubtful lungs and appeared to be wasting away, a process which now seems to have gone into reverse. It was clear that I would have to look for a job in the war, that of a divorce barrister not coming within the category of a 'reserved occupation'.

I did my best to enjoy what was left of Oxford. Encouraged by my mother I had always drawn a little and I went to the Slade School which had been moved to the Ashmolean Museum, and sat in the life class before large nude ladies who were pink on the side nearest the radiator and blue with cold on the other. Occasionally the teacher, a small grey-haired man in a bow-tie, would sit beside me, smelling faintly of Haig and Haig, and do a perfect drawing of the radiator aspect and leave without comment. I met a girl at the Slade and we became engaged. When I showed her my art work she suggested that I stick to writing. I realized that this was sound advice and took it. Apart from this strongly-held opinion she was very quiet and gentle and came from Wales. I took Elizabeth and her mother out to dinner at The George and, overcome with excitement and too much Algerian wine, seized a silk-stockinged leg to fondle under the table. I looked up to see the mother glowering at me over the grilled spam. I had chosen the wrong leg.

My engagement, like my enthusiasm for Oxford, wilted. Jack Beddington, son of a barrister my father knew, and a neighbour in the country, was in charge of propaganda films at the Ministry of Information. Mr Beddington, many years before, had seen me do a 'Punch and Judy' show in my puppet-theatre and took the view that the performance showed just the talent needed to wage the movie war against Fascism. He offered me a job for when I came down from Oxford. I got a 'war degree'. It was given with no ceremony and luckily for me there were no classes. It was just one more utility BA 'in a nutshell'. I left Oxford station for the last time and went up the line to London, scene of all excitement, to the Blitz and to the Swiss Pub and the Coffee Ann, to the bookshops in the Charing Cross Road and to the Ministry of Information with the girls with pillar-box red lipstick and padded shoulders and Betty Grable curls, and silver barrage balloons floating over gutted terraces in a blue sky, and to Winter's Pacifist Service Unit in Paddington.

The pacifists used to take turns in cooking, and the quality of the stew, when I went to visit Winter, depended on the varied talents of the pacifists on the rota. However bad the cooking there were always bitter arguments about the size of the helpings, on which subject the conscientious objectors, before my astonished eyes, almost came to blows. Only Winter remained imperturbably calm. After dinner was over and washed up he would fill his pipe and play the Brahms Fourth and tell me that he had seen so much of man's mayhem in the Blitz that he had decided to qualify as a doctor after the war. Although his education had been entirely classical, and his decision would mean his starting again with elementary science, he was prepared to work as a hospital porter and put in the necessary five or six years' study.

He also told me that he had fallen in love with the red-haired girl-friend of the leader of another Pacifist Service Unit. Her name was Lillian and one night after supper, and a movement of the Brahms, we went to visit her in a bed-sitting-room in a tall grey house left standing like a solitary tooth in the decayed mouth of a crescent behind Westbourne Grove. Lillian was strikingly handsome, but whilst we were talking to her quite innocently, she heard her lover come up the stairs and she told us to go out and hide on the fire-escape as his visit would only be a short one.

As we did so, a small, stocky pacifist in ARP uniform erupted into the room. He heard some stirring behind the black-out curtains and immediately opened the wardrobe, pulled out an army rifle and, loading it in a practised sort of way, advanced on our hiding-place at the top of the fire-escape. When he saw us he accused us both of the gravest misconduct with Lillian and offered to 'wing' us both in a sensitive area. Winter took the pipe out of his mouth and smiled reasonably.

'You can't possibly do that,' he said. 'You're the head man of a Pacifist Service Unit. You totally rule out the use of force. Isn't that what you told your tribunal?'

I saw no future in a political argument about violence in public and private situations. I could see that the collapse of Western Civilization might seem of lesser importance to the irate pacifist than the suspected gang-bang of Lillian. I dragged Winter away down the iron stairway and didn't stop running until we had got to a safe bar in Notting Hill Gate. There was a great deal in the incident which should have given me a clue as to the future of Henry Winter.

8

FILMS, THERE IS NO DOUBT ABOUT IT, HAVE AFFORDED ME over the years many such things of value as experience, laughs, foreign travel, disappointments and lessons in the transience of human hopes. If working for the movies has brought me only a few great satisfactions it is probably my fault, or the fact that satisfied writers in the film industry are about as numerous as black Africans in the South African government. The writer, in the eyes of many film producers, still seems to occupy a position of importance somewhere between the wardrobe lady and the tea boy, with this difference: it's often quite difficult to replace the wardrobe lady.

The films that were being made by the Ministry of Information during the last war were largely documentaries. Why a childish aptitude for the 'Punch and Judy' show, a form of drama involving fictional executions, ghosts, crocodiles, and married relations of a savagery which make Strindberg's plays look like 'The Archers', should have led Jack Beddington to believe that my talents were best suited to the 'Documentary Cinema', I don't know. However that was the view he took, and had he not done so my lifelong, maddening, frustrating but somehow irresistible love affair with moving pictures might never have started. As it was, it began, in the least romantic way possible, when I went to live in Slough, a place handy for Pinewood Studios and the 'Crown Film Unit'. I lodged with an aircraft fitter and his wife. When I started as a fourth assistant film director I was on a salary of £2 a week; for thirty shillings the fitter gave me a room and the run of my teeth.

The title 'fourth assistant' director may sound impressive. The duties connected with it are not, however, of an artistic nature. I had to get the director's tea, buy him cigarettes, park the lady producer's car in the mornings and call 'Quiet please!' at the start of each 'take'. It is always hard to know where to be on a film set; you are forever treading on a cable or in immediate danger of being in the shot. Those fears added to my natural diffidence to produce an almost inaudible, 'Quiet please!' during which the technicians went on hammering, pushing heavy lamps about or placing bets. Rebuked for this I once yelled, 'Quiet, you bastards!' in a sort of hysteria, as a result of which the whole unit threatened to strike.

'Once the film bug bites you,' said the Head of the Crown Film Unit, a man called Ian Dalrymple who smoked cigarettes through a white paper holder, 'you never recover.' In the days when I bumped the producer's car short-sightedly into the petrol pumps, or watched the aircraft fitter asleep in his armchair all the evening, his mouth open and his top row of teeth fallen, as often as not, on to the bottom, or lost fifty electricians on a train journey to Liverpool, or when the camera crew set fire to their table in the Adelphi Hotel by lighting cigarettes with strips of film, I thought that if enthusiasm for films was a disease it was probably curable, at least as far as I was concerned. I didn't know how right, in fact, Ian Dalrymple was.

Documentary films, during the war, reached the peak of their prestige. They emerged from small beginnings, being based on the theories of John Grierson, a puritanical Scot with a contempt for Hollywood, and the early work of the Post Office Film Unit, for which Auden wrote scripts and Benjamin Britten wrote music. Documentaries were called upon to play a major part in the propaganda of war. One director of genius emerged, Humphrey Jennings, who had been a surrealist painter and whose films were poetic and touching in a way that our more orthodox products never were. In fact most of the films we made were conspicuously lacking in human interest. Their great concern was with machines, usually bombers or other engines of death, which were shown rising slowly into the air to the music of Dr Vaughan Williams. Human beings were treated with less respect. They never said much to each other except, 'Roger and out,' or, 'What about a brew-up, George?' or, 'Gerry's a bit naughty tonight'. They sat stolidly on tractors or watched the return of the herring fleet with dogged patience or, if women, toiled at the assembly line with their hair tied up in scarves. I don't remember any of our films in which the characters complained about the war or tried to fiddle extra expenses on the fire-watching or had love affairs with the wives of soldiers posted to Burma or the Western Desert, although these seemed to be the chief occupation of the carpenters, plasterers and electricians with whom I spent my time. For a great deal of it we played Pontoon in a disused prop-room, among the thrones and four-posters of Korda's pre-war film empire, totally unaccompanied by the music of Dr Vaughan Williams.

'Seen the King last night, John?' Charlie, the prop-man, used to call out as he spotted me lurking in a corner of the 'Ops Room' set, trying to avoid the camera or the all-seeing eye of Doris, the lady producer with the fur coat slung over her shoulders, khaki trousers and short cheroot, who might, if she spotted me, bark an order to fetch her car or the director's vitamin pills. At first I didn't know whether Charlie's daily question was based on a misconception of my social status. Did he think Old Harrovians were in daily contact with Royalty? Then he would repeat the formula more slowly, making the words clearer.

'Had it in last night, John?'

I tried an enigmatic smile, not wishing to admit that I had spent the evening dozing on the leatherette settee opposite the aircraft fitter.

'Didn't spend out on her I hope.'

Charlie was as anxious as I was about my financial situation.

'No, I didn't spend out on her.'

'Never invest a penny piece till she's given you one. That's the rule, boy. Then you can run to a half of mild and bitter between the two of you.'

It was a new approach to courtship. At Oxford I had bought books on credit and sold them immediately second-hand to take 'Home Students' out to dinner at the Mitre, with nothing at all to show for it. I was in a new world, from which, in my one-class, one-sex schools and the isolation of my father's house and garden, I had long been segregated. It was a world full of sauce sandwiches and fiddled petty-cash vouchers and playing Solo with the 'Hourly Boys' and tea-breaks and Union get-togethers when the sense of the meeting was put by Brother Chair, and girls who were known generically as 'smiggett', and where the expression 'having your greens' no longer meant finishing up the cabbage and making a clean plate. They were days which began in the cold light of dawn in a mocked-up gun emplacement and ended in the public bar of the Crooked Billet at Iver Heath, singing *Roll out the barrel*, or in an Uxbridge cinema watching Alice Faye or Carmen Miranda. They were times when I first experienced the only sort of group loyalty I have ever been able to manage, to a collection of people tirelessly engaged on one piece of work, producing a film, or a play, or a television programme or, perhaps later, defending a man accused of murder.

64

'With Venus entering your birth sign this is a good week for you to make up a long-standing dispute with a partner.' Jill, the continuity-girl, used to read the horoscope from her *Woman's Own* and I kept up the pretence of having a partner, a bit of 'smiggett' next door perhaps, or a little woman in St John's Wood. Jill also taught me many of the mysteries of the film business. When shooting in a street she used to put down five shillings on the expense sheet 'To buying a penny whistle', because there was a mythical child near all locations who wouldn't stop ruining the sound by playing this instrument until it was bought up at an exorbitant price. Jill also showed me how film scripts were set out on a page. It was information which later brought me trips to Honolulu and Hollywood and enabled me, on one happy occasion, to write a scene which brought all the traffic round Notre Dame Cathedral to a prolonged standstill.

INT. SET OF SUBMARINE. STUDIO. DAY.

LONG SHOT, establishing TWO ABLE SEAMEN sitting at a table in the confined quarters of the submarine. They are wearing white sweaters and drinking cups of char. Around them mill members of the Film Unit, including the DIRECTOR, DORIS, JILL, CHARLIE the prop-man, and ME. The CAMERA TRACKS into a TWO SHOT of the ABLE SEAMEN whose names are PETE and JIM.

PETE: What do you reckon's going to happen when this lot's over, Jim?

JIM: I dunno, Pete. What do you reckon's going to happen?

PETE: I reckon there's going to be some changes made.

Background SOUND, hammering, whistling, an outburst of tap-dancing from an elderly Scots CHIPPIE. The CAMERA ASSISTANT has his arm round JILL.

CLOSE UP   DORIS

DORIS: Keep it quiet now. This is a rehearsal not a bloody knees-up at the Crooked Billet.

CLOSE UP   JIM

JIM: What sort of changes, Pete?

CLOSE UP   PETE

PETE: Well, the kids. I reckon the kids are going to get a better
                chance this time. We're all going to get a bit more
                equality. I mean, that's what we're fighting for, isn't it?

TWO SHOT   PETE and JIM

JIM: What are we fighting for, Pete?

Pause

PETE: (looking thoughtful) Well. I suppose it's ... it's this
                thing they call democracy.

MID SHOT   the DIRECTOR with the FILM UNIT in the B.G.

DIRECTOR: Wonderful! Why don't we risk a take on that one?
DORIS: All right. Going for a take. You happy, Dick?

C.S. CAMERA MAN (whose name is DICK)

CAMERA MAN: Quite happy, Doris.

C.S. SOUND MAN
The SOUND MAN takes off his headphones, and looks aggrieved as no
one ever asks him if he's happy.

SOUND MAN: Sound reloading.

C.S. DORIS (She looks intensely irritated)

DORIS: Bugger sound! All right. Quick as you can, Sydney.

MID SHOT   the DIRECTOR, JIM and PETE

DIRECTOR: Wonderful, chaps! Tremendous! Just give us a little more
                wonder, Jim, on this thing they call *democracy*.

TWO SHOT   JILL and ME

ME: Look, Jill ...
JILL: Bugger off, I've got work to do.

MID SHOT   the DIRECTOR, PETE and JIM

DIRECTOR: Puzzled but *sincere!*

MID SHOT   JILL and ME

ME: What about the Uxbridge Odeon tonight? It's Betty
                 Grable in *Sweet Rosy O'Grady*.

The CAMERA tracks back to the THREE SHOT.
JILL and ME and CHARLIE the prop-man, who is loitering about with
smoke coming through his fingers and a cigarette burning the palm of
his hand.

CHARLIE: Lovely bit of smiggett, isn't she, John?

C.S. DORIS

DORIS: All right. Settle down now. We're going for a take.

C.S. DIRECTOR
He is talking to JIM and PETE

DIRECTOR: *Democracy*. That's the word you've got to *hit*!

Background noise, hammering, tap-dancing, etc., as before.

C.S. DORIS

DORIS: Where's John? Can't you get a decent bit of quiet? We're
                 going for a take!

C.S. ME
I sound far too apologetic.

ME: Quiet everyone. I say, quiet, could you?

C.S. DORIS
Impatient.

DORIS: Let's get on with it or they'll have won the bloody war
                 before we finish the picture. You happy, Dick?

MID SHOT   CAMERA CREW
They appear to be taking the camera to pieces.

CAMERA MAN: Sorry, Doris. There's a hair in the gate.

C.S. DORIS
She looks resigned.

DORIS: All right. Relax, everyone. There's a hair in the bloody gate.

LONG SHOT   the UNIT as they resume hammering, etc. The ABLE SEAMEN are both stroking the MAKE-UP GIRL, who is dabbing their foreheads with a large powderpuff.

C.S.   JILL and ME
JILL: Terribly sorry. I can't tonight. I've got to write to my gran.

SLOW FADE TO DISAPPOINTMENT.

It is, you see, a tedious and laborious way of writing, but it can be profitable if you stick at it.

In spite of our bland official films and the movies made by private enterprise, in which Jack Warner looked dogged as the Sarge, and Corporal Gordon Jackson was terse and determined, and the young Dickie Attenborough always had the screaming hab-dabs in the bottom of the long-boat; in spite of *In Which We Serve*, in which Captain Noël Coward found non-commissioned John Mills snogging in a *first-class carriage* and merely said, 'Carry on, Petty Officer Whatever' ('Thank you, sir'), the war was undoubtedly going on unscripted and far from the cameras. And yet the time which I had looked forward to as the execution of that sentence of death which had haunted my childhood dreams, was in fact the first moment when I felt I had come fully to life, a situation which filled me with a perpetually nagging sense of guilt then, and more so when the war was over. It was entirely a side result of the European catastrophe that people in England then seemed more united, even more cheerful, than they have since. All the hatred which we now reserve for one another was, I suppose, directed against Hitler; and the English, with their perpetual gift for understatement, sang a song in which they called him a rabbit.

Blown by the wind of these great events, lodged on the roof of Pinewood Studios where I sat fire-watching with a thermos of tea and a group of extras, I was, in spite of all my schoolboy foreboding, inordinately happy.

From time to time a sweet, melancholy music could be heard in the corridors of the Crown Film Unit. It was the poet, Laurie Lee, playing on his recorder. Laurie Lee used to lean against the wall, bronzed from his walks across Spain, his long sojourns in Gloucestershire, looking like a small, sly Pan, piping endlessly, and the secretaries would open their doors and hope to speak to him. He was the official script-writer of 'Crown', not that he could be blamed for the dialogue of our more pedestrian films which was usually cobbled together by the director with the help of the amateur actors and a few ideas thrown in by Doris after an evening in the pub.

'You see, Laurie isn't really very keen on this war. He was much more interested in the war in Spain.' One of the secretaries, whose name was Mavis, told me this. She was a hugely desirable girl with a face the colour of brown, farmhouse eggs and her eyes were like their hard-boiled whites with dark centres. I invited her home and broke all Charlie's rules by treating her in all the pubs in the neighbourhood, and I filled her handkerchief with glow-worms when I walked her home across the common; but she did nothing but talk about Laurie Lee. After the weekend Charlie asked me if I had seen the King and I replied with a silence I hoped he might take for an embarrassed confession.

Laurie Lee is an enormously talented writer who can find more ingenious ways than most people of putting off the appalling moment of putting pen to paper. When he has made coffee, filled his pipe, changed his typewriter ribbon, moved the furniture, telephoned his mother, had a sleep, gone for a walk, he is often reduced to copying out the newspaper. I don't know if he found this rate of progress perfect for poetry, but his poetic prose created difficulties in the documentary film world. Perhaps his heart was still in Spain where he had walked the dusty roads from village to village, drinking with the soldiers and playing his fiddle to pale girls with tragic eyes. At any rate the sound of his recorder was heard less often in the corridors and in time it was learned that there was to be a vacancy in the script department.

After what seemed a lifetime as an assistant director I was called into the office of the new Head of the Crown Film Unit, an extremely kind man who looked at me sadly.

'We were wondering', he said gently, 'whether you were exactly cut out by nature to be an assistant director. I mean, Doris says you're having a bit of trouble saying "Quiet please".'

'Just a bit.' I had to admit it.

'When I was an assistant director I was on my toes the *whole* time. I mean, are you quite sure *you* are?'

'Well. Not the whole time. No.'

'Bit of trouble, Doris tells me, getting the electricians to Liverpool?'

'I did find them in the end.'

'But you shouldn't ever have lost them. Isn't that the point? You know, it seems very hard to me to actually *lose* an electrician.'

I might have said that if he thought that he didn't know our hourly boys. Instead I looked suitably contrite.

'Doris and I have gone over the situation from every possible point of view and the conclusion we've come to is that you're not exactly a "natural" as an assistant.'

'Not a "natural", perhaps.'

'Look, you are a writer, aren't you?'

I had had one story published in the *Harrovian* and one in *Lilliput*. I secretly cherished half a novel about the Crown Film Unit which I was writing between takes. 'Oh yes,' I said. 'I'm a writer.'

'There's going to be a vacancy in the script department when Laurie goes. The idea we've arrived at, that is Doris and I have arrived at it, is that we should all be a great deal better off with you in the script department. Script-writers have almost never been known to lose the electricians. Look, we'll send you off somewhere to write a script and then you can show it to Laurie and if he passes it you're on.'

I went to the door in a sort of dream. My first novel may have been unpublishable, but now I was a writer; my pay-packet would say so just as my battledress shoulder-flash said 'Crown Film Unit'. Only when I got to the door did a doubt cross my mind.

'Where will you send me off? To write a script, I mean.'

If the Head of the Unit was laughing to himself he had the mercy not to show it. 'I don't know,' he said. 'What about Watford Junction?'

I went to Watford on a bicycle and spent a day staring at the railway lines and the rolling-stock without inspiration. Then I went home and wrote a script, based on the movies I had admired (*La Femme du Boulanger* and *La Bête Humaine*), about a station-master's wife and her unhappy love affair with a GI in charge of an American Army Transport Post. I sat by the fire after dinner and read it aloud to my father, doing the characters in various voices.

'When the war's over,' he said when I'd finished, 'I think you ought to take the bar exams. I think that would be a wise precaution.'

Jill typed out my script very neatly and I gave it to Laurie Lee, who vanished with it. I didn't see him again for a number of years. However he must have given it his seal of approval, or my 'Quiet please' must have deteriorated even further, because a month later I was posted as an official writer, with a salary which rose to the almost unthinkable height of eleven pounds a week. The time had come to say goodbye to Slough and the aircraft fitter. I moved to London.

Time, like short sight, improves every view, but there is no doubt that London, a place I now inhabit only under compulsion, was a better city then. There were no tower blocks, Soho was full of food shops and Italian restaurants, and only a very occasional and apologetic grimy window displaying Durex, trusses and a volume of Krafft-Ebing, hinted gently at the distant coming of the 'Pornorama' and the 'Boutique of Sexual Aids'. It seemed a perpetual adventure to buy second-hand books in the Charing Cross Road, or drink in the Swiss Pub or the York Minster or stand outside Goodge Street Underground Station in that long silence, filled with infinite possibilities, between the moment when the buzzbombs cut off and the thud as they fell somewhere else.

So I lived in London and went on journeys in blacked-out trains to factories and coal-mines and military and air force installations. For the first and, in fact, the only time in my life I was, thanks to Laurie Lee, earning my living entirely as a writer. If I have knocked the documentary ideal, I would not wish to sound ungrateful to the Crown Film Unit. I was given great and welcome opportunities to write dialogue, construct scenes and try and turn ideas into some kind of visual drama. I had the pretext, which the law has also given me, for talking to an endless variety of people and asking them impertinent questions. But my aims and interests were far from the documentary ideal. Drama to me meant the lines of Shakespeare that my father recited with relish, the nervous elaboration and distinctive music of Gielgud's 'Hamlet', Laurence Olivier rolling down a flight of stairs as dead Coriolanus, Donald Wolfit bringing tears to my eyes as Lear in lunch-time Shakespeare played in front of tabs with minimal support. With my head full of such miracles I found it hard to reconcile myself to lines which always had to be played with a stiff upper lip, like 'Roger and out'.

And the writers I admired, an ill-assorted gallery now peopled by Dickens, Chekhov, Firbank (for the dialogue), Evelyn Waugh, P.G. Wodehouse, Raymond Chandler and Lytton Strachey (who still seems to me to have had the best prose style of any writer this century, and to be the only true genius of the Bloomsbury Group), could hardly be said to

71

have had the documentary approach. What they all had in common, I suppose, apart from an admirable determination to entertain, was a belief in the importance of style and a preference for trying to catch some fleeting truth in a web of artifice, rather than bashing it on the head with a camera and a tape-recorder.

What obsesses a writer starting out on a lifetime's work is the panic-stricken search for a voice of his own. His ears are full of noises, a cacophony of sweet airs from the past and the even more delightful sounds of the present. When I sat in dark trains and wrote the novel I had planned about the Crown Film Unit, I thought I could, and for the first time, hear some noises that didn't come straight out of other people's books. My novel was called *Charade*, and reading it again it does seem to have some personal sound, which got lost later, and didn't reappear until I had spent ten years listening to other people's problems, and had learnt much more about dialogue in Law Courts and Legal Aid Centres, and met a lady called Nesta Pain, a radio producer of undoubted genius, who made me write a play in which the sound of my own voice would at last become consistent and audible.

9

'PENSOTTI'S OUT OF THE ARMY.'

Whatever became of us all? Tainton was killed in a ridiculously brave, fated commando raid on a French port; it may be that he alerted the enemy by his practice of blowing a hunting-horn before he went into battle. Martin Witteridge went into the Pioneer Corps. His brother Tom went into the Guards and was found by Major Witteridge, their father, in bed with a surrealist poet in the Witteridges' Sloane Street home wearing nothing but a Guards officer's cap and an Able Seaman's hat respectively.

'You two men', Major Witteridge was reported as having said, 'are a disgrace to His Majesty's uniform!'

'I don't think he would have minded half so much', Tom told me later, 'if we'd taken our hats off.'

The head boy at Harrow survived the war to become an English butler in Hollywood, a profession for which his education had prepared him admirably. Weaver, whose parents had committed the solecism of having side-plates at dinner, died with extreme gallantry in Normandy. And Henry Winter? Winter's death was still far ahead, lost in the mists of peace. He sat with me now in a North London pub where he had been gently putting me right on such matters as the effect of Passive Resistance and the Universal Value of Art, and why Mozart is a more satisfactory composer than Brahms. He had corrected some of the wilder grammatical constructions in *Charade*, which he received with cautious approval; and then he gave me the news of Oliver Pensotti's premature demobilization.

'But the war's not over yet. Hasn't he heard?' I wondered.

'They got rid of him. They turfed him out of Army Intelligence.'

'Why?'

'He told them he'd fallen hopelessly in love with his Sergeant-Major.'

'Had he?'

'No. It was a ruse. Pensotti's a very devious character. Probably

73

something to do with that school you were both at. He had to get out of the army because he'd fallen desperately in love with Lillian.'

'Lillian? *Your* Lillian?' I had still to get used to the tendency of life to move in ever-narrowing circles.

'She's not *my* Lillian.' Winter sounded, as always, philosophic. 'I had absolutely no right to possess her.'

'But how on *earth* did she meet Pensotti?'

'I asked him round for a vegetable stew at the Pacifist Service Unit. He came in his military uniform.'

'With dark glasses?'

'Yes. Apparently Lillian told him that she might feel quite passionate about him if it weren't for this military thing. I don't really know what happened. I think he took her to the Dorchester.'

'But what about her lover, the Leader of the Bayswater Pacifist Group?'

'Oh, he fell for a huge blonde WREN. He's volunteered for the Navy. Pensotti and Lillian are moving into a house in Flood Street.'

'It's rather strange.'

'What?'

'All the most sensational events of the war seem to take place among the Pacifists. But don't you *mind*?'

'Mind? What's the point of minding? It was pretty inevitable.' Winter was refilling his pipe.

'You mean "It is written", as the Asiatic characters in Somerset Maugham stories always seem to say.'

'Written by something. Certainly not God. Anyway, I've met the person I think I'm going to marry.'

It seemed that Winter had met a girl who served in a cigarette kiosk which he often passed on his way to bomb-sites. She stood in a small window and was invisible from the waist downwards.

'We talk every day. She's extremely intelligent and she smiles nicely. And she has splendid tits.'

'You haven't taken her out?'

'I've only spoken to her, when she's been in the kiosk.'

'And you want to see more of her?'

'That's the sort of joke that you ought to restrain yourself from putting into your books.'

We were interrupted then by a girl called Angela Bedwell who came into the pub to ask if we'd happened to have seen an Australian airman

74

called 'Benny' who sometimes bought us a Guinness. We hadn't, so we asked her to come to the house-warming party which we decided that Oliver Pensotti would have to give the following Saturday to celebrate his departure from Intelligence (Military) and his unilateral Treaty of Peace.

The London I had known from my childhood was in the North, the Wrong Side of the Park, the remote uplands of Swiss Cottage and the heights of Hampstead.

When I left the aircraft fitter I had a room with an engineer in a Haverstock Hill house where the going was extremely tough. His Irish wife was often unhappy and sometimes desperate. Strong-minded toddlers, reared to an alarming state of physical fitness by frequent doses of Ministry of Health cod-liver oil and orange-juice, tramped about the kitchen with their plastic pants and dirty nappies clinging to their knees or, barebottomed, lurched across the living-room to shred copies of *Penguin New Writing* or the 'Left Book Club' George Orwell which they tugged from the shelves. The infrequent meals were mounds of grey rice covered with grated carrot. On the day I found a used Tampax under the piano I decided to emigrate, Southwards if possible. Chelsea seemed a remote region, where the climate was different; where people no doubt had siestas and lay about eating grapes and playing the guitar. Meanwhile the only way to deal with life in Haverstock Hill was to spend as much time as possible visiting Northern Coal Mines for the Crown Film Unit or down the pub. Oliver's house-warming party in Flood Street marked an enormous change in my way of life. I moved to Chelsea and fell painfully, anxiously, ecstatically, and for what seemed like about a century, in love with Angela Bedwell.

'I heard about you leaving the Intelligence Corps.'

'Oh really, is that what you heard?' Oliver Pensotti looked amused. He was no longer in uniform, but wearing a silk scarf, a green velvet jacket with evening trousers and his balding suede shoes. We had a conversation along these lines:

'Well, it's true, isn't it?' I asked him.

'Is it? You seem to know so much about it.'

'Winter told me.'

'Winter only knows what I told him.'

'Well, what did you tell Winter?'

'I really can't remember now. Why don't you remind me?'

'The one about falling in love with the Sergeant-Major.'

'Oh, *that*! I thought Winter might appreciate that one.'

'You mean you didn't say you fancied the Sarge?'

'I certainly said that to *Winter*.'

'But is it true?'

'What is truth, said Jesting Pilot?' A little late in life Oliver had started to write *his* novel in the style of Aldous Huxley.

'Come on, Pensotti. Don't tell me you're still *in* the Intelligence Corps.'

'Well, if I was I wouldn't be able to tell you, would I?'

'Why ever not?'

'Intelligence.'

He smiled at me with great amusement. From then on I was never sure if I hadn't been entirely misled about my friend Oliver Pensotti. Was it all a gigantic cover, his stormy life with Lillian, his visits to undisclosed addresses in the country ostensibly to write his novel, a work he composed at the rate of about a page a month? Was he in fact engaged on some Top Secret assignment, dangerous but vital to the country? Could you get out of the army by pretending to be in love with the Sergeant, and if this were so why didn't unhappy conscripts embrace their non-commissioned officers in droves? Was the truth simply that Pensotti had been kicked out of the army for some quite different reason, or that he hadn't been kicked out at all?

'But *really*, about the Sergeant . . .?'

'Shall we say an excuse? Even if excuses sometimes happen to be true.'

The house Pensotti had acquired in Chelsea was tall and extremely comfortable. The whole of the top floor was a studio in which the house-warming party was being held. Lillian was a publisher's secretary and she had invited a number of her authors, and Michael Hamburger was there among the poets. Pensotti had prepared great bowls of some opaque mixture in which leaves and slices of fruit were floating, but this cup, usually so uninteresting, had a kick like a mule.

'I can't think where you got all the gin from.'

'Oh, you can get plenty of spirits', Pensotti smiled and I knew he was mocking me, 'when you're in the Service.'

'And I thought you'd left the Service.'

'You can get even more when you've left the Service. Now you tell *me* something, if it's not entirely secret.'

'The more secret it is the more likely I am to tell you,' I said. I have never had Pensotti's talent for concealment.

'Why did you insist on my giving this party?'

'You're enjoying it. Also I wanted to ask this girl.'

'Now we're getting at the truth,' Pensotti said, as if he valued frankness above all things. 'What's her name?'

I told him and he laughed. I didn't think it was as funny as all that.

The truth was that I longed for Angela Bedwell with a yearning so acute I didn't even like to think of the strange accident of her name, which seemed to make her a walking advertisement for the pleasures of others. I wanted to think of her as living quite alone in her room near Hampstead Heath, travelling alone to the Air Ministry where she read a book during her lunch hours and never spoke to a man in the canteen. In my wildest fantasies I thought she only came into the pub because of the loneliness of her bed-sit and that she spoke to the Australian airman only because she had been introduced to him at work and wished, in a purely platonic manner, to further goodwill towards the Dominions. Even as I talked to Pensotti I knew with a sick feeling that she wasn't going to turn up at the party.

Angela seemed to me to be all I wanted and all I was ever likely to want. She looked small and quite fragile, like a brunette Veronica Lake with long hair, green trousers and a shoulder-bag; and yet she was surprisingly athletic and spoke in the clipped, sensible tones of a modestly efficient officer in the Brigade of Guards. Her background was military; her father was a retired General who lived in Dorking, her mother enjoyed a high rank in the wvs. On some nights she used to look round the door of the pub, provide us with a second of nervous beauty and then vanish. On other occasions she'd let me buy her a drink and sometimes a sausage. Then she'd tell me about her father who once shouted at a heavily-bearded man he saw sitting in a tea-room, 'You bloody awful-looking creature, can't tell if you're a man or a woman!' She also told me about her Uncle Arnold, and said he was a charming but very elderly bachelor who often took her out to dinner at the Ritz and would advance her money if she were ever really broke. I told her about my job, which I made sound a great deal more exciting than it was, and the book I was writing, and the friends, like Mrs Cox, whom I knew in the country. I told her about nights in the Swiss Pub and the York Minster and how once, when too drunk to remember much about it, I had had tea with Stephen Spender. I mentioned my father to her, but not the fact that he was blind.

On the nights when she didn't come into the pub I hoped that Angela was writing to her father, washing her hair or, at worst, out to dinner with her Uncle Arnold. I had never invited her to anything before and, as Lillian refilled my glass and introduced me to Rodney Ackland, a successful playwright who, for some reason, she had managed to lure to the party, I was quite sure that Angela wouldn't come. Then an even worse fear overcame me. She would come with Benny, the Aussie airman. He would be carrying a bottle of whisky which they would drink together in a corner, and rather early in the evening he would shout, 'Thanks a bundle, cobber!' and take her off to the Strand Palace Hotel. She would reappear a week later in the pub looking frail and more beautiful than ever. Perhaps – my thoughts grew gloomier by the glassful – she would eventually let me take her out to lunch and ask me to lend her fifty pounds for an abortion.

When any middle-aged or even, let's face it, old person talks about the promiscuity of the young, I wonder what they were doing forty years back. Today, teenagers seem determinedly monogamous, sticking to their steadies, however unsatisfactory, with unbelievable devotion and fidelity. Their mothers, perhaps their grandmothers, thought little of packing their overnight bags and fighting their way through the blackout to another shared flat, another tolerant hotel, to keep in touch with a floating and transient population of lovers. Neither was love as safe and harmless as it is today. In the years before the Pill, every month brought days of anxiety followed by unexpected relief or incredulous despair.

'You thought we should have a party for a dream of yours, a kind of fantasy?' Pensotti danced past me with a Free French AT, displaying her so that I should have no doubt about her reality.

'It's still early,' I said. 'Angela may have missed a bus.'

'She may have missed a party. Don't you miss one as well. Why don't you go and talk to Lillian. She looks lonely.'

On my way to Lillian I met Peter Brook, who had been at Oxford with us. It was a time of his life when the aloof OUDS never invited him to do a production, but he did make a film of *Tristram Shandy* which was full of his talent. He had the most fascinating things to say, I'm sure, on the movies he had seen, the books he'd read and on the disastrous state of the English theatre. Had I been listening attentively I could have written them here, but my eyes were fixed on the door. I felt sick in my stomach, having organized a party for a reason which would never start to exist.

It was then I heard a sentence to which I was to grow accustomed. 'Terrifically sorry I'm late. I had to have dinner with Uncle Arnold.'

10

'THE ART OF CROSS-EXAMINATION', MY FATHER TOLD ME, 'IS not the art of examining crossly. It's the art of leading the witness through a line of propositions he agrees to until he's forced to agree to the *one fatal question*.'

When I got to know about it I realized my father was a cross-examiner of brilliance and any ability I achieved in that direction was learnt entirely from him. But in those days I was hardly listening. We were going on one of our long Sunday walks, down a steep field towards the woods and Turville in the valley below us, the village where he is now buried. As we started down the hill he would say, 'You've heard of the gatherers of eidelweiss. On this hill we're gathering momentum.' It wasn't one of his better jokes.

'Opinions vary as to whether you should ask your most devastating question first or save it up as a *bonne bouche* at the end.'

'Do they?' My mind wasn't on the art of cross-examination. I was carrying an extraordinary weight of happiness, like some bowl filled with a precious liquid which you hold and walk carefully lest it should spill. The fact of the matter was that I was sharing a room at the World's End with Angela Bedwell.

'My advice to you is to go in with your guns blazing. See if you can't knock the stuffing out of a witness in the first five minutes,' my father said, as I helped him climb a stile into the woods.

It had happened, amazingly enough, at Oliver Pensotti's house-warming party. Angela and I had talked and sat on the stairs and kissed occasionally. It was a Saturday night and she said she didn't have to be at work until Monday morning and had nowhere particular to go until then. People came up and started to talk to her. Peter Brook, if I remember, came to invite her to the movies, and Pensotti moved up to her and whispered, 'I hope, when you remember this party, you'll decide the whole thing has been *worth while*.'

By keeping a firm grip on her wrist I managed to prevent Angela from straying more than six inches from my side the whole evening. When I asked her if her plans included the possibility of her staying the weekend in one of the spare bedrooms in Flood Street she said, 'But wouldn't your friends take a frightfully dim view of a chap?' It was the way of the fragile Angela to refer to herself in this tantalizingly masculine way. Anyone who had left the Services, I told her, for the reason volunteered by Pensotti, was hardly entitled to take a dim view of anything. Terrified that she might change her mind I steered her into the nearest bedroom, which happened to be the place where the guests had dumped their coats. I can remember nothing about that night but happiness, and the distinguished playwright, Rodney Ackland, standing at the door and saying to the departing guests, 'Better not go in there. I think someone's having his greens.'

'I always ask a husband, or a wife, as the case may be,' my father told me, 'is there anything you have done in the course of your married life of which you are now thoroughly ashamed? The witness usually finds that a tricky one to answer.'

'Why?' We were walking through Turville now, towards Fingest and the pub where we should have tea and a slice of seed-cake.

'Well, if the husband, or wife, says "Yes" then he or she has made a damaging admission.'

'But if he says "No"?'

'He shows himself up as a self-satisfied hypocrite and has lost the sympathy of the Court. By the way, what've you been doing?'

'I went to Liverpool.'

'Liverpool?' My father gave the word a remote glamour as if I had said Popocatepetl or Persepolis. 'What led you to *Liverpool*?'

'I was looking for Chinese seamen.'

'*Chinese* seamen? Not for their opium, I do hope. Remember the constipation!'

'We want them to act Japanese soldiers. I'm writing a script about the Menace of Japan.'

'Rum sort of business, the show business. I say, do try and get the hang of the art of cross-examination.'

The first day I spent with Angela was Sunday, the day after Pensotti's party. We got up late, had lunch in a pub and went to see *The Magnificent Ambersons*. Then she said she had to get back to her room in Hampstead. I felt unreasonably cheated, ridiculously disappointed, I already regarded a happiness I had never expected as my right, its continuance forever was the least I was entitled to. After all, she had said she didn't have to be at work until Monday morning. But of course she had to wash her hair, write to her father, prepare for the overland safari and huge adventure of turning up at the Air Ministry at nine o'clock. As we parted at the bus-stop I asked the sort of idiotic question which showed I knew less than nothing about the art of cross-examination.

'By the way,' I said, 'how's Benny, the Australian airman?'

'Oh, he's away for the weekend, actually.' She smiled at me tolerantly. 'I thought you realized that.'

I spent a sleepless night groaning in Oliver Pensotti's spare bedroom. Lillian didn't help by saying, 'Gone already, your little friend?' In a black moment before dawn I hoped it was the end of my seeing Angela. The feeling of going around with a high temperature and the hourly expectation of doom was too much for me. I'd go back home and live in the country. I'd take up water-colours, read Thackeray and write the definitive history of Lord Byron's school-days. I began to list Angela's imperfections. Weren't her chin too large and her shoulders rounded? Her father was a General in Dorking and she was probably a Conservative. What on earth did I want with a Conservative with a huge chin, and as for Uncle Arnold, a person would have to be a member of the Flat Earth Society to believe in the existence of Uncle Arnold. She also ordered exotic drinks like large whiskies and water when Charlie the prop-man's sensible rules suggested that she should have been content with a half-pint of mild and bitter, preferably shared. I had decided all these things by six o'clock in the morning and by nine fifteen I had already rung the Air Ministry four times. When I got Angela at about eleven she ruined all my carefully-laid plans by saying, 'I say, what about a chap coming to supper with you in Chelsea tomorrow night? Is that a good idea?' Of course I agreed to the suggestion with the enthusiasm of Duncan accepting an invitation to stay the weekend with the Macbeths.

Angela came to stay with me occasionally at Oliver's. I never went to her room in Hampstead; I simply didn't want to see the letters, the possible presents from lovers, the photographs on the mantelpiece. The time came when I could no longer stay at Pensotti's. He said he needed the spare room. 'For a friend?' I asked him. 'Possibly for an enemy. It's best to be able to keep a constant watch on those sort of people.'

We had had a friend at Oxford called Watkins. His father was a butcher and Watkins had worked very hard to get to Oxford. Once he was there he was overcome with an extraordinary lassitude and found himself quite unable to read anything at all. He would tell us about his father's and mother's marriage, which was in a frightful way as his father saved all the best cuts of meat for his mistress. About this time Watkins called on us and said that his mother had left his father and taken a house at the World's End. Mrs Watkins offered me a room and Angela offered to move in with me, except on the nights when she was writing to her father, washing her hair or, of course, having dinner with her Uncle Arnold.

It was a good room. It had very little furniture except for a big table to write on and a rather jaundiced-looking copy of the Hermes of Praxiteles which I had been carting around with me since Oxford (soon after I was married one of my stepchildren pushed it out of a window in Swiss Cottage and the yellowish god shattered into a thousand pieces). Half-way up the stairs was a bath with a geyser which made a sound, when you lit it, like an early warning for the destruction of Pompeii. As an addition to the Greek statuary, Angela brought some trophies of the chase which she said had belonged to her father. There were heads of shot wildebeeste and Thomson's gazelle which she hung on the walls for decoration.

On the good evenings, the wonderful evenings, we would play bar billiards in the King's Head and I would admire Angela, bent over the table neatly sinking her shots whilst I blundered about and knocked over the mushrooms. Later we went to drink in the Cross Keys and staggered home to jump, as quickly as possible, between the icy sheets. In spite of the breakdown of her marriage, Mrs Watkins still had connections with the meat trade and, as a particular treat, she would cook various items of off-ration offal for our breakfast in bed. So fried liver, sweetbreads or heart would be balanced on our recumbent bodies in the faint light of a chilly dawn.

Mrs Watkins, who was a cheerful and extremely hospitable woman, had an elderly gentleman friend called 'Uncle Jim' who kept a small, but prosperous Durex shop somewhere near King's Cross Station. When we had a party Uncle Jim would, for no discernible reason, dress up as a Chinaman with a black skull-cap and a pigtail and go round serving tea to the bewilderment of the guests. When Christmas came near, Mrs Watkins bought a tree and Uncle Jim blew up some of his stock to act as balloons and give an impression of festivity in a time of shortage.

In the bad times, when her shampoo, or her correspondence, or her relatives kept her away, I would sit alone with Hermes and change the girl in *Charade* into Angela. 'In my dreams', I wrote, 'that rather long, wistful, childish face hung always in front of me, filling me on that night, as on every night since, with the same feverish excitement composed, in almost equal parts, of melancholy and hope.' As I sat alone writing this about Angela, the Thomson's gazelle stared down at me, glass-eyed, their lips curled contemptuously over their bright yellow teeth.

Nothing stands still and the flood of history, Auden said, if I remember rightly, held one moment, burns the hand. I could, I felt, have inhabited that room at the World's End for ever, grateful for the nights when Angela rang from the Air Ministry to say she was free. Then she would arrive with her overnight bag and her little black dress, as though for cocktails in Kensington, to play bar billiards and drink at the Cross Keys. One night she said, 'I told my Uncle Arnold I was going to marry you.'

In all my thoughts about Angela, occupying as they did about 99.9 per cent of my waking hours, marriage had not, up to then, been included. Our family lives were kept strictly segregated. I spent most weekends at my father's house in the country and most weekends, she told me, she spent with her father in Dorking. Marriage would mean her meeting my father and my being looked over by the General. I also feared that marriage would mean a lifetime worrying if she were really washing her hair.

'What made you say that?'

'Well, I've told my Uncle Arnold lots about you. Actually I lied and said you were in the Pioneer Corps. I don't think he can quite take script-writers. Not that it's not extremely clever of you to be one.'

'Yes. But is there any particular reason why you should tell him now?'

'It's just that I happen to be feeling most frightfully pregnant.'

I looked at her and saw a sight I had never seen before: Angela Bedwell crying into a small crumpled handkerchief. 'Then we'll get married,' I said. 'Of course we'll get married.'

'No. You don't really want to. I mean, I'm not sure I really want to. The best thing for a chap is a hot bath and half a bottle of gin,' she sniffed. 'A most stupid girl called Rachel Hacker in the Air Ministry poured the gin into the bath and sat in it. Then she wondered why nothing happened.'

It was, perhaps, a rare moment of choice, and if I took a decision it was one I was to regret bitterly in the months to come. I said, 'The gin's easy. The hot bath may be more difficult.'

'Not if we light the geyser before we go to play bar billiards. We could do that, couldn't we? I mean, wouldn't that be marvellously *efficient* of us?'

We did light the geyser in the most capable manner and came back to fight our way upstairs through a cloud of steam and a noise like the breaking up of the Titanic. Angela was boiled to a light shrimp colour and then we drank the gin together, solemnly and in almost complete silence. Then she stood up, carefully put a cigarette between the lips of the Thomson's gazelle and lit it. Soon all the decapitated animals on the wall were smoking heavily. There was a species of elk who had, as I vaguely remember it, a cigarette in each nostril. After this fierce burst of activity Angela fell into a heavy sleep and then, as I lay beside her, she peed in such a prolonged manner that I was almost washed into the King's Road. I got out of bed, had a long, and by now tepid, bath and sat watching her. Her oval face had a look of extraordinary innocence. I loved her, I thought then, more than I should ever be able to love anyone ever. And I had stupidly lost her.

One day at Pinewood Studios I saw something other than the usual crowd of chippies, prop-men, directors, electricians and members of the Army and Air Force Film Units. There were not only the Boulting Brothers in khaki and Richard Attenborough and Jack Clayton strangely dressed in Air Force blue, and even Garson Kanin in American officer's uniform, but a number of visitors who looked even more remarkable. The canteen was full of nuns. As I queued up behind one particularly devout-looking Sister for my plate of beans and bacon, she turned round and whispered, through a delicate cupid's bow of a mouth, 'It's being a virgin that makes you so bloody hungry!'

The war, of course, had ended and Pinewood, after its flirtation with the facts, was returning to the honest pursuit of fiction. The nuns were extras in the film of a Rumer Godden novel called *The Black Narcissus*. Elsewhere the piping times of peace were being ushered in by movies of sensational happenings during the Regency, usually starring Margaret Lockwood armed with a hunting-crop and James Mason. The safe war years, when most of the decisions had been made for us, were over. It was time to think of the future.

What on earth was I going to do? Get a job with the Rank Organization? Write a costume drama for Patricia Roc and Stewart Granger? Marry Angela? But then Angela had been remarkably busy during the last weeks. Uncle Arnold was staying in London and seemed to demand her company nightly. She had only a few days over for washing her hair. I spent most evenings alone, working on the last pages of *Charade*.

However we had a journey planned. Since I was a schoolboy I had been confined to England, as Soviet citizens are now confined to Russia. I can't say I had felt any particular claustrophobia, but now the seas were open and it was possible to go abroad. In Dublin, they said, you could order an enormous steak or even, and here was a delicacy I hadn't seen for years, a banana. Mrs Watkins and Jim were planning a holiday in Ireland and Angela and I were going with them. We would rent a car and drive to the blue mists and white beaches of Connemara, drinking Guinness all the way and eating ourselves silly.

'I hear you're not coming to Ireland,' Mrs Watkins said one morning as she plumped my breakfast, calves' liver on toast I think it was that morning, and strong tea, down on my solitary bed.

'Oh, who did you hear that from?'

'From Angela. She said she was bringing Peter instead of you.'

'Peter? Who's Peter?'

'Peter Pargeter. Don't you know Peter? I think Angela's really keen on Peter. So we shall have two love-birds with us on our trip to Ireland, won't we?'

'And who the hell', I said when I got through to the Air Ministry, 'is Peter Pargeter?'

'Please', said Angela, 'don't be angry.'

'But who is he? And why should he be getting my banana?'

'He's just someone terribly sweet who's come back from India. As a matter of fact, this'll interest you. He used to work in films.'

I said I found that absolutely riveting and I supposed she had told her Uncle Arnold that she was going to marry Peter Pargeter.

'Well, yes,' said Angela. 'As a matter of fact I did. Look, a chap can't go on talking in the Air Ministry's time. There *is* a war on.'

'The war's over,' I said. 'Or hadn't you heard?'

'There's a war', she said, putting me right with a good deal of quiet heroism, 'in Japan.'

The Crown Film Unit had a new director whose name was Alexander Shaw and he looked like the nicer type of Roman Emperor. 'I thought you might like to go up to Glasgow', he said, 'and write a script about a new attitude to town planning.'

'No thanks,' I said, 'I don't think I will.'

'It's an important subject for peace time.'

'I think I'd better go away', I told him, 'and be a barrister. That was what I was always meant for.'

'Don't tell me', Alexander Shaw looked genuinely concerned, 'that you haven't been happy here?'

'Oh yes,' I said. 'I've been very happy. But not any more.'

'You're back,' my father said. 'That's good. You can give me a hand with the earwigs.'

I installed a paraffin heater and a card index full of leading cases in my bedroom. I reopened *Potted Torts*, I memorized the case of the unfortunate woman who found a snail in her ginger-beer, I wrote short notes on 'easements' and I defined murder; I distinguished 'Justification' from a 'Plea of Fair Comment' and I defined 'Malice'. Now and then, in the silence of my room, I opened my mouth and yelled, 'Angela!' very loudly. As a way of exorcizing pain it was totally ineffective.

II

I FINISHED *CHARADE* AND SENT IT TO VARIOUS PUBLISHERS. My heart sank regularly as it came thudding back through the letter-box. Daniel George was then art editor at Jonathan Cape and he wrote me an encouraging letter and even took me out to lunch at the White Tower, but he wasn't able to publish the book. As the rain fell on the sodden garden and dripped in the shrubbery, as my father felt for the knob on the wireless and my mother looked at me with infuriating pity and said, 'Poor boy. He's had his book back again. He seems to take one step forward and one step back', I fell into a mood of bleak despair and grief. My life, so far, seemed to have been a complete fiasco. I had lived twenty-three endless years and what had I to show for it? An unpublished novel, an inglorious war and a disastrous love affair.

I had no courage to go to London so I spent my time on the common and in the local pubs. I went to tea with Mrs Cox and 'Bill' Baker and there saw an improbable sight. An old friend of theirs, the French cook, playwright and *bon viveur*, Marcel Boulestin, had died and in some way and for some reason which wasn't entirely clear to me, had managed to bequeath his entire wardrobe to 'Bill'. Clothes were then in short supply so Mrs Cox's friend, a tall and angular woman, was glad to wear the outfit of a small, stout *boulevardier*, striped trousers and a coat with an astrakhan collar, as she went about her gardening or shopped in Henley-on-Thames.

I made other friends who lived near to us. There were two artists both called Jim: Jim Fitton and Jim Holland. They not only had a great deal of talent in common, but they had been influenced by Grosz cartoons and drew in a satirical and realistic manner. We used to go with their wives to dances in village halls and do the 'Hokey Cokey' and the 'Palais Glide'. Jim Holland was especially kind to me; he introduced me to various magazine editors for whom he drew and, when the Great 1951 Exhibition came, he got me a job writing captions for the 'Hall of Coal', which was undoubtedly my least glamorous commission ever. There was a magazine called *Our Time* edited by a remarkable poet called Edgel Rickward for whom I began to write film reviews. Naïve as ever, I didn't realize that it was a Communist magazine and when I got letters saying that 'The Party in Wimbledon' didn't like the tone of what I wrote I thought that some people in the suburbs had met for a few Saturday-night drinks and taken the opportunity of discussing my notices.

So I read the leading cases on Contract and got deeply into Criminal Procedure and drove my father's Morris Oxford round the narrow lanes to visit the Jims, or Mrs Cox or, with increasing frequency, a place which could usually be relied on to produce an eventful evening, Wyn's Cottage. The story of Wyn Henderson might provide a novel in itself, written perhaps, by Joyce Cary. Wyn and her cottage became, just after the war, a large part of my life: and it was due to a meeting there that I was transformed, in a remarkably short time, from an unhappy young scriptwriter and novelist to a middle-aged professional man with an overdraft, a family of four and very little time to wonder if I were happy or not.

But let me try and describe Wyn Henderson. I have no idea how old she was then, in fact I never knew her age. She had the face, bright-eyed with a tip-tilted nose, of a pretty child and the waddling, ungainly body of a fat, middle-aged woman. She had been part, if she were to be believed, a vital part, of the Bloomsbury world; but she had abandoned London and her friends in the Charlotte Street pubs to work with the Pig Board in Henley. She had been, again if she could be believed, the mistress of many notable people, millionaires, surrealist painters, actors and musicians. She had been a close friend of Havelock Ellis, who taught her to pee standing up, an art she often used to practise as we staggered out of the White Hart at closing time. She must have been an unworldly woman because from all those relationships she had preserved no money, no presents and certainly no fur coat. She moved about her cottage, which was lit by candles and a smouldering wood fire, wearing an old black dress and a string of large amber beads, cooking bowls of spaghetti and pouring out little 'drinkies' of the Algerian wine her visitors brought her. She was always cheerful and could talk endlessly of her friends and conquests in the thirties. Mrs Cox took all her stories with a grain of salt and viewed Wyn Henderson with a certain wariness and suspicion.

Wyn Henderson's later years were no less dramatic than her prewar prime. After Dylan Thomas's death she became a close friend of his widow Caitlin, with whom she travelled round Europe and lived for a while in Italy. At last, ill and exhausted by an eventful life, she returned to England and went into a hospital, I think it was in Cambridge, to die. Before she died she decided to be received into the Roman Catholic Church and a comparatively young Dominican monk visited her to give her religious instruction. The sight of this monk had a totally revitalizing effect on Wyn. She made a rapid recovery, left the hospital and in almost no time at all had married the monk, who applied to be released from his vows.

Many years later the ex-monk was teaching English at Chichester. Hoping to see Wyn again I drove down to talk to his students. I found her, mountainous but not looking very much older, sitting immobile in the corner of the room, still bright-eyed, still telling endless stories of the writers and the painters she had known. He was then in his fifties, and as we parted he told me that Wyn meant everything to him and that she was the only woman there had ever been in his life. He died before she did.

All of this was in the future, although it might have encouraged Wyn if she had known about it as, at the end of the war, she moved through the hospitable gloom of her tiny cottage. I met her two sons, both in the Air Force, one of them married to a niece of Virginia Woolf, a thin and remarkably silent girl who sat in the shadows like an echo of the Great Days of Bloomsbury. Other visitors were the sculptor Naum Gabo, and Harry the local poacher, a man who managed to bear a close resemblance to Lady Chatterley's lover, and often arrived with gifts of venison and pheasant. He would help Wyn out of the pub at night and support her as she did a 'Havelock Ellis'. Another visitor to Wyn's cottage was a poet and novelist called Randall Swingler. We used to go in my father's car to Watlington, a place which combined the distinction of being the smallest town in England with having more pubs per head of the population than I believed possible. Randall Swingler told me a great deal about a friend he had who lived in Oxford. She turned out to be that Mrs Dimont whom I had visited years before with Henry Winter and who, it seemed, was now separating from her husband.

So, in those first days of peace we drove with the car's mudguards brushing the white cow parsley in the hedges, and drank in the beer tents at local shows and gymkhanas, and took a bottle of wine over the dark fields round Henley and swam in the sour, reed-filled river and waited for the Brave New World.

My father had told me about the Great Liberal Landslide before the 1914 war and the joy he had felt as the Government seats fell. After our war we had our election. The Jims and I had volunteered as drivers and I trundled my father's car through remote villages and round the suburbs of High Wycombe pulling out Labour voters. There was an extraordinary feeling of hope and suppressed excitement. Were the clichés about the age of the Common Man about to come true? Were peace and justice to be ushered in by *Penguin New Writing* and Army Education? These simple-minded beliefs could almost have been justified on the morning after the election, when the Labour victory reminded my father of his beloved Landslide. The history of politics in England since that heady moment now seems, in spite of some achievements, to be a record of disappointment. The fruits of victory turned out to be the Age of Austerity, with the gaunt Sir Stafford Cripps telling us all to tighten our belts. The entry into the promised land was indefinitely postponed and 'The Just City', we were told with increasing irritation, would prove far too expensive to build.

In that curiously unmemorable period after the war I wasn't, I'm sure most people weren't, thinking about tightening my belt or even about bread rationing. I was enjoying, in a small moment of triumph, the fact that the Bodley Head had agreed to publish my *Charade*. I waited as patiently as I could for the year it would take to get printed to be over, for the certain future when its success would make me rich and cause Angela Bedwell to ring up and say it had all been a most ridiculous mistake, marriage to Peter Pargeter was unendurably dull, and could we meet and play bar billiards? My father said, 'I felt just like you when the fellow agreed to publish *Mortimer on Probate*. Don't let it put you off the exams, dear boy. That's the great thing. Always have something to fall back on.'

So I continued to fall back on the law, that great, Gothic structure of authority, with its stone buttresses of power and its ancient ecclesiastical ornaments, as though it were a mattress. I went to lectures in a basement under Chancery Lane and sat at the back of the class re-reading the proposed blurb of *Charade* while a small red-faced barrister yelled at us about the elements of the criminal law.

'If you climb down my chimney, Mortimer, during the hours of darkness, simply to gain entry, what offence have you committed? And now I add a gloss. Let us suppose,' (here he addressed the class at large) 'as seems highly probable, Mortimer climbs down my chimney by night with the felonious intent of *raping my cook*, what offence has Mortimer committed then?'

I gazed at the lecturer, my mind filled with the blurb of my book which I was re-reading for the ninetieth time. Was this really what being a barrister was all about? I tried to picture my soot-stained self struggling with a huge, aproned Irish woman on a kitchen range. The mind fortunately boggled and it was left to the rest of the class to cry, 'Housebreaking with intent to commit a felony.'

In due course I passed some exams and while waiting to do others I went to Paris. The Age of Austerity followed me there, wine and cigarettes were on coupons in France. But I was elated by my first post-war escape from England. Having missed my Irish banana with Angela I had to make do with other new experiences, bleeding steaks criss-crossed with burns and Portuguese oysters in La Coupole, which has remained, since I ate there in those days with Tommy Motte-Smith and his far more masculine mother (I had discovered them both in some strange Parisian exile), my favourite place to eat in the world.

Later I managed to get myself a job teaching English to a number of Parisian models who wanted to get work in America. I used to sit on a small gilt chair at the back of the fitting-rooms and try to get the girls to concentrate on Somerset Maugham's short stories. Their attention was hard to retain. They were excited by the distant sound of the austere ice breaking and the coming tide of long skirts, frilled petticoats and flounced umbrellas which was to be that year's noticeable contribution to the Brave New World.

So it was a time for long walks from the dress-salons of the Right Bank to La Coupole, where the oysters and mussels and sea-urchins nestled in their beds of seaweed. More often I stayed alone in my bleak hotel bedroom in St Germain and drank rationed *vin ordinaire*, opened a tin of sardines and tried to get some sort of tenuous grasp on the law of Resulting Trusts.

The art director at the Crown Film Unit had been Teddy Carrick and he had given me an introduction to his father, that creator of never realized theatrical dreams, Gordon Craig, who had been the hero of my toy theatres, and whose designs were always in my mind when I tried to do theatrical drawing in the art room at Harrow. I found him, an old man with long white hair, some sort of a shawl round his shoulders, in a dusty studio where the Nazis had not disturbed him, surrounded by his models and drawings for vast, brooding, epic productions. He sat surrounded by his memories of Irving and his mother, Ellen Terry, on the gas-lit sets of the Lyceum, and of his love affair with Isadora Duncan.

I brought him English tobacco and for a while breathed in the smell of old theatrical magic, the excitement of a stage-struck childhood I seemed to have lost and wouldn't recover for more than another ten years.

Then I left Paris and went back to face the Law of Real Property.

Charade came out eventually with a jacket designed by Jim Holland and got the sort of enthusiastic notices which would amaze and delight me now; then I supposed it was what always happened. Daniel George wrote a review in the *Daily Express* saying 'Not for thirteen years have I found so certain a touch', and I was ungrateful enough to wonder what he had been reading for thirteen years. The notice I remember most clearly was written somewhere by Val Gielgud, who was then Head of Radio Drama. 'The book', he said, 'contains the sort of fumbling round the skirts of sex which passes for sophistication in adolescent minds.' Mr Greenwood of the Bodley Head told me that *Charade* was selling well and I suppose I must have made about a hundred and fifty pounds out of it altogether. I sent a presentation copy to Angela with an inscription, nicely combining tenderness, courage and irony, which I had dashed off in a couple of months, but received no reply.

The book was out, but nothing seemed to have changed. It's often said that my old schoolfellow, Lord B., awoke and found himself famous. I feel sure that he woke up and didn't find any huge improvement in the quality of life. His sister Augusta was still having trouble with her husband, one of the housemaids was pregnant again, there was a good deal of anxiety about the overdraft and the mortgage on Newstead Abbey, and his Lordship was unable to catch the waiter's eye in the coffee-house. The success of *Charade* was transient and it removed few anxieties. However it did mean that from my early twenties I have been able to think of myself as a professional writer, and I haven't had to wait long and heart-breaking years for publication. The troubles came later, in years when my writing seemed to be advancing nowhere, when I felt myself bumping painfully up against my own limitations, when I despaired and thought that the voice in which I had once spoken was lost forever.

Life became enormously uneventful. I took to riding about the common on a small and extremely docile horse. It was a hot summer and, as my father recorded in his log, he took the first prize for peas and pom-pom dahlias at the local flower-show. 'Peaches are very fine (though only about two-and-a-half-dozen on both trees). Splendid runner beans. We made 13 pounds of plum jam (Czar). We noticed one of the Neapolitan cyclamen in flower for the first time at the north of the copse.' It was some time during that summer that I rode past Wyn's cottage and, peering over the hedge, saw Mrs Dimont crouched in the front garden, painting a coal-scuttle.

No marriage I could possibly have contracted could have been more inconvenient from my father's point of view. He was the doyen of the Matrimonial Bar, and I couldn't marry Penelope Dimont without being dragged (as people used to say in those far-off days, when co-respondents were kept off the Queen's Lawn at Ascot lest they might scorch the turf) through the Divorce Courts. In addition she had four young daughters who menaced my father, to whom all visitors were unwelcome, with a mass invasion of ready-made grandchildren. Clearly he had to do something about these threats to his peace and security, and with the mixture of guile and effrontery with which he had managed to settle so many heavily-contested Probate actions, he chose to proceed, not by pointing out to me the dangers of marrying Penelope, but by persuading her that I was a hopeless proposition. He took her for a walk and told her that I had no money, few prospects and no sympathy for anyone who got ill. With her assets, a fine and attractive family, some bits and pieces of furniture and her own small car, he was quite sure that she could find better fish from a wider and richer sea.

Penelope's father was a Rector in the Cotswolds. It was in his greystone Rectory that I watched her dish out the huge lunches, the great roasts and mounds of vegetables, which her children consumed with wide-eyed determination. My future father-in-law was small and stout. He grew depressed after services, when he was troubled by the thought that he could no longer bring himself to believe any one of the Thirty-nine Articles. In time he gave up preaching sermons and took to showing short religious films in his church instead. I remember him stumping off wearing Wellington boots under his surplice to insulate himself against any electric shock provided by the projector. He ruined his health by smoking and eating too many heavy puddings, but I was always fond of the Rector and got on well with him. He told me that I should be hopelessly lost in my future marriage to Penelope unless I could 'keep a firm hand on her tiller'. Each of our fathers seemed to have hit on the same expedient, to play up the hopeless deficiencies in their own children's characters.

In a very short time my father grew fond of his family of ready-made grandchildren, and they had an easy access to him which I had never claimed at their ages. They climbed over him, felt in the waistcoat pocket where he kept mints and wine-gums for them, and blew on his gold watch causing it to fly miraculously open. They took at once to the garden I had seen built and then slowly discovered, and they cantered up to their knees in daffodils or rolled down into the copses. They showed no patience with the hunt for earwigs. My father's entry for 28 January 1948 ran: 'Today is mild and sunny. Smith has finished planting the rhododendrons and camellias against the hedge. John was called to the bar on Jan. 26th.'

There was no possibility of my marrying Penelope until she could get divorced, for which we had to supply evidence. We went, at ruinous expense, to several Brighton hotels but, on being questioned later, the staff quite failed to remember us. We went to even more expensive hotels and did our best, by burning holes in the sheets or screaming during the night, to make our visits memorable. We had no success, our appearance and personalities were clearly such that we created no impression. Finally we suggested a private detective. One afternoon we looked from the windows of the cottage we had then rented and saw a respectable-looking person in a bowler hat walking slowly up the front garden. He introduced himself as Mr Gilpin and we showed him up to our bedroom where he was delighted to find male and female clothing scattered.

In my first days at the bar I often saw Mr Gilpin in the Divorce Courts. He greeted me respectfully, but made no reference to his afternoon visit. Many years later he was engaged in an entirely justified action against the police, who had wrongfully and frivolously arrested him when he didn't get out of the way of a Panda car on a zebra crossing. Mr Gilpin needed a character witness for the purpose of these proceedings, and I was glad to be able to say that I had known the 'Private Eye' for many years and always had found him a person of the greatest respectability whose evidence had been, when I had occasion to test it, totally reliable.

Thanks to Mr Gilpin the divorce at last went through. 'August 27th, 1949,' my father dictated for the record. 'John and Penelope's wedding for which we cut all available flowers which Penelope arranged with great effect.' I had fled from the loneliness of my childhood into a large and welcoming family, but I was back where I began, in a flat in the Temple, playing with the children in Temple Gardens, and being looked after by my father's clerk.

12

THE SIMILARITIES BETWEEN THE BAR AND THE STAGE HAVE
been frequently noticed, and if there has never been a more
authoritative-looking judge than the actor, Felix Aylmer, there has never
been a greater performer on his day and in the right part than the
criminal defender, Sir Edward Marshall Hall. My father remembered
Marshall Hall and it was not his classic profile that he described to me,
nor his flamboyant oratory ('Look at her!' Sir Edward once said to a
Jury, pointing to his trembling client in the dock, a young prostitute
accused of murder. 'God never gave her a chance. Will you?'). It was
Marshall Hall's dramatic entry into a courtroom that impressed my
father. His head clerk would come in carrying the brief and a pile of
white linen handkerchiefs, then came a second clerk with the water
carafe and an air-cushion (lawyers and pilots, as a result of sitting for
long hours, are martyrs to piles). Sir Edward himself would then burst
through the swing-doors to be installed in his place by a flurry of
solicitors and learned juniors. He would subside on to the inflated rubber
circle and listen to the case for the prosecution. If the evidence against
Marshall Hall's client looked black he would, so my father assured me,
slowly unfold the top handkerchief and blow, a clarion call to battle.
When the situation became desperate he would remove the air-cushion
and reinflate it, a process which always commanded the Jury's undivided
attention.

There is no art more transient than that of the advocate, and no life
more curious. During his working days the advocate must drain away
his own personality and become the attractive receptacle for the spirits
of the various murderers, discontented wives or greedy litigants for
whom he appears. His is the fine-drawn profile, the greying side-pieces,
the richly-educated voice and knife-edged pin-striped trousers which
everyone accused of crime allegedly wishes to possess. The advocate
must acquire the art of being passionate with detachment and persuasive
without belief. He must be most convincing when he is unconvinced.
The advocate has this much in common with the religious mystic, he can

only operate successfully when he is able to suspend his disbelief. Indeed belief, for the advocate, is something which is best kept in a permanent state of suspension. There is no lawyer so ineffectual as one who is passionately convinced of his client's innocence.

So, in growing into a way of life as a barrister who wrote, or, as I wanted to think of it, as a writer who did barristering, I was stretched between two opposite extremes. The writer cannot help exposing himself, however indecently. Every performance he gives, although cloaked in fiction, reveals his secret identity. And yet in the biography of Sir Edward Marshall Hall the great advocate's 'self' seems to have vanished. The props are there, the collection of revolvers and precious gems and the taste for rare claret; but the voices are those of the prisoners in the dock, such people as Robert Wood, the artist accused of the Camden Town Murder, and Madame Fahmy, who shot her husband in the Savoy Hotel. They borrowed his personality to escape death and left him, as perhaps he always was, hollow. His life is merely their lives and nothing is left of Sir Edward but a list of 'Notable Trials' and a few anecdotes about his outrageous way with an air-cushion.

I suppose most barristers, even those condemned to a life in the Chancery Division, were once infected with a slight case of the 'Marshall Halls', just as the actor who has settled into an unambitious round of voice-overs for breakfast cereals once yearned to play Hamlet. I have never been able to go into a court-room without that twinge of excitement and dread which actors feel as they wait for their entrances and, although I have never owned an air-cushion, I was once accused of cracking Polo Mints loudly between my teeth to the distraction of the Jury. All advocates have their acting mannerisms. When I started off my career in defended divorce cases I greatly admired the smooth and elegant advocacy of Lord Salmon, who seemed to me to win his cases with all the noise and bluster of a perfectly-tuned Rolls-Royce coasting downhill. Cyril Salmon would take out his more valuable possessions, his gold watch and chain, his heavy gold key-ring and cigarette-lighter and place them on the bench in front of him. Then he would plunge his hands deep into his trouser pockets and stroll negligently up and down the front bench lobbing faultlessly accurate questions over his shoulder at the witness-box. Here, I thought, was a style to imitate. For my early cross-examinations I would take off my battered Timex watch, lug out my bundle of keys held together with a piece of frayed string and pace up and down, firing off what I hoped were appropriate questions backwards. I continued with this technique until an unsympathetic Judge said, 'Do try and keep still, Mr Mortimer. It's like watching ping-pong.'

Despite this early discouragement, my methods of advocacy remain distressingly flamboyant. Years later, when I had taken up a life of crime, I was representing a highly-talented lady singer accused of passing dubious cigarettes through the Customs at London Airport. The case took place, as do most airport offences, in the Uxbridge Magistrates Court, not a notoriously soft-hearted or easily swayed tribunal. The lady, who had arrived at Court in a purple Rolls-Royce, stood in the dock wearing a simple black frock, a model of contrition. I stood addressing the Bench and listened to myself with considerable surprise, not to say distaste. 'Give her justice!' I heard myself say. 'Justice is what she has been waiting for and praying for during these long months of suspense. Yes, give her justice. But let it be justice tempered with that mercy which is the hallmark of the Uxbridge and Hillingdon District Magistrates Court!'

The tone was unmistakable. The ghost of Sir Edward rode again. How long would it be before I too vanished into oblivion, becoming nothing but a string of improbable anecdotes?

Not, of course, that the High Court of Justice, Probate, Divorce and Admiralty Division (Divorce) gave great scope for forensic fireworks of the Marshall Hall variety, at least not during my early days of practice.

Our staple diet, our legal bread and butter, was the uncontested divorce case known simply as the 'undefended'. The 'undefended' was the way in which consenting married couples, anxious to be free of each other's company as expeditiously as possible, obtained their 'Decree Nisi' or order for release. Such people, it might be thought, should be allowed to go their separate ways in peace. Fortunately for those who earned their living by doing 'undefendeds', this was not so. Freedom was only possible if the complexities of an unhappy life could be fitted into the neat pattern of a divorce law still founded, to a large extent, upon the morality of the medieval Bishops. Furthermore the so-called 'innocent party' had to perform in the witness-box to the satisfaction of what seemed to us then a collection of excessively irritable old Judges, some of whom apparently satisfied a wry sense of humour by keeping intolerable marriages alive on some obscure legal pretext. When some of these Judges granted divorces they were often so moved by imagination at the alleged offences of the 'guilty party' that they would utter resounding and alliterative judgments; so suburban housewives would find themselves stigmatized in the evening papers as 'A Mitcham Messalina who treated her husband without mercy or remorse' or 'A Catford Cleopatra, careless of her marriage vows, who sinned shamelessly'.

Those barristers who practised outside the Divorce Division tended to think that doing 'undefendeds' was an easy option, like shooting foxes or playing cricket with a tennis-ball. As a matter of fact an 'undefended' could be extremely tricky, although it bore the same relation to a legal contest as a ten-minute review sketch does to a three-act play. Years of dissension, decades of matrimonial disharmony had to be reduced to such pithy one-liners as, 'The Fish-Slice Incident' or 'The Matter of the Hairgrips in the Waistcoat Pocket' or 'The Day She Pawned my Masonic Regalia'. There was no time for character development, only for a quick punchline, Decree Nisi and Black Out.

Moreover the client in the 'undefended' had to be rehearsed, in a brief meeting outside the Court, to put on the desired performance and make a complex saga of human relations legally acceptable and comprehensible to the Judge. As time went by and my practice went up the social scale this task became easier. Divorcing doctors, politicians or West End actresses could at least be understood by the judicial handers-out of Decrees. When I set out on the 'undefended' trail, the clients seemed to be all stone-deaf monoglot Poles and the difficulties were enormous. Even the hard-done-by working-class housewife shared no common language, in those days, with the learned Judge. After he had pronounced upon her case she would look confused, uncertain as to whether she had been awarded damages or divorced or sentenced to a term of imprisonment. It was often a painful task to explain that she was, after all the embarrassing questions and legal argument, still inextricably married to her husband.

The advocate in the 'undefended', I found, was most useful as an interpreter between the Judges, who tended to form one class, and the clients who fell into another. In a reasonably short time I became bi-lingual and able to speak both 'Judge' and 'Client' and I formed a sort of glossary of useful phrases with their translations. This is an extract:

The Judge's 'sitting-room' is the client's 'lounge'.
The Judge's 'dinner' is the client's 'tea'.
The Judge's 'lunch' is the client's 'dinner'.
The Judge's 'magazine' is the client's 'book'.
The Judge's 'furniture' is the client's 'home'.

Thus the phrase 'My husband ran off with the home', if untranslated, might leave the Judge with a nightmare vision of an entire semi-detached being removed by articulated lorry, when all that was meant was that the ruthless spouse had made off with the G-Plan suite when his wife was out shopping.

'Falling for a baby' always meant becoming pregnant and never described, as some of the more rarefied Judges might have thought, an act of tumbling to amuse an infant.

Armed with these and similar equivalents it was possible to build a career in 'undefendeds' and avoid any major disaster, provided you could learn to fit each and every marriage into the three immutable categories of adultery, cruelty and desertion. As one or other of these elements appeared to be present in most homes, the legal side of the work was not hugely demanding, particularly as 'cruelty' became extended to cover almost any activity in which even the best-intentioned husband might engage. If a man made frequent love to his wife he could be accused of 'unreasonable and exorbitant sexual demands' and if he didn't he was 'denying her sexual intercourse and causing her deep humiliation and distress'. If he chattered to her he could be guilty of 'nagging', if he didn't you could allege 'long periods of sullen silence'. Sex, in anything but the missionary position, could be described as 'perverse and unnatural demands' causing, of course 'humiliation and distress'. So remote and long-forgotten acts of love were re-enacted in the witness-box to bring tired marriages to their legal termination.

The strangest element in the then current matrimonial law was the 'Discretion Statement'. All cases had to have an 'innocent party' but some parties, of course, were more innocent than others. If a divorcing husband or wife had ever been unfaithful this fact, in an act of contrition which must have derived from the confessional, had to be revealed in a sealed document which was torn open for the Judge who could then, in his discretion, refuse a decree of divorce. One lover could usually be explained away, but when the numbers rose to two or three the atmosphere in court became grave and disapproving. However, Judges always received the sealed documents with an air of interest and expectancy, perhaps hoping to find in them the names of old friends or prominent members of the bar. Between the Decrees Nisi and Absolute, a period of six months, the innocent and successful party in a divorce case was required not to commit adultery, otherwise the 'King's Proctor' might intervene and send everyone back to square one.

'What happens', I asked my father before I started in the divorce business, 'if the innocent party's living with someone else? Do they have to separate?'

'No. But you must advise them to stop sleeping together.'

'For six months?'

'Why ever not?' My father seemed to find this perfectly acceptable.

'How do you put it exactly? To the client?

'You tell them to exercise a self-denying ordinance.'

So I saw my father, the doyen of the divorce bar, in a rare role, that of the confessor, imposing a few Hail Marys and a period of abstinence. This was the sort of law I was engaged in during the first years of my married life.

After paying the costs of the divorce, Penelope and I had £11 left to spend on our honeymoon. We went to Brittany, sat in the rain, ate lobster at dinner and quarrelled out of financial anxiety. When we came back to London, considerably earlier than we had planned, we set about living within our means which were then £5 a week which my father gave me for drafting his less sensational divorce petitions. 'Five pounds should be just about all right for you,' he said vaguely. 'Any more than that and you're liable to have problems about income tax and so on.' I knew that an incautious expenditure on rare shrubs, Japanese cherry trees, gardeners, sacks full of daffodil bulbs, cigars and barrels of oysters had left him with an overdraft which was the subject of frequent, carefully-phrased letters to his bank manager in Bristol. 'Who steals my purse steals trash' was a quotation which figured often in this correspondence, together with promises that all would be well if only he could be paid for '"Merrydew v Merrydew and Simpkins", a long dogfight over adultery and a good money brief during which I managed to clock up *twelve refreshers*!' Although the distant manager of the West Country bank was usually mollified by this correspondence, I knew that any request for a rise on the £5 would cause my father to change the subject and criticize the latest opinion I'd done for him on the law of domicile, or invite me down to the country for the weekend to 'help out' with the earwigs. 'You'll get more briefs of your own eventually,' he reassured me. 'Once solicitors get to like the cut of your jib.'

Solicitors, however, seemed slow to appreciate any breezy and nautical way I might have with a Decree Nisi. I would look out, from our reasonably expensive flat in the Temple, over a sleeping city and think of the innumerable homes in which adultery, desertion without cause and conduct causing deep humiliation and distress were no doubt occurring with monotonous regularity and wonder when just a little of it all might be expected to land on my mantelpiece, neatly tied up in that pink ribbon which signalled the longed-for 'undefended'. The children I had taken on ('You're like a railway train,' my father had said with relish. 'Pause at the next stop to take on children.') would, I knew, be awake in the morning to renew their extraordinary demands for Farex, Ribena, Johnson's Baby Shampoo and knicker-linings, luxuries which, in the far-off days when I shared a room at the World's End with Angela Bedwell, I had been quite able to do without.

Oliver Pensotti, my school friend, came to visit us and emerged from the kitchen wreathed in smiles.

'What are you laughing at, Pensotti?'

'Your grocer's bills! They're hanging on a hook beside the cooker. You must be feeding an army!'

'It seems like that sometimes,' I agreed.

'Well, you made your bed, you must lie on it,' Pensotti said. 'Or not, as the case may quite possibly be. I mean, I know you had a lonely childhood but haven't you *over-reacted*?'

Sometimes I crossed Fleet Street to pawn a silver cigarette-case (a birthday gift from my father after a particularly long 'mental cruelty'). More often I went into the bank to cash small cheques and tried not to break into an undignified run if the cashier came across with the money. I was once at the counter when the manager (I remember rimless glasses on a rimless sort of man) came up and said, 'Drawing out are we today, or are we paying in?'

'Drawing out actually,' I admitted. 'I mean, we've got to live.'

'No "got to" about it,' the manager said sharply. 'In fact many people have to learn that living is quite unnecessary.'

It gave me no satisfaction to hear that, the following week, my bank manager had fallen off the platform at Charing Cross and been killed instantly by an oncoming 'Northern Line'. I don't know if it was an accident, natural justice or even if he had been contemplating suicide when he spoke to me at the counter. All I have learnt is that it is very unsafe to prophesy other people's deaths. I got to know a superstitious criminal lawyer who once consulted, at huge expense, a fashionable fortune-teller. After the usual opening pleasantries about dark women and financial advantages, the seer looked pained and embarrassed and, when pressed, said, 'I'm sorry to have to tell you I can see nothing at all after the end of September. I'm afraid that the future is totally blank after that.' My friend went away convinced that his imminent death had been horrifyingly foreseen and he made his Will and unhappily arranged his affairs. However, after my experience with my bank manager it came as no surprise to me to learn that on 1 October the fortune-teller died.

Getting a start in the world of divorce seemed the more difficult in that the work was shared out among a small circle of lawyers who had thus consolidated their hold on matrimonial disharmony. My father was one of the leaders of this group, another was a senior member of our chambers called 'Father William'. William Latey had two sons, one now a Judge and the other a distinguished broadcaster, who were big boys when I was a small child in the Temple. He was a small, fat, extremely clubbable man who wore pince-nez and had been, as a journalist on *The Illustrated London News*, posted to Russia in the days before the revolution. He would often describe to me nights when the troika was loaded with champagne and he was 'off to the gypsies'. 'Father William' was extremely kind to me and took me to dinner at the Savage Club where he would explain that it was useless to hope for a brief in your first ten years at the bar. 'We used to sit in chambers doing absolutely nothing. Then my wife would lend us balls of her wool and we would practise safe cricketing strokes with them in the corridor outside the clerk's room, sending the knitting wool for six with our rolled umbrellas.' Later 'Father William' developed this reminiscence into a speech which he would make annually at the chambers' Christmas party, and describe the first lean years at the bar when 'we had absolutely nothing to do but play with our balls'. It was clearly not a prospect which was going to help a growing family.

The old divorce lawyers seemed to stretch back into history, almost to the Ecclesiastical Courts where they talked about 'Vera Copula' instead of complete intercourse and a 'Divorce a Mensa et Thora' (from bed and board) instead of Judicial Separation. One of my father's friends was called Victor Russell who, as a child, had been frightened by Bismarck when his father was Ambassador to Berlin. Victor Russell had also met his grandfather, Lord John Russell, a Prime Minister who had, as a small boy, been held up to see Napoleon standing on board the *Bellerophon* before sailing from Portsmouth Harbour. I also knew a somewhat dissolute old solicitor who said that once at tea, Hilaire

Belloc's mother had told him that she hadn't tasted cucumber sandwiches since Lady Byron died. These old lawyers, rooted in the past, seemed so firmly entrenched that it was difficult to know what I was going to do for a crust, as they say in Australia.

As old as the lawyers and a great deal more alarming were the first divorce Judges I encountered. One thing to be said for spending a few years at the bar is that the Judges do get younger. In those days they exercised the old middle-class male prerogative of being permanently in a most filthy temper. One of them was a Catholic convert who seemed to be against divorce on principle, not a happy position for one whose crust earning consisted of handing out Decrees Nisi to anxious applicants. This Judge would rap on the desk with his fountain-pen and announce, as was no doubt the fact, 'We are a Court of Justice, we are not a stable!' if anyone so much as stirred on an aching buttock during the administration of the oath.

My father, of course, was more than a match for these old Judges, about whom I would dream and wake up screaming in the night. He once made my mother lead him banging out of the President's Court in a gesture of entirely simulated rage. There was, as I now remember it, one Judge who never stopped talking, with barely suppressed fury, about the children of broken homes. 'They are innocents,' he would often say. 'They have committed no matrimonial offence. Yet they are the ones that suffer.' My father appeared before him when he was acting for a husband who had left his wife after years of misery and married again; the question was one of maintenance for the first family.

'What I have to consider, Mr Mortimer,' the Judge said bitterly, 'are the innocent children! They are the sufferers. I suppose your client [heavy sarcasm] has *some* sort of concern for his blameless children. *Has* he?'

'Let us assume', said my father, 'that he has none. Suppose he absolutely loathes the little brats. Be so good as to act on the assumption that he can't stand the sight of them and wishes to God they'd never been born. And then let us approach the practical question of how he's going to keep two homes going on an agricultural wage of four pounds seven shillings a week.' It was an effective gambit, but one I've never dared to imitate.

Worst of all was a temporary Judge who ruined, for himself and everyone else, the divorce cases he tried, by becoming greatly overexcited by the evidence. He was a tall, gaunt, bright-eyed person with the rusty black plumage and greedy expression of an ageing, but still amorous, vulture. A witness had only to touch lightly on what he called the 'sexual allegations' for him to quiver eagerly. 'Did it look like that, madam?' he would say and draw a hurried diagram of a hugely erect member which he would ask the usher to hand to the appalled Petitioner. In one of the makeshift Courts that were used for 'undefendeds' after the war, he once became so excited during the course of a nullity case that he stood up and his wig attached itself to a low lamp-bracket above his head. He sat down bald and breathing heavily to ask further questions about some long-past night of sexual débâcle. Needless to say he was soon put out to grass. With Judges as with advocates detachment is all; and what is to be aimed at is the state of lucid indifference.

13

IN ORDER TO GET SOLICITORS TO LIKE THE CUT OF YOUR jib you had to meet some solicitors. This could only be done by appearing in Court, something that you wouldn't be asked to do until you'd met a few solicitors who liked the cut of your jib. This was the sort of difficulty which could last a lifetime, as with some unfortunates it did. My father told me of one barrister so briefless that, when a pupil came and paid him £100 for six months' instruction on the mysteries of the law, both the senior barrister and his clerk decamped with the money in the general direction of Boulogne and were never, either of them, seen again.

Other less ruthless, but equally unsuccessful barristers would spend a lifetime, supported by small private incomes, dutifully sitting in their chambers reading the Law Reports, having lunch in the Inns and discussing other people's cases. They knew exactly who was going to 'take silk' or be appointed to the bench. They became obsessed by a world from which they were arbitrarily excluded, like social climbers who know all about the latest Hunt Ball, but only from reading *The Tatler*.

Resolved to participate in the legal world, I started doing 'Poor Persons' Divorces' and going to a Free Legal Aid Centre in the East End of London. Neither of these sources could be relied on to produce what my father called 'money briefs'; but they might yield appearances in Court and introductions to solicitors. So I sat in the Legal Aid Centre in the evenings longing for a murderer to come rushing in with a dripping knife, begging me to conduct his defence. All I got was a succession of bewildered old ladies in trouble with their pensions and their rents, ushered in by a tireless, chain-smoking, underpaid and uncomplaining Administrator who only really cheered up when she could produce a husband accused of outrageous cruelty, or a young fairground boxer faced with ten paternity summonses. 'He's certainly innocent,' she muttered persuasively past a strong Capstan and a haze of smoke. 'He was in strict training at the time.' Never an expert on rents or pensions, I was of limited use to my clients at the Free Legal Aid Centre, but they taught me never to show surprise at instructions, however unlikely. One completely credible and highly respectable lady sought a divorce, but had to admit that her son, a young Post Office worker whom she brought with her, was not her husband's child although he had been born during the marriage. It took a good many visits and some close questioning before she admitted that she had been impregnated by the spirit of the late Ramsay MacDonald who came at her over the wireless waves as she was passing Bush House. In the end, I remember, she got her divorce and proved, on all other subjects, a most sensible and reliable witness.

So, by the way of the 'Poor Persons' and Free Legal Aid and by courtesy of a few 'undefendeds' which fell from my father's table on the days when he was in a Probate action or 'laid up with a cold' or had wisely chosen to stay at home, wearing his straw hat and pricking out antirrhinums, as a preferred alternative to slogging up to London in the train for one short act of adultery, I got into Court and managed, in the course of time, to meet that great source of money briefs, the Solicitors' Managing Clerk.

Managing clerks of the old school were, it seemed to me, the main prop and buttress of the legal system. When qualified solicitors were too busy conveying office blocks or attending funerals to bother with the daily grind of the High Court of Justice, their unqualified managing clerks, equipped with an old raincoat whose pockets were stuffed with writs and summonses, a cunning way of getting round the Clerk of the Lists and an experience of life which started by being an office-boy at the age of fourteen, escorted mink-coated actresses through the Divorce Courts and cajoled greedy beneficiaries into accepting settlements in Will cases. I remember particularly Mr Wyvern, with a plume of grey hair over a bald pate, spectacles as thick as the bottoms of beer mugs and a head worn always tilted to one side, who would pull the essential, and disgraceful, facts out of a divorce case with the delicate enthusiasm of a bird extracting a juicy worm from a dry garden. There was also Mr Bertram, small and very fat, with a purple nose and a hat turned up all round, which made him look like a north-country comic, a deceptive appearance because he was both legally astute and deeply puritanical, believing that all women in divorce cases were reincarnations of 'La Dame aux Camélias' and destined for a tragic death if they didn't reform. 'You seem a decent enough woman at heart,' Mr Bertram would say to some twittering actress with a 'discretion statement' which ran into several pages. 'Why can't you give up your horrible way of life and try and turn out a reasonable Yorkshire pudding?' We once joined in divorcing a distinguished lady novelist to whom he said, 'Why don't you give up writing that pornographic filth. Your books are an embarrassment to open up in the Tube. If you can't write decent stuff you'd be far better off spending the time with your kids.' Curiously enough both the actress and the lady novelist seemed to find Mr Bertram entirely reassuring and they would go off to buy him a Guinness in the Cock Tavern feeling that with the forces of morality so strongly on their side they had little to fear from the most censorious Judge.

Finally there was Mr Evelyn, with his drooping moustache, stiff collar and dangling watch-chain. He was a man who spoke in a soft voice of incurable sadness, whose marriage to a brutal hospital matron was so wretchedly unhappy that he could only find some sort of peace of mind during his day's work in the Divorce Court. He was gentle with his clients and suffered deeply if they weren't able to obtain their freedom. Mr Evelyn lived life at second hand, enjoying nothing more than the knell of Decrees Nisi tolling to terminate other people's marriages.

Mr Wyvern, Mr Bertram and Mr Evelyn and others like them were the men whom I had to get to like the cut of my jib, and I proceeded to woo them with a grosser flattery and more assiduous courtship than I have ever used on a lady. I drank endless cups of coffee with them in the crypt under the Law Courts. I paced up and down the corridor outside the summons room with them, waiting to do a spot of custody, or I travelled with them on the Tube to doomed confrontations before the Uxbridge Magistrates. I enquired endlessly after Mr Wyvern's tomato plants and the health of his begonias. I asked for daily bulletins on Mr Bertram's daughter's progress in the small but cut-throat world of Croydon figure-skating, and I discovered unhappily just how many years it had been since Mrs Evelyn had agreed to accompany her husband on an evening at the pictures. When Mr Wyvern asked if I and my good lady would care to be his guests at one of his Masonic occasions I lacked the courage to refuse immediately. So much Farex, so many knicker-linings depended, I knew, on the likeability of my jib.

It was often said that a life at the Divorce Bar leads to cynicism, disillusion and despair at the frailty of human nature, and yet the cases I did with the tireless managing clerks showed, as often as not, men and women trying to behave decently against appalling odds. They also showed the respect that most people have for the institution of marriage, indeed they only got divorced in order to marry again immediately, usually to a partner who bore an extraordinary likeness to the spouse they had been at such trouble and expense to abandon.

I also discovered that husbands and wives don't rush into divorce. They will put up with the most appalling home conditions rather than apply for the order of release. I discovered couples who hadn't spoken for years and who communicated solely by means of laconic and unfriendly notes left on the boiler, or on the kitchen table with a plate of congealed stew. 'Let her down at the office heat this up for you, she seems to do everything else' or 'Your conduct last night with the hall light just about beat the band! I take it you're now going all out for my financial ruin' were common phrases in this sort of correspondence. I heard of a General who used to address letters to the furniture his wife's family provided, leaving on the articles concerned notes like, 'You are a very vulgar little sideboard. Go back to Whiteleys where you came from' or 'Gentlemen's homes have rugs over polished boards. You are a nasty common fitted carpet and your presence here is *no longer required*.' The wonder was not that this sort of conduct led to the Divorce Court but that it was tolerated for so long without complaint.

This toleration is no doubt due to a reluctance to admit defeat. It also comes, I'm sure, from a terror of loneliness. Any human relationship, however painful and absurd, even if it is reduced to a trickle of abusive little notes in a desert of silence, can seem preferable to the unchartered desert of divorce. Better, perhaps, a life of choked-back fury and a companion to hate than the loneliness of the bed-sitter and the silence of a book in the corner of a holiday hotel.

These were the sort of discoveries I was making during the years when I first worked as a barrister, facts vital to a writer which I neglected then and didn't use. In the absurd world of the old-style Divorce Court I was treating life in the law with peculiar seriousness, enjoying the hunt for briefs and a practice. I behaved more like a lawyer than I have done since, and bought a bowler-hat, an umbrella and a pair of striped trousers. Clad in these I met Henry Winter for lunch in El Vino and allowed him the privilege of watching me do a 'separation order' down at Tower Bridge. When we came away from the case, which I had lost, I saw him staring at me with amusement.

'What're you looking at?'

'Your barrister's set.'

'My what?'

'It's like those cards with bits of costume stuck on them that children used to get for Christmas. A "Ticket-collector's set" and a "Nurse's set" and a "Red Indian set". They just have the hat and the main essentials like the ticket-punch or the thermometer. Your's is the barrister's set.'

'You mean you don't think I'm *really* a barrister?'

'I don't know. Do you?'

I suppose I did. When success can be clearly imagined it is easy to succeed. If your ambition is to have as many 'undefendeds' as possible that can be achieved simply by persistence, a reasonable amount of good luck and sufficient strength to stand on your feet and ask for Decrees Nisi at regular intervals. I continued to flatter Mr Wyvern and Mr Bertram and Mr Evelyn and, as my father spent more and more days in the country, I found myself taking over more of his practice. Members of the Forces and their wives became able to get divorced under a scheme which meant that the barrister got paid a guinea for an 'undefended' and if you were lucky you got them in batches of five or even ten. In my struggle to provide a satisfactorily affirmative answer to Winter's question Penelope gave me every support. She used the machine on which she had written her first novel to type my divorce petitions, tapping out paragraphs of wilful refusal to consummate, or desertion without cause, or particulars of deep humiliation and distress, the long litany of broken homes which I had learnt at my father's knee.

14

SOMEONE, WHO MIGHT WELL HAVE BEEN THE FRENCH FILM director Jean-Luc Godard during a lucid interval, said that while he agreed that every story should have a beginning, a middle and an end they need not necessarily be in that order. Looking back down a long corridor of years at that serious, prematurely middle-aged figure in the wig and gown, or the bowler-hat and pin-stripes, I seem, for one hallucinated moment, to be looking at the future and not the past, seeing one complete version of what I was going to be when I grew up. I had become, perhaps too easily even for him, what my father had in mind, the ambitious barrister of the Probate, Divorce and Admiralty Division, the professional product of an English education. In our twenties we embrace middle age with enthusiasm, enjoy discussing mortgages and school fees and acquire a taste for mowing the lawn. The years which follow can bring the courage to return to the essentials of childhood, a state of carefree individuality which can only be completely recaptured at the moment of death.

Not, of course, that the simplicities of professional life can be separated from a deep basis of private confusion. Billowing up to his client outside the Court, resplendent in the barrister's set, aloof in the fancy costume, the professional has no difficulty at all in picking out the vital points in other people's marriages and deciding that it was what happened in the summer of 1943 that caused the breakdown. At the same time he may have no idea why his own home is a daily battlefield, the scene of a war whose origins have long since been forgotten. Just as miraculous cures are brought about by doctors who are themselves suffering from fatal diseases, great issues of life and death are decided by Judges who, in their daily lives, can't make up their minds when to play out their trumps and whose existence is entirely in the hands of resolute wives or implacable sisters. To the professional adviser nothing is easier to decide than other people's problems, and I found no difficulty in telling men and women twice my age how to regulate their finances or to 'exercise a self-denying ordinance'. I knew just what provision they ought to be making for their tax and what would be best for their children. I often had the satisfaction of leading them through the dark maze of the old divorce law into some sort of daylit sanity. I could only hope that they never saw me breaking into an undignified run as I left the Westminster Bank, or returning home with a nightly feeling of bewilderment to face again the perpetually insoluble complexities of married life.

We had gone to stay in Ireland before we were married and Penelope had stood on the beach in Connemara looking at the sea, tempted, as she sometimes was in those days, by thoughts of death. Our temperaments differed in that while I looked at life, a good deal of the time, with the facile optimism of one who sees a steady increase in the number of his 'undefendeds', she got her strength, and I sometimes thought her pleasure also, from the undoubted awfulness of the human situation. She contemplated an increasingly desperate plight with a gloom which was frequently expressed with humour and a kind of glee. This attitude, so painful to her that it became, at times, heroic, provided the source from which she was able to produce her novels and short stories. She would lie stretched out in front of the fire filling notebooks with her neat handwriting, or sit in the sun with her typewriter clicking endlessly whilst the growing band of small girls galloped through the unmown grass astride short sticks which they made believe to be horses and fed, under the hedges, with small plates of cornflakes. Meanwhile I was writing out further and better particulars of intolerable conduct leading to the breakdown of the marriage, or, as time went on, preparing to fight the case of the Methodist minister whose wife ran away with the District Nurse.

Life was not made easier, in those early days of marriage, by the extreme generosity of friends. A temporarily wealthy friend of Penelope's presented us, in a moment of extraordinary kindness, with a farmhouse in Essex, and added the gift of a huge shooting-brake to transport the children there. It was something of a struggle to afford the petrol but when we did, and had loaded the great van to the rafters with plastic pots and toys and gumboots and carry-cots and Ostermilk and shopping-bags full of spare knickers and balding Teddy bears, we were faced with a house which demanded more devotion than we had time for. I sat on the floor of a shed trying to start the electric light engine with a piece of string. I would pull and pull with no result and then the engine would start purring, the house would be lit up like a Christmas tree for about five minutes, but then the machinery would cough, splutter and fade away, the lights would dim and I would be left in the dark, hopelessly pulling the string and wondering how my ambitions to write got diverted into this extraordinarily frustrating activity. Once, in a magnificent gesture of despair, Penelope threw an entire bowl full of washing-up out of the kitchen window and into the uncultivated garden. The growing army of children looked on politely, and in mild disbelief.

It was Jim Holland, once again, who came to our rescue. We managed to swap our house in Essex for his in Swiss Cottage. It was a tall, narrow and crumbling Victorian building which then attracted a rent of seven pounds a week. It was a huge, it seems now totally appropriate, family house with dark corners in the basement and unvisited rooms in the attic where children could hide, laugh and run to sulk or cry unnoticed. The rooms had moulded ceilings and the staircase stretched up into remote areas, which in twenty years we never finished painting. So distant were some of the floors that, years later, a notable Polish actor, who had made friends with one of my step-daughters, managed to live upstairs for a week without either us or his anxious Embassy, who suspected defection, ever being aware of it.

There was also, in the Swiss Cottage area at that time, a wonderful sadness which seemed, for some reason which I cannot entirely recall, well suited to our mood. There was a sort of late Viennese melancholy, promoted by the large number of middle-aged refugees who sat drinking *Kaffee mit schlag* in the Finchley Road tea-rooms and then returned to their bed-sitters to listen to Mähler on the wireless and work out chess problems. They were the lost families who, during the war, felt particular terror when they were able to shout at an approaching aircraft, 'It's one of ours!' In time the quiet streets round Swiss Cottage would be torn down to make room for offices and blocks of expensive flats. When we started to live there the rows of bells beside each front door were identified by engraved, Central European visiting cards. On summer evenings the crumbling terraces would come to life with the sound of exiled string quartets, rehearsing for concerts which might never be arranged.

The Swiss Cottage house contained the lifetime of our marriage. It was the setting for the Christmases when the children were kept waiting outside the sitting-room door, breathless with expectation, and for the New Year's Eve party where a literary County Court Judge tried to persuade a despairing young poet not to hang himself because it would be so embarrassing for His Honour to have to give evidence at the inquest. It was the place we were glad to see when we came home from holidays abroad and where, on many occasions, a strong feeling of doom was passed round the huge nursery lunches with the roast potatoes.

It did us for almost twenty years, and put up with the vagaries of fashion, from the austere fifties to the more affluent sixties. At first we had single walls painted in distinct poster colours in the manner of the Great Exhibition on the South Bank, a small flourish of culture now almost forgotten, which left a memory not of the Crystal Palace but of the Guinness Clock. Then we had ivy-leaved wallpaper and rubber plants during the early Expresso Age and the Great Sanderson Revival. Finally we installed a kitchen designed by Terence Conran with a room divider, orange cupboards and concealed lighting. By that time the destruction of the area was almost complete, the new apartment blocks were forming up around us and the moulded ceilings had begun to tremble and crack and shower plaster down into the hall. The Terence Conran kitchen stood, cheerful and functional, in the centre of a disintegrating house and marriage. As the cracks spread we evacuated the house and, in the course of time, new lives were started. We didn't expect the house to survive our departure, but unexpectedly it has and stands almost alone among a forest of North London towers of cubby holes, places where there is no room to put the books or for the children to hide. It is still a beleaguered witness to a Victorian ideal of family living.

In her stories Penelope kept her log of these years with wry precision, but in the early fifties she had not yet achieved her great success. Not even the rising tide of 'undefendeds' and the occasional contested divorce with 'refreshers' could keep the great, leaky edifice of the Swiss Cottage house financially afloat. I went on writing, finishing two or three novels quickly, anxious for the hundred pounds advance, conscious that, perhaps due to the premature onset of middle age, I had not found my voice, or that my head was still too full of the voices of admired talents. I was also invited to write stories for women's magazines and, because of the close scrutiny of the cashiers at the Westminster Bank, I accepted the invitation.

I was taken to lunch at The Ivy by serious, blue-haired ladies, to have the essence of 'Women's Magazine Fiction' explained to me. Everything, they said, must happen by chance, the dark and handsome stranger (a doctor, perhaps, or a farmer, never, please God, a dentist or a divorce lawyer) should ideally pick the girl up in the street after a passing motorist has knocked her off her bicycle, although meetings in lifts or at concerts in the Festival Hall were not ruled out. The idea of life as a series of random accidents appealed to my view of the universe and the money promised seemed to me princely and likely to keep the Inland Revenue at bay for at least a month with something left over for Farex and bikkipegs. I wrote several stories at great speed which appeared, lavishly illustrated with pictures of sun-tanned characters with amazingly white teeth, and I made the mistake of reading one to my father during a weekend in the country.

'Writing *down*?' he said. 'Stick to divorce, old boy. Far less humiliating.'

There was surely, however, some source of wealth and recognition which could be tapped, apart from adultery and cruelty, to meet our more pressing needs. I thought of my knowledge of the technique of film writing, so painfully gained during my years in the Crown Film Unit. Was such expertise to be allowed to gather dust or had the time come for me to make a fortune in pictures?

Whoever or whatever is in charge of our accidents provided a swift answer to this foolish request.

I came back to chambers after a particularly testing 'undefended', one in which the marriage was less dissolved than slowly hacked to pieces before the Judge's eyes, and my father's clerk told me that a Mr Moxer had rung me. He had no idea who Mr Moxer might be, but he said that he didn't sound much like a legal gentleman.

When I dialled the number there was a sound of heavy, suspicious breathing.

'Hullo,' I said. 'Is Mr Felix Moxer there?'

The breathing stopped, appeared to be painfully held and a suspicious voice finally said, 'Is *who* there?'

'He wanted me to ring ...'

'Here. Give it to me.' I heard a female order and then an excited buzz as of amateur actors bickering behind a first-night curtain. Then there was silence as though a hand had been put over the mouthpiece. After a long wait the curtain rose on the female voice, aloof and efficient.

'Films of Truth and Reality.'

'Is Mr Felix Moxer there?' I asked.

'Mr Moxer is in conference. I don't think he can speak with you.'

'That you, Mortimer?' Almost at once the voice I was to know as Felix Moxer's broke in. He sounded, I thought, in almost mortal terror. 'Doris is always talking about you. Says I ought to use you as a writer. Look, can you come round at once? You remember Doris, don't you?'

Could I ever forget Doris, with the cheroot dangling from her scarlet lips, wearing flannel trousers with a cheap fur coat slung over her shoulders, swearing at the hourly boys like a trooper? Doris was the *Obergruppenführer* of the Crown Film Unit and it seemed improbable that she should have had anything as human as a brother-in-law and incredible that she should have recommended me to him.

'Come round? Where are you?'

'In the City. Not far from where you are now.'

I found 'Films of Truth and Reality' in a side-street a short walk from my father's chambers. I pushed open a purple front door and I was in a passage leading to a small, but well-equipped, studio. I saw the familiar sights, the lights producing continuous sunshine, the one-dimensional walls and swaying backcloths, the electricians playing Solo and a nervous assistant waiting by an urn for the director's tea. It was a world I had hardly thought to see again, one which I then realized I missed very much.

I was shown into an empty office, the door of which bore the inscription 'Felix Moxer, ARPS. Private'. After about five minutes I felt I was being watched, but before I could enjoy the full discomfort of the situation Mr Moxer burst in at the door, giving an extremely poor imitation of a man who has just returned from a long journey.

'Glad to see you, old man,' he said. 'Have a cigarette?'

He produced a gold case, found only one cigarette in it, looked at it with dismay and then pressed it between his lips. He was a large man whose features, undistinguished in themselves, seemed to be on the point of drifting apart.

'My God,' he said. 'My wife's got a touch of the nervy. They get it in this business, you know. It's the uncertainty. And a woman's life can be very hard, old man, after a certain age.'

I started to say that women no doubt had many difficulties at all ages, but he interrupted me severely.

'You mustn't keep me gossiping, old man. Now then. Feature-length film. Subject? Diamond smuggling. Budget? Open-ended. Your fee? Generous. First day of principal photography? Three months' time. Can you leave for Africa next week?'

'I suppose so ...' I thought of the bush, far from Swiss Cottage and the Temple. Above all I thought of the generous fee.

'Just word out a short treatment, old man. Something to show the punters. Bring it in on Monday and I'll have your contract ready.'

That weekend I abandoned the Petitions and laid aside the Further and Better Particulars of Cruelty. I wrote a story about diamond smuggling which included an eccentric Dutchman, a beautiful Zulu girl and a cynical South African policeman who was given to quoting Swinburne. It was something, I felt sure, that Mr Moxer would enjoy and it should even keep the punters happy. It would pay the rent for a year and give me a month away from the Law Courts, with a film unit, in a tent, under the stars, where I could smell the dry, dusty veldt and watch the animals move out of the shadows around the water-hole at night.

That year I saw no lumbering elephant or delicate antelope come to drink. I missed the jeep bumping across the dry landscape and the excitement of gumboot dances in the mine-workers' compound. When I got back to 'Films of Truth and Reality' on Monday I thought at first I had mistaken the address. But the purple front door was unchanged, only the inside of the building had altered. There were no lamps, no electricians, no tea-boy and no make-up department. There were only boxes of bananas, apples and oranges. Felix Moxer's name had been removed from his office door and the room was occupied by a man in a brown overall who wore a trilby hat. Like this insubstantial pageant, Mr Moxer had faded, leaving behind him nothing but a wholesale fruit business.

The movies, of course, provide a perpetually frustrating occupation, not unlike the search for the Holy Grail, or the passionate pursuit of girls who never keep any appointment and finally turn out to have left for New Zealand with no forwarding address. In this way films have always seemed to me a world apart. When I wrote novels they appeared, however temporarily, in print. When I wrote plays none of them failed to be performed. As a lawyer, my cases came on for trial. Films are different. Films evaporate. After weeks of excited work they vanish into thin air. Now you see them, now you don't and often, when you don't, it comes as a merciful release.

That, however, was the only occasion on which an entire film studio eluded me. It was symbolic, perhaps, of my pursuit of the drama at that time. I stood with treatment in hand in front of a fruit shop, and 'Films of Truth and Reality' had melted into the world of fiction.

15

WHEN HE NOTED THE DEATH OF KING GEORGE VI IN HIS garden diary my father had embarked on the last decade of his life. 'Went up to chambers', he dictated to my mother, 'and found it rather a strain. Everywhere the weeds are growing rank, but we are determined not to mind.'

His interest in the law had faded a little and every moment seemed wasted spent away from the garden whose ceaseless activity he learnt of by hearsay from my mother. He would then repeat to her the news she had given him and she would note it down in her neat art-school handwriting, in a narrative in which she appears as a character. 'Kathleen released a sparrow entangled in the grass of the West Field,' she wrote, or 'This evening Kathleen saw a hedgehog drinking the cat's milk.' This, however, is a rare instance of my father's reporting that my mother alone had seen something. Usually events are recorded as though they had been visible to his sightless eyes also.

'We saw two brimstone butterflies and a peacock,' he reported and, in April 1952, 'Anemone Blanda are improving, about 40 blooms. The first daffodils in flower are the Lenten lilies. Rhododendron Thomsonii is in flower, beautifully but sparingly.' 'On the 2nd of May', the chronicle continued, 'we had our first dish of asparagus and the first cockchafer flew in. There is much apple blossom in the orchard. A thrush's nest in the rhododendron border contains 3 or 4 newly born chicks. We have had to have a new outer cover on the spare wheel, the second tyre this year!' That summer it became extraordinarily hot and my father recorded the fact that he had taken two cold baths a day, and 'Smith has planted nemesias, asters and snapdragons in the border. Unknown to us (but guessed at by Kathleen) scything has been going on in the West Field. Three wasps nests were destroyed in the orchard. The Crinum Powelli has sent up four spikes which are now in flower. A homing pigeon has taken up residence with us since August 1st, completely tame. He comes into the house and sits on the table heater and the ice chest.

On August 6th we had our first ripe peach. John and Penelope came down to stay with the children and we had a treasure-hunt.'

Now Sally, my own small daughter born in May 1950, a month when my father noted that the camellias were flowering well, staggered after the other children. They were sent off on the hunt my father had planned, with the clues in verse leading from the fowl-run to the stile in the West Field, back to the orchard and on to a dozen other hiding-places, to end where a string, tied to a bush, could be pulled, to drag from the brackish leaves and sour-smelling mud of a tea pond a biscuit tin containing the treasure, a humming-top, perhaps, or a bag of mint humbugs.

So through all times of doubt and boredom, during the gloomiest custody cases and in moments of deep frustration, when the film studio vanished or the half-completed novel felt as though it should never have been begun, my father's house and garden were there as a show that never closed, a solace and a kind of drug. Life in the garden was never uneventful; drama of a kind was always taking place. An owl might be trapped in the fruit cage, or my mother, veiled like a widow, wrapped in a Burberry and carrying a puffing funnel of smoke, would be going bravely through the orchard to delude the bees into thinking their hive was on fire and to rob them of their honey.

In April 1955 my father was able to dictate: 'We pricked out the blue salvias and potted up the seedling dahlias. John telephoned us to say that Penelope had a baby boy born at 8 a.m. Smith has made up a hotbed in the cucumber frame and sown grass on the old rose beds. We bought hoops for the children who are coming to stay and went on planting out rhododendron seedlings.'

It was Penelope's sixth child, her and my first son after a long line of daughters, an event to take its natural place in the chronology of the garden.

Apart from my father's house and garden, stability in a shifting world was provided for me by Henry Winter. He had gone back to Oxford after the war and started the slow process which led to his qualifying as a doctor and he was now a GP in a quiet West Country village. He had a pretty wife, children whom he treated with unfailing courtesy and helped with their Latin, and a huge collection of gramophone records.

When I visited Winter he would drive me on his rounds and I would sit in the car or in village pubs while he reassured the old men, cheered up the young mothers or carried out endless, minute inspections of ailing children. Everywhere he was welcome and, as with all good doctors, his presence alone caused relief from sickness. When he had finished work we would drink beer together and discuss the old days in the Paddington Pacifist Unit. In the evenings he would play Mozart or Haydn (Brahms's Fourth Symphony had receded, with some embarrassment, into our romantic past) or part of his huge collection of Blues records.

> Went down to St James's Infirmary
> Saw my baby there . . .
> Laid out on a long white table . . .
> So white so cold so bare.

The mortuary lament would ring out from his house, and Winter would light his pipe and tell me about the extraordinary pregnancies and the gossip from the cottage hospital. I enjoyed my visits to Winter, but was never sorry to get back to London. One of my novels had been selected, to my amazement, by the Book Society. I was writing another (which turned out to be my last) in which I seemed, after some misspent years, to be rediscovering some sort of identity. Penelope and I had been asked to write a travel book about Italy; it was a necessary commission because it was the only way we could afford to go there. There was, I was beginning to feel, a world outside. Although I admired Winter's life of obscure professional dedication and total peace of mind, I knew I couldn't share it. In his presence this knowledge of my different ambitions made me feel vaguely tarnished and I was glad to get away.

The house we rented in Positano was exactly up four hundred and thirty-six steps from the beach. The town, too small to be spoiled even today, is shaped like an opera-house and at night the houses glitter like stage boxes round the horseshoe of cliffs. We had to climb from the orchestra stalls, from the bar of the Bucca di Bacco with its intimate view of the beach and the crowds passing by, up to the gods, to our small, square, bougainvillaea-covered house in the cheapest part of the auditorium. From there we could see far, far down the stage of grey volcanic sand, the backdrop of sea and the big white steamer passing slowly and with imperturbable punctuality on its way to Naples or Amalfi.

We had put our noses out of the door of beleaguered England before, clutching what always turned out to be too few travellers' cheques. I once got paid an extraordinary £100 for a brief. Much to my clerk's horror I tore open the envelope containing my fee ('I don't think your father would ever have opened a letter addressed to his clerk, sir') and we went straight to Paris, which I was determined to enjoy and was disconcerted by the deep pleasure Penelope took in finding fault with the Champs Elysées and the 'Nouvelle Eve' club where I suppose the girls might have looked better-tempered and which saw off, anyway, most of the fee for my divorce. We had driven to Rome and crashed the car in a valley of Romansh-speakers in Switzerland. We had stayed in the South of France and lain out on a beach unwisely and spent the next three days shivering with sunstroke in a dark room, spraying the mosquitoes and counting our money. We had driven through the Camargue in the hope of seeing a flamingo, but we were quarrelling at the time and when my wife spotted the flamingo she kept it to herself. Every trip abroad seemed to end sitting on a bench in a public park, clutching small presents for the children with nothing left to buy a drink. Sealed up in England during the long wartime years had made us ineffectual travellers.

Positano was the first foreign town we lived in, the first place out of England where we kept house and learned a new language to buy groceries, order meals or manage a simple and boring conversation without jokes. The older girls drifted away from us with doubtful Italian Counts or on the back of waiters' Vespas; the eldest became so enchanted and so expert at the language that she spent most of her adult life in Rome and became one of the few English people to discover the existence of a small, discreet bar somewhere behind the High Altar in St Peter's. The younger children sighed in the sun and my daughter confused the place with Scotland. I carried my infant son up and down the four hundred and thirty-six burning steps to the beach daily. He wore the sort of white hat which old men put on for playing bowls, he was covered with mosquito bites and seemed extremely grumpy. When the children became ill we called in an Italian doctor who came puffing up to the house, sat down, borrowed our clinical thermometer to take his own temperature, swallowed a handful of our Disprin imported from the Swiss Cottage Boots and went away, apparently feeling a good deal better.

Seeing me staggering up the stairs with my arms full of child, Tennessee Williams, pressing back against the wall, would look at me with large eyes full of pity and genuine concern. He was staying at Ravello, in the Villa Cimbrone, with Arthur Jeffries, who came from an American cigarette-manufacturing family and was one of the few inhabitants of Venice to run his own gondola, complete with gondoliers wearing his

My father about to avoid doing
anything too heroic

My mother as a young woman

The Sloane Square Wolf Cubs. I am in the front row on the left

Duelling with *The Times* music critic

Turville Heath when my father built it

A MEMENTO OF 'BOOTH. V BOOTH'
MORTIMER ' IN EXPEDITIONE'

MORTIMER DE PROBATIONE NOVA ÆTIS

A recently-excavated fragment
dug up near Dr Johnson's Building.

Doing battle in the Probate
Court

My father, when he could see,
ready to do battle in the
Divorce Court

About to be deposed in the prep school production of *Richard II*

One-man band

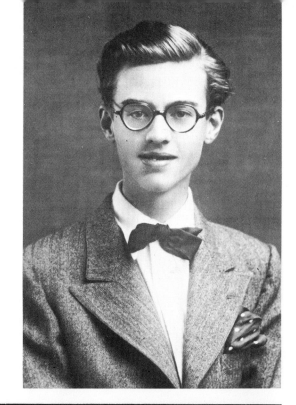

Leaving Harrow

At Oxford, simulated
study of law

Wedding group, 1949

Having caught Arthur Jeffries' gondola

An extended family, 1958: Madelon stands next to me; sitting from left to right: Caroline, Penelope, Jeremy, Sally and Julia; Deborah is lying on the floor.

Encore

ERIC BENTLEY   WAYLAND YOUNG

TOM MILNE   IAN DALLAS

Theatre Survey: NEW AUTHORS

SEPT.-OCT. 1958

2/-

'Into the New Wave as the tube doors were closing'. Back row, left to right: Arnold Wesker, Erol John, Bernard Kops and David Campton; front row, left to right: N.F.Simpson, Harold Pinter, Ann Jellicoe and me.

Jeremy as a Roman
soldier in discussion with
my father

Reading aloud, stories of cruelty, adultery and wilful neglect to maintain

OPPOSITE Keeping down
the mutiny in the garden

RIGHT In my 'barrister's
set'

BELOW An encounter
with Rumpole

Turville Heath today

Working at Turville Heath today with my daughter Emily – 'years of unlooked-for happiness'

personally designed yellow uniform. His gondoliers were in constant rivalry with Miss Peggy Guggenheim's gondoliers, who wore a uniform of a different colour and lived on what Mr Jeffries persisted in calling 'The Wrong Side of the Canal'.

In spite of our manifest heterosexuality and the position of our house on what was, on any showing, the Wrong Side of Positano, Arthur Jeffries befriended us and, in due course, we received an invitation to his pocket-sized palazzo in Venice. He was an endlessly generous host; every day the gondola would be made ready, a long and elaborate process, and we would be taken over to the Lido where lunch would be served, by the gondoliers wearing white gloves, in the shade of a yellow-and-white-striped tent. Arthur Jeffries would ask us politely about our writing and then tell us long, unhappy stories of his short-lived love affairs with Able Seamen from various visiting British battleships.

One day a balding, good-looking man came across the sand towards us, limping slightly. He was someone whom I had noticed the other passengers shunned on our motor boat journeys to the Danieli Hotel. As he sat down to lunch with us, Arthur Jeffries introduced Oswald Mosley. Accustomed from childhood to denouncing Fascism, certain that he was at one with the enemy who had made the war a reasonable necessity, I should of course have got up, protested, and stridden indignantly away to a restaurant. So ingrained are our English attitudes and so deep the anxiety to avoid a scene that I sat on, and in no time at all Mosley was talking entertainingly about French and English architecture and the house he owned outside Paris. I felt, as I listened politely, a new awareness of our good fortune in never having been put to the test like Frenchmen, who may have found it all too easy to stifle a protest in the presence of a cultivated Nazi of undoubted charm.

Life at the Villa Jeffries brought other humiliations. I had at that time a rather squalid pair of swimming-trunks, well used and somewhat gnawed around the crotch by moths. On leaving the Lido after one of our visits, I forgot my Jantzens, leaving them on the roof of the yellow-and-white pavilion where Arthur Jeffries took his lunch. Months later, in the middle of a damp London winter, Mr Jeffries invited us to dinner in his house in Eaton Square. There were his fine collection of primitive paintings, his priceless Oriental rugs and his solid-gold dinner-service off which a party of about twenty-five murmuringly sophisticated people ate. Half-way through the meal he struck a bell which produced silence and the entry of a footman bearing a salver with a heavy gold cover. 'A little something', our host announced to the assembled company, 'which Mr Mortimer left behind in Venice.' The cover was removed and the footman bowed to present me with my bathers, looking singularly inappropriate on the gold platter and more moth-eaten than ever.

If I didn't live in the English countryside I would prefer a North Italian town to anywhere, although Venice has never been my favourite city. To me it has the dead feeling of places which live entirely on tourists, and from the first visit to Arthur Jeffries I found a sort of claustrophobia in Venice and a limited pleasure in sitting in the Piazza San Marco listening to ten bands outside ten different cafés playing selections from *Oklahoma* in ten different tempi. On our last visit I lost favour by not waiting for the gondola to be got ready, and by setting out on foot to various churches and arriving maddeningly ahead. However Arthur Jeffries' hospitality remained superb. Feeling that, perhaps because of our socialist views, we must come from the North of England, he got his cook to make what she proudly described as 'Il Hotpot Lancastero'. Later, when our heterosexuality seemed to set us apart from his other guests, he said, 'Cheer up, Mortimers. Next week a *honeymoon couple* are coming to stay. Then you'll have someone to discuss baby food with, won't you, dears?' In due course the honeymoon couple arrived. He seemed like a nice, straightforward young lawyer fresh out of Harvard and she was the handsome product of an English girls' boarding-school. We formed a splinter group at dinner and, ignoring the other guests who were gossiping about the latest visit of the British Navy, we went into breast-feeding, private education and infant jealousy in considerable depth. We smiled at the honeymoon couple with secret understanding when they announced they were going to bed early and went up the marble steps of the Palazzo Jeffries hand in hand.

A couple of hours later we were alone with Arthur Jeffries, drinking Sambucca. He was at his most sympathetic, describing the sad results of his sexuality which made it impossible for him to form satisfactory relationships. Indeed his tastes ran to young sailors who, once back in home waters, were perfectly contented with their wives to whom they no doubt gave the gold cigarette-cases with which our host invariably presented them. He was going to travel the world in search of someone, a Japanese perhaps, or an Indonesian, with whom he might manage to spend a second night. Permanence is, of course, the advantage of heterosexuality, we thought, feeling smug on behalf of ourselves and the couple upstairs.

At that moment there was a cry of, 'This is the *real* me!' and the young Harvard lawyer appeared at the top of the staircase. He was wearing high-heeled shoes, a sequined evening dress, lipstick, mascara and elbow-length gloves as he tip-toed down the stairs and came pirouetting across the tessellated marble. After him, frowning malevolently, came his young wife, wrapped in a Jaeger dressing-gown calling dolefully, 'Ronald! You're wearing my clothes *again*.' And this, we remembered, was only the honeymoon.

We left Venice the next day and took the boat to Dubrovnik. Drinking plum brandy in the walled city beside that pellucid water, life suddenly seemed to lose its complexity. There was nothing to buy, nothing much to do and in those days, few tourists. I remember sitting in a garden after breakfast, listening to the buzz of wasps who seemed too amiable to sting and starting to work out a play. The young men and girls of Yugoslavia looked remarkably handsome and not at all inclined to borrow one another's clothing.

Arthur Jeffries, in spite of the affair of the bathing-trunks, is a man I remember with great affection. I can see him now, reclining outside his tent on the Lido, working out the list of acquaintances he would ask to his London dinner parties, for I think he had no real friends although he was generous to many people. He was asked to leave Venice when his use of it became too scandalous even for the Italian police to tolerate. He toured the Far East in search of a companion but found no one. Years later we heard that he had committed suicide when he was staying, alone as usual, in 'L'Hôtel' in Paris; the refurbished and redecorated scene of the death of Oscar Wilde.

'Someone I know in London keeps talking about you.'

I was in the bar of the Bucca di Bacco in Positano some years later. It was littered with the friends we had made, including the tall painter who lived in a house full of doves and canaries where everything was beautiful except his works of art, and the blinded American ex-pilot who was noted for his speedy seduction of visiting Swedish girls; his dog was able to pick out the most beautiful and together he would quickly lure them aboard his boat for a trip to his house in the next bay. The band was playing the syrupy Italian hits of the time, and a retired Admiral from Naples was announcing his plan to include a life-sized model elephant in that year's pageant of Positano history. This animal could be made to walk up the beach with the Saracen invaders and drop a realistic plastic turd onto the sand. Wide-eyed children were peering through the straw screens, and on the dark sands beyond them, beach-boys were trying to earn enough foreign currency to see themselves through the winter. The Mayor was sitting surrounded, as usual, by a group of young English visitors whose Sloane Square voices rang out above the music and the clatter of Italian. It was a man from this group who had spoken to me and my stomach contracted with a kind of dread as he repeated,

'She's always talking about you. Angela Pargeter. Angela Bedwell, as was. Rather appropriate name, don't you think?'

'Yes,' I said. 'I do think,' and whispered, 'I suppose you don't happen to have her telephone number?'

I wrote it down on the corner of a paper tablecloth, tore it off and kept it for a long time. One day I rang the number and heard Angela's voice, apparently unchanged. 'About time,' she said. 'Why didn't you ring up a chap?'

We met for lunch. She had had two children and was living with them in a house in Kensington where she let out rooms. Peter Pargeter had been killed in a car crash in Ceylon where he was working on a film. We talked a lot about our children and their schools and the impossible character of her lodgers. We had several such lunches and then went to bed together one afternoon, comfortable and without discussion. In that considerate embrace much of the past seemed to be buried.

16

THE SHADOW OF THE CROWN FILM UNIT SPREAD ITSELF OVER the years which followed the war. The English, battered by the Age of Austerity, suffocated by the tightening of belts, bewildered by the loss of Empire and quite unable to explain why their defeated enemies gave every appearance of having won a tremendous victory, were clinging to the proud memory of war in fear of finding something worse. War movies continued to be made, and war books written. Men with short-backs-and-sides, blazers and cavalry twill trousers stood in saloon bars on Sunday mornings ordering pints of bitter, still saying, 'Roger and out'. Public life in the decade after the war now seems to have been curiously muted, habits of obedience persisted and demonstrations and marches, everyday events in the sixties, were unknown in the bland, forgettable decade that stretched between VJ Day and the Suez adventure. Severely shaken by the Blitz, the assured middle-class world into which I had been born remained intact until the mid-fifties; then, like the ceilings in our Swiss Cottage house, cracks and fissures began to be noticed and, in no time at all, the plaster was falling. Those who had been children in the war, and so had not been called upon to declare their patriotism, had found their voices. Nourished on Ministry of Health orange-juice and cod-liver oil, they had grown up to find themselves unimpressed with the Battle of Alamein, and not particularly interested in the sight of Corporal Dickie Attenborough having the screaming hab-dabs on the night before the attack on the Pinewood lot. Bill Haley and the Comets, although themselves chunky, mature-looking men in tartan dinner-jackets, had played *Rock Around the Clock* and caused the young Teddy Boys to riot down at the Elephant and Castle. James Dean had announced himself as a causeless rebel and been immolated in his Porsche. Whoever was young in those days it certainly was no longer me.

We did our best, of course, standing as the police horses advanced upon us at the time of Suez and shouting for Eden to go. Penelope was better at demonstrations than I, more determined in Downing Street and much more resolute in Grosvenor Square. There was really no need to shout because the unfortunate Mr Eden was on his way out of his own accord, victim of the fantasy that we still had an Empire and could live the heroic days of 1939 all over again. The Prime Minister retired appropriately to 'Goldeneye', the somewhat Spartan house in Jamaica where Ian Fleming wrote his dreams of a clubland hero, licensed to kill. But the voice of protest, once found, could scarcely be silenced. Far from being without a cause, the Rebels were supplied with an almost embarrassing superfluity of causes. Within a year you could march for nuclear disarmament or sit down for it in Trafalgar Square. Time stretched on down a never-ending line of marches, for Women's Rights and Gays' Rights, for Abortion on Demand and Women against Rape (marches for rape were fairly unusual), an endless stage army began then and stretched to the Children's Libbers lining the road to the *Oz* trial and demanding their birthright of a daily orgasm. A whole generation plodded along, perhaps nostalgically echoing the footsteps of those who had marched with equal confidence and simplicity to war.

If political life was tame and obedient for those ten years, the theatre was conformist also. Incessant revivals interspersed with Eliot's somewhat rarefied later verse plays and the plays of Anouilh, dealing with such comfortable themes as the pathos of lost innocence, made writers feel that the theatre would not welcome them. All this changed in 1956 with the production of *Look Back in Anger*. Although conventional in form there is no doubt that this play provided a theatrical revolution. For the first time the voice of someone not born to keep his upper lip stiff and take it with Britain could be heard raised in a violent soliloquy of discontent. More important to authors was the fact that the play made managements prepared to back contemporary writing. None of us who lived through that time can fail to be grateful to John Osborne, and my own childhood fantasies of performing and showing off on the dining-room staircase, the theatrical dreams which made me shut myself away in the bedroom making sets for a model theatre, might have remained a well-guarded secret but for the change his success brought about.

It has become fashionable to disparage Mr Osborne and he has naturally had to pay for his early adulation with a good deal of under-valuation of his later work. He is also mistaken for the eloquent but embittered characters he has written so well. This is a great error. Shakespeare was described by all who knew him as a singularly sweet and modest person, although he could rail with the best of them when he took it upon himself to be Timon of Athens. When, in the course of time, I got to know Mr Osborne, I was, like most people, surprised to find a gentle and unembittered man who lived in a stockbroker's house in Kent, went to Evensong and gave parties attended by those who administered to his spiritual, physical and financial needs: his bank manager, his vicar and his fishmonger. One of the happiest evenings I can remember was when I gave a poetry reading in his local hall. We drank a good deal of champagne and then Mr Osborne, wearing a boater and a striped blazer, made a long introductory speech in which he referred to what he suggested was the immorality of my life. I then entered, flanked by two actresses, from a door marked 'Gents', the area we had been allotted as a Green Room, and we read a great quantity of poetry. I felt like a wayward undergraduate who was being generously introduced by the local squire. It was a scene I never imagined possible when I first went to see *Look Back in Anger*.

My own entrance into the theatre was on a smaller, not to say a minute, scale.

Through Robin Denniston, then at Collins, who had published my last novels, I met, to my lasting benefit, Nesta Pain. She was a producer at the BBC and she asked me if I'd write a play for her to do on what my father always called 'the wireless'. Not only did she ask me once, but she went on asking me when I showed no signs of doing any such thing. Nesta Pain turned out to be a remarkable woman. She talked precisely, but with a slight stammer, and seemed like an enlightened, extremely intelligent headmistress, a marked contrast to the expansive grey-haired men in knitted ties and the hard-drinking poets who stood around her in the bar of The George in the great days of steam radio. She had dramatized Fabre's works in a series of programmes, and there was little that she didn't know about the merciless world of insects.

I had once gone, on the instructions of the Free Legal Advice Centre, to London Sessions to defend an elderly man on a charge of receiving stolen fish. For many years it remained my only criminal trial. London Sessions is stuck in a despondent area of South London, a sort of urban desert without a reasonable pub to go to in the lunch-hour. While a hint of sunshine often touches the gilded figure of Justice on the dome of the Old Bailey, it always seems to be raining round the London Sessions. It's a sad sort of place with all the cheeky Cockney sparrows waiting silently for the burglary to come on in Court No. 2, and the Juries look as if they rely on the work to eke out their Social Security. It was in that Court, as I defended the fish-receiver, that I saw a row of old barristers waiting for the 'Dock Brief'. Unwanted criminal practitioners had an option not open to their unemployed learned friends in the Probate, Divorce and Admiralty Division. In those days, before Legal Aid, penurious, un-represented criminals could pick out any robed figure in Court to defend them; there would be a quick consultation in the cells and then the trial, for which the winning barrister received, I think, a guinea, was off to the races. Busy barristers, men with cases elsewhere and a diary full of engagements, would duck out of Court bent double when a 'Dock Brief' was about to be chosen. Those who were less in demand would sit on, preening themselves like a line of elderly, wigged wallflowers, in the hope of being selected by the all-powerful figure in the dock. It was quite contrary to legal etiquette to wink, wave or try and attract the attention in any way of the alleged criminal upon whom so much depended; the 'Dock Brief' had to be, like so much in the law, a matter of pure chance.

I invented one such unsuccessful barrister for my radio play and paired him with an equally unsuccessful criminal. I wanted to say something about the lawyer's almost pathetic dependence on the criminal classes, without whom he would be unemployed, and I wanted to find a criminal who would be sorrier for his luckless advocate than he was for himself. Whether it was the new freedom of writing for actors whose voices would come out of the air unattached to a realistic set I don't know, but I found myself working with ease at a new level of reality, one that was approximately two feet above the ground. It was a style which had come naturally to me when I wrote my first novel, but which had become lost in the pursuit of more literal models. Since then I have not aimed to write dialogue which is entirely realistic, although I have always believed that comedy writing, like comic acting, must be based on some recognizable truth. If this is so, then it is possible to take off and break the sound barrier of pure naturalism. One of the great joys of writing in this way, for me, was that it would have been considered a complete heresy in the old world of the 'documentaries'.

The barrister I wrote then was, perhaps, a distant ancestor of a far more extrovert creation, 'Rumpole of the Bailey', whom I wouldn't begin to think about for another fifteen years. I had no trouble in catching hold of the whirling and confused thoughts of the Dock Brief barrister and reproducing them in suitable rhythms, but the criminal came out extremely flat. Then Nesta Pain said, 'That sort of character would speak very elaborately. He'd never use one word when six would do and he'd always plump for the longest words possible.' It was an obvious thing to say, but I remember it as one of the moments in which I was able to learn something of lasting value from a director. In the years to come Jack Clayton taught me how to forge links in a story and how the end of one scene can echo the beginning of the next. Jacques Charon, who came from the Comédie Française to direct a Feydeau play I had translated, gave me invaluable lessons about the nature of comedy. But Nesta Pain added a new note to my dialogue when she told me something which I should, of course, have been perfectly able to work out for myself.

I knew how my clients talked in divorce cases. Every day I heard involved sentences, staggering painfully under the weight of clichés got from the reports of police evidence in *The News of the World* or off bottles of sauce. I knew all the comfortable phrases designed to conceal the reality, and how death is always referred to as 'a blessed release' and sex as 'intimate relations'. I knew it all but I hadn't used it, and, when I wrote, I had not been listening hard enough.

Radio plays have many advantages. They are not subject to the technical mischances and distractions of the theatre and television. They call on the audience to make a great effort of imagination and in them words must be used, as they were in the Elizabethan theatre, to paint scenery or suggest changes of light. They also appear in decent obscurity. Last night's radio play is hardly ever front-page news and I never had to fear 'Mortimer Lays Egg on Third Programme' as a headline in the *Daily Express*. Where *The Dock Brief* was noticed, however, it seemed to be liked and the BBC paid me an extra £20 for it, a gesture of goodwill which I was told was almost unknown in the history of the Corporation. My father said, 'When you first read that play to us I thought it was poor fooling, likely to come very "tardy off". But much to our surprise, when we listened to the wireless, it really came across quite well.'

Michael Codron had just come down from Oxford and decided, as an alternative to his father's cement works, to go into theatrical management, where he became the greatest patron and promoter of new writers and now enjoys great commercial success. His then partner, David Hall, had written to me and when I called on Mr Codron he appeared to be rather young and very silent. In the years to come I discovered that this silence was an effective technique for conducting interviews; if you can keep quiet for long enough your interviewee is bound to make some rash promise if only to save the occasion from becoming boring. In this way patients apparently blurt out bitter self-truths to avoid boring the analyst who sits couch-side and silent. In my case the commitment was to write a companion piece to *The Dock Brief* which Mr Codron wished to stage at the Lyric Hammersmith in the course of a season which was to include the first production of Harold Pinter's play, *The Birthday Party*. If I failed to produce a second play in about two months, Mr Codron threatened to do *The Dock Brief* with something he called an 'Ionesco', a word I thought, in my appalling ignorance, denoted an educational branch of the United Nations.

Ignorant of the terrors of playwriting and its technical difficulties, I wrote a companion play called *What Shall We Tell Caroline?* surprisingly quickly. I managed to persuade Michael Hordern, who had given an impeccable performance as the hopeless barrister, to play a banjolele-twanging prep-school master, a character who also stepped, obediently, out of the shadows of my past. The plays came on in the season at the Lyric and my father, having potted nineteen dahlia plants, was driven up to London to, as we all said, 'see' the play. He seemed to have forgotten his first impression as his diary notes that the play was a success and 'John pointed out Harold Hobson who, to our surprise, is quite small.' He had an excellent dinner at the Clarendon Restaurant in Hammersmith. The next morning, he noted, the newspaper reviews were 'surpassingly good'. He planted seed pans and pots of stocks, arcotis ipomea, marigolds and blue and pink salvia. On the whole life continued, in spite of the notices, to go on much as usual.

17

THERE'S NO BUSINESS, AS I HAD LEARNT EARLIER IN MY LIFE, like movie business, and there's nothing like having had a small success with two miniature plays about an unsuccessful old lawyer and an eccentric prep-school master, to make the movie moguls prick up their ears, reach for their synopses and decide that you are just the person to write a three-hour epic about the Conquest of Mexico, or the love life of Genghis Khan. The period after *The Dock Brief* marked the start of my second love affair with the art of the film, a relationship as frustrating but rather more exotic than my first.

The two plays transferred to the West End of London where, despite the 'surpassing' notices, they didn't live for very long, this being due to various theatrical diseases such as the fact that it was raining, or too hot, or Holy Week, or the news was bad, or there was a bus strike, or it got dark at night. All the same I enjoyed, in my mid-thirties, all the pleasures of being a new, young writer (although Harold Hobson did point out, among many kind and flattering remarks, that at my age Racine had been dead for at least five years). Just as old character actors are the better for having had a period of acclaim as a *jeune premier* to look back upon, it's as well for an ageing author to be able to remember a period when he was thought of, no doubt mistakenly, as being of the avant-garde. This was the situation in which I found myself after five novels, some of which it must be admitted clung firmly to the middle of the road. A couple of years later when Michael Codron put on three short plays in an evening which I shared with Harold Pinter and N.F. Simpson, I remember that Emlyn Williams, who acted in all of our pieces and is not a man to mince his words, took a look at me during the first rehearsal and said, 'Well, you just got into the New Wave as the Tube doors were closing.' The metaphor might have been mixed, but there was a good deal of truth in what he said.

At the time *The Dock Brief* opened, Penelope and I rented the nursery wing of an enormous manor-house in Norfolk, to which we would go for long weekends and family holidays. The climate there was what they call 'bracing', that is to say it was a few degrees up on that in which Captain Oates took his final and heroic departure. There were big empty beaches and cliffs which the children slid down in an avalanche of sand, and with rare courage they sometimes swam in the treacherous waters of the North Sea. Then we would build bonfires of driftwood on the shore to cook shrimps and sausages and still their chattering teeth. The conditions were Arctic and I remember seeing a seal under the pier in the local town.

When the children became ill a Norfolk doctor recommended that we tie dirty socks round their throats, treatment from which generations of infants may well have died in the nursery wing, and ours might have followed them had we not fallen back on newer-fangled remedies. I sat, on days of pale sunshine, in the garden and wrote with pen forced between freezing fingers. The importance of failure and critical attack is that it may rob a writer of confidence. It is like riding a bicycle and being told you can't do it: if you listen to this verdict you immediately fall off. The small success of *The Dock Brief* had given new confidence to the voice I had found. New stories came to me easily and almost uninvited, I wrote quickly and with great happiness. In another part of the garden, wearing gumboots and a fisherman's sweater, Penelope typed without interruption, charting the sea of marriage and its hidden rocks and shallows. The children discarded their sock chokers and played happily in the house, losing themselves in the long corridors and dust-sheeted drawing-rooms of the part of the manor we did not inhabit.

It was in those days that I heard from Mr Anatole de Grunwald, known to his many friends as 'Tolly', and was invited once more to write for the movies.

When I first met Mr de Grunwald he was asleep on a small gilt sofa in the sitting-room of his suite at the Ritz Hotel. His shoes were off and a pale toe stuck through a hole in his sock. He was a handsome man whose hair, face and moustache wore a uniform tinge of grey. When he awoke he lifted the lid of a silver chafing-dish which had come up with the room service at the same time as my arrival. 'Something I can only get in England,' he said joyfully, and fell hungrily on a plate of sardines on toast.

Tolly de Grunwald had produced many distinguished films, including *Henry V*. When I met him he was about to start work on another great movie. His problem was one little project which, for obscure and political reasons, he had to do first. If I would join him in getting through the preliminary chore the world, he always told me, was at our disposal. We could do *The Possessed*, perhaps, or *Nostromo* or had I, perhaps, a little story of my own in the bottom drawer? Meanwhile there was this subject to which he was committed for the sake of a number of important people, including the head of the studio to whom he was exceedingly close. It was a job which, 'At the speed you write will take you four weeks maximum,' Tolly said, adding, 'I would be prepared to make you a promise to that effect, but I have only ever made one promise and that was to my wife on a purely personal and private matter.' This one film, it seemed, would solve all Mr de Grunwald's financial problems. I only had to say 'yes' and give him four weeks of my life. 'What's four weeks, after all, a drop in the ocean,' he said. After that a bright new future stretched before me, filled with exotic parties and films which would make movie history. Not feeling that the time had come to reject all the kingdoms of the world, I followed Mr de Grunwald down a primrose path which led after months and months of discouraging work to a quite awful movie.

I moved, during my early film life, from Pinewood to Pacific Pallisades, from Slough to Los Angeles, towns which seemed to me to differ mainly in climate. Driving to work in Hollywood, a distance of never less than twenty miles, was much like negotiating a familiar stretch of Western Avenue; there was the same mess of scrubby garages and supermarkets, but in the somnolent atmosphere of Los Angeles the traffic seemed to go much more slowly. Between the buildings tall palm trees stretched up to the sky and in their branches you could hear, on still evenings, the rustling of rats. Stranger animals like mountain lions came in from the desert in which the long streets ended. I got to know a producer whose roof was seriously gnawed by a possum. He rang the City Sanitation Department, who came with a possum trap, a heavy iron cage which they placed on his roof. During the night the cunning possum ate neatly round the trap, which then fell through the roof, injuring the producer's wife.

Later I found the beautiful parts of Los Angeles, Malibu and the Italianate landscape of Topanga Canyon, where the houses were built of wood and plaster and hung perilously to the space between the precipice and the road. 'I had a bad situation here,' a girl who lived in one of these houses told me. 'Two idiots in a Buick, they must have been stoned out of their minds, missed the corner and drove straight into my bedroom. Knocked the bed clear across the room. Since when this house lets in air.'

Writers, in the first days when I visited Hollywood, suffered even greater risks than those of falling possum traps or head-on collisions between a Buick and a brass bedstead. They were put in small, similar offices in the studio and were not supposed to go 'off the lot'. Nothing, I found, stifles creative endeavour more quickly than a desk in an air-conditioned cell, piles of yellow pads and stacks of sharpened pencils with a secretary waiting eagerly to type out 'the pages'. Every twenty pages had to be shown to the producer who first read it with deeply sincere admiration, and then having shown it to his wife, a number of old friends, three or four guys from the front office, his children and his devoted grey-haired secretary, found that it was sadly lacking in drama, was too literary, contained too many words, contained characters who were as flat as a pancake and many another fatal flaw. The most unnerving producer in this regard was Mr Sam Spiegel who would receive pages of pure gold in the evening which, like some Rumpelstiltskin in reverse, he would cause to dwindle to a small pile of rubbish by the following day.

Another great handicap for a writer was the 'story conference' where as many people as possible were supposed to sit round joining in the discussion, with the result that the plot, out of sheer boredom, crept away and died. The story having been decided in committee, the characters in the drama were meant to follow it faithfully and never had a chance of changing its course without the producer's consent. Successful fiction writing, which depends on privacy, secrecy and a writer's occasional ability to take himself by surprise, was impossible under these conditions. In fact the ground rules of Hollywood script-writing seem to have been designed to ensure that the film, unlike the theatre, radio or even television, can never be mistaken for a literary art, and the cinema has not yet produced a memorable writer.

With all this to contend with I was surprised to find my fellow-prisoners in what was appropriately called 'The Writers' Block' reasonably contented. As producers didn't read books they had to have scripts written in order to find out that no one wanted to make the movie. So a handsome and extremely safe living could be made from writing films that never went into production. There were also writers who had perfected the art of remaining on the pay-roll of a film which was, in fact, being written by someone else. They could then spend relaxing days taking their children to Disneyland or picking up girls in Schwabs' Pharmacy, and if the film got made they could enter into a fierce struggle for the credit. In Hollywood it seemed to be a basic rule that it is better to have a credit on a bad film you haven't written than to have no credit at all. No doubt such recognition gave the script-writers the feeling of being loved; it was as though they lined their mantelpieces with invitations to parties to which they never went and which they certainly wouldn't have enjoyed.

Movies in those days were more remarkable for the trips than the work in hand. The old-style film producers regarded the world as their oyster, a quite manageable setting for any drama they felt inclined to stage. For the writer, imprisoned in so much solitude, the idea of a medium which could take him anywhere in the world at the drop of a contract provided a strong temptation. In due course Penelope and I were asked to write a quite effective film for Mr Otto Preminger. *Bunny Lake is Missing* was a thriller set in and around a nursery school in Swiss Cottage where we lived, yet to write it Mr Preminger summoned us to Hawaii, where he was restaging the Japanese attack on Pearl Harbor. We walked on the beach among blue-haired American matrons who wore plastic grass skirts, we breathed in the seductive perfume of pineapple-canning factories and we watched a pool full of charming dolphins who rang bells and danced the *Merry Widow* waltz. We did our best to recapture the life of NW6 from the eighteenth floor of the Ilikai Hotel. I remember that the best thing to eat in the hotel restaurant was a dish, rather like swordfish, called 'Mai-Mai Steak'. What on earth was 'Mai-Mai'? Mr Preminger, who had a somewhat merciless attitude towards actors, assured us that we were eating those dolphins who failed in their performance of the *Merry Widow* waltz.

Later still we were employed by the greatest of all the tycoons, Mr Sam Spiegel, whose home was a private yacht, about the size of a small Channel steamer, which wandered lazily about the Mediterranean Sea. Once a writer was lured aboard there was no escape, the yacht might up anchor during the night and make off in the direction of St Tropez. All the boats which might put you ashore were in Mr Spiegel's command, and there was no alternative to sitting in the stateroom, drinking Bullshots and trying not to pay too much attention to the producer's alternate praise and abuse of your script.

There were two highlights to life on Mr Spiegel's yacht. One was when the walkie-talkie which he used when on shore to summon the ship's motor boat to take him on board failed after he had visited a Casino. He was unable to call the yacht from the beach at Cannes and seemed marooned. However the man who had produced *Lawrence of Arabia* was not easily deterred from his purpose. He rose to the occasion and hired a pedalo and the great producer, in a dinner-jacket, sat in the small craft while his chauffeur in uniform, his cap firmly on his head, pedaloed them both across the moonlit Mediterranean.

On another occasion I asked Mr Spiegel if I could swim from the yacht. This appeared to be a somewhat unusual request, but in due course a gangway was lowered, sailors brought towels and the steward stood by with a huge Bullshot should I need reviving. The Captain stopped the engines, other guests lined the rails and I walked slowly down to the sea. And then, as I entered the clear water, a sailor flushed a lavatory somewhere in the steerage. As I swam I was suddenly surrounded by floating lavatory paper and even less attractive material. Such were the splendours and miseries of a life in show business.

On my first visit to Hollywood I pursued Mr de Grunwald's story through a number of changes, doing my best to camouflage its basic improbability. I met George Cukor, the charming, waspish director of great actresses, the old wizard who wheedled unforgettable performances out of Garbo and Katherine Hepburn, in his quiet house and Italianate garden with its lawns and white pillars just behind the line of 'Topless' and 'Bottomless' bars on Sunset Strip. I went to a party in the ruins of a palace in Bel Air which William Randolph Hearst had built for Marion Davies. The swimming-pool was built round the house like a moat, but its walls were cracked, trees had fallen into the water and the place had been taken over by a group of abstract painters who sat on large cushions in the ballroom smoking and drinking iced tea. 'It's wonderful to be in such a historical place,' one of them said. 'This was a house built of pure love. You do feel that, don't you?'

I sat by the pool in the Beverly Hills Hotel, a place where actors paid their agents to telephone them often so that their names might be heard repeatedly over the Tannoy. I had a sudden nostalgic longing for the High Court of Justice, for the great hall in which it is never quite daylight and where the secretaries come out of their small offices to play badminton at night. I wanted to see the old barristers climbing like black beetles up the marble staircases again. I even longed to meet a client and deal with the plots and dramas of real life, matters which could be proved to have happened instead of flawed speculations from the producer's office.

'I think I'd like to go back to England,' I said to Mr de Grunwald. 'It's the divorce, you see.'

'The divorce?' Tolly de Grunwald looked genuinely concerned and put an arm about my shoulder, holding me in an increasingly bear-like hug as he said, 'That's never going to happen to me. I've made my wife a promise, you see, of a purely personal and private nature. All the same, if you're going to have a divorce I'd better let you go. Pity. The last pages were just perfection.'

I got back to England and comforted myself with the simplicities of the law. Mr de Grunwald followed me later and his film, which might with any luck have followed 90 per cent of such projects into oblivion, was unfortunately made. From time to time Mr de Grunwald rang my chambers and asked, in hushed and reverent tones, if I felt any happier. Then he would ask me if I could think of a good new ending for our story. 'We're shooting the last scene tomorrow,' he said once with a kind of unearthly detachment. 'You got any ideas about what it ought to be?'

Before the film came out a miracle occurred. An old Hollywood writer who had once done some work on it long before claimed, to my enormous relief, the sole credit. He was, Mr de Grunwald told me, prepared to pay top lawyers and argue the matter at length before the Screen Writers' Guild, so determined was he to accept responsibility for my failure. I gave it to him without making the smallest trouble.

18

IT WAS A RELIEF TO RETURN TO THE THEATRE, WHERE I
had undertaken what seemed to me the superhuman task of writing a
full-length play, one which could occupy the audience's life for two and
a half hours, including the intervals when they fought to wrest a warm
gin and tonic from an overworked lady in black bombazine.

I had enjoyed, up to then, writing short plays for the theatre and for
television. I have to confess to a low threshold of boredom. At one
distant Edinburgh Festival I recall that Kenneth Tynan called us the
'Half Time Mortimers', and though I have often been with Saint Joan
when she picks out the Dauphin I have not always been among those
present when she makes her posthumous return to his sleepless bedroom.
I have some sympathy for the Victorian Liberal, Sir Charles Dilke, who
never saw more than one act of any play. He loved the theatre deeply
but enough, he no doubt felt, was as good as a feast. I have even more
sympathy with that member of the House of Lords who fell asleep during
his own maiden speech. The only rule I have found to have any validity
in writing is not to bore yourself.

So, with a good deal of trepidation, I began a 'full-length play'. The
central character was our house in Swiss Cottage and I called the play
The Wrong Side of the Park. Michael Codron presented it, and it was
directed by Peter Hall, who was married at the time to Leslie Caron. I
used to sit in his house which was filled with the gilded cherubs and
strawberry-coloured velvet of the Belle Epoque and discuss NW6. When
he married for the second time the décor changed dramatically and
became Italian functional, not to say futuristic; the cherubs were replaced
by automatically rotating abstract sculpture. I have always liked Peter
Hall and we have remained friends over the years. He has an admirable
determination which led him, inevitably, from the station-master's house
to directorship of the National Theatre. He told me that when he first
arrived at Cambridge with a scholarship he paused, in his walk from the
station, to book the Arts Theatre for the production he knew he would

be doing there in two years' time. Like many people in the theatre who came from relatively poor backgrounds, he was anxious to enjoy his prosperity: it was only the directors with comfortable bourgeois backgrounds who seemed, in the sixties, so doggedly anxious to appear working class.

Among the putti of Peter Hall's Montpelier Square pad we got the news that Margaret Leighton had agreed to play the wife in *The Wrong Side of the Park*. She came back from Hollywood, a beautiful, nervous, strong actress who ate, apparently, nothing at all. She was married, then, to the actor Laurence Harvey and they lived in a lavishly converted squash-court somewhere in Mayfair. Mr Harvey used to ride about on the pillion of a chauffeur-driven motor-scooter. He was a man of considerable charm and did surprisingly good imitations. He always seemed to treat his wife very badly and in restaurants he would call out to the wine waiter for 'another drink for my mother'. However I noticed that if he stopped mistreating her she would turn on him and insult him with far more imagination than he could command. Although it was an improbable marriage they seemed well suited and I was sorry when it broke up. When it did so, in return for her superb acting in my play, I conducted Miss Leighton's divorce. She arrived at the High Court of Justice in full mourning, very pale, supported on the arm of Terence Rattigan who also seemed to be dressed for a State funeral. It was one of the most theatrically effective 'undefendeds' I have ever done.

The play, at the time, appeared to be a success. In a way that time marked the beginning of the end of our living in the house, because although we stayed on for a number of years we had begun, perhaps unconsciously, to make secret preparations for our departure. It was the last play of mine that my father 'saw'.

In the last years of his life my father's garden became mutinous. He depended on a changing stream of gardeners and garden boys whose attendance was sporadic. In their absence the weeds took over more and more territory and a large part of the fruit cage collapsed. He went less and less often to his chambers and occasionally, in a strange reversal of our roles, he did the paper work and drafted the legal pleadings which I had no time to do.

His diaries speak of the number of people who worked at the house. There was Dora, a fat cook, who came by bicycle from a nearby village. She was walking out with a man to whom she had been engaged for some thirty years and she was waiting for his younger brother to die before she felt they could marry. Dora helped my father fill in his football coupons. The pools seem to have occurred to him as a source of income in his seventies when the chance of a good 'money brief' grew slimmer. Otherwise the diary records his frustrations as he waited for 'Gerald' or 'Thomas' or 'Allan' or 'Mr Long' or 'Mr Richards' to call and do battle against the weeds. Gerald's name appears the most often. Gerald's visits were unpredictable and when he came he often spent hours 'fiddling with the lawn-mower' and no grass was cut.

Ever anxious about the world, and hungry for literature, my father persuaded my mother to read him Harold Pinter's *The Caretaker* and, to her intense embarrassment, *Lolita*. In the year we did *The Wrong Side of the Park* he had a heart attack. The doctor came in the middle of the night and gave him two injections of morphia and later sent a male night nurse called 'Hare', a somewhat sinister figure who didn't expect my father to live. After a while my father banished Hare from his bedroom, so the sullen nurse sat in the kitchen chain-smoking and telling me how long it would be before the end. I think it was mainly to irritate Hare that my father made a determined recovery and ordered a kidney for his breakfast.

Later the diary records with great satisfaction that Gerald came to work and that Hare was driven to the station in Henley. This ill-tempered harbinger of death was not seen in the house again. For a long time my father's recovery seemed complete.

My Uncle Harold having died, my Aunt Daisy arrived with her dog and her shrubs to stay with my parents. Later she bought a house near to them and kept them company. My mother was always a little in awe of her younger sister, perhaps because she was richer and had become independent. My parents got a small income from my Uncle Harold's Will, which went on a new boiler and the wages of a constantly floating population of gardening mercenaries. And every day my father noted the moments of triumph, as when they walked down to the West Field to admire the wonderful show of crab-apple blossom, or when the berrying shrubs, in particular the cotoneasters, 'did marvellously'. He also recorded the moments of frustration and near despair, as when Gerald announced that he was going to join the RAF: 'We were tremendously taken aback.'

Gerald's threat seems to have been of a temporary nature and no doubt my father, summoning all his skill as an advocate, managed to persuade him that his real enemy was nearer at hand, growing hourly and threatening to strangle the rose bushes. The next week Gerald was back in the garden, weeding sporadically and 'fiddling with the lawn-mower'. Later Gerald buckled the scythe.

In the July of his last year, my father had raspberry pie from his own raspberries and the peas were demolished by jays. Gerald was kept busy tidying up by the white seat and round the camellias. Someone called 'Bartholomew' was weeding on the terrace and in front of the borders. And then, at long last and after much fiddling with the mower, 'Gerald cut the grass and was paid.'

August was cold and miserable. My mother read *Waiting for Godot* aloud, and they wasted time trying to extricate a peach net from the loft and discovered that Gerald had been paid twice for one lot of grass cutting. By the end of the month my father was eating his own tomatoes.

Suddenly the weather changed and became hot and stifling. It took four men and two Allen scythes to cut the long grass in the West Field. Towards the end of September my father was troubled with a pain in his left wrist which the doctor diagnosed as gout, an affliction he suffered from whenever he ate strawberries. Two or three days later he became very ill and I went to stay in the house. My mother had been left with oxygen cylinders and a mask which she was to put on my father's face to help him breathe.

The night was very hot when he died. The doctor called and said there was nothing more he could do, but that we should try to keep my father awake. The huge and unwieldy garden surrounding the small house seemed unnaturally silent and I could hear nothing but the sound of my father's assisted breathing. At the last moment he wanted to get out of bed and cried out angrily because we wouldn't let him have a bath. When my mother protested he said, 'I'm always angry when I'm dying.' I don't know if it was something he had prepared for a long time, but those were the last words I heard him say. I held the mask over his face until he no longer had need of it.

When my father died I hoped that, liberated from her extraordinary bondage, my mother would find a new life and perhaps draw and paint again. She never did, but devoted her years to living as though my father were still alive, to keeping the house and garden exactly as they had been, doing *The Times* crossword puzzle when he had done it and following the Law Reports.

She kept on writing the diary, which continues in her handwriting after the brief entry, 'On September 29th Clifford was very ill and on September 30th at 3.30 a.m. he died. Oct 3rd. Clifford's funeral.' The next day she went shopping and was called on by a local architect who talked to her until she 'felt frozen with boredom'. A few days later Gerald called and said that he had not bothered to come and mow the lawn during the last two weeks as he thought that my mother and father 'had been on holiday'.

My mother continued to battle with the weeds and occasional gardeners, to plant flowers in the places my father had planned for them and record the performance of the flowers he had planted. But just after my father died she walked round the enormous garden and then came indoors to write, 'I was very lonely and sad and nothing could quench my regrets.'

19

MY FATHER HAD BEEN SPARED THE SIXTIES, WHICH WERE held to be, for those few people who met regularly among the low-hanging lights and lavatory tiles of the Italian restaurants in the King's Road, Chelsea, an era of gaiety and swinging delight. It was probably the last period in which England and English matters were of much interest to the rest of the world but, as has been said, when history repeats itself it usually ends up as farce. My father had been a child of the Empire. He had survived a couple of world wars, in the second of which England might, without injustice, have been thought to have saved Europe. What he missed was the new decade when to be English meant to have a Union Jack shopping-bag from Carnaby Street and to know the words of all the Beatles' numbers. The sixties were meant to be the decade in which young people enjoyed going to bed together, although in this I don't think it differed noticeably from the forties or the fifties or the swinging 1410s. It was a time when the theatre and movies discovered that there was an enchanting, new, uncharted area somewhere to the north of Watford, and when RADA-trained actors did their best to flatten their vowels and scowl a good deal. Girls who had never been far east of Sloane Square started to say 'innit?' and 'didni?' In the old-fashioned forties, when the West End was ruled by glossy revivals and homosexual managers, a young actor was asked at an audition if he wasn't, perhaps, heterosexual. 'Well yes,' he admitted and added eagerly, 'but it doesn't show from the front.' Among writers during the sixties, matters like having been born in the Home Counties or having gone to a public school were kept as similarly embarrassing secrets.

Nothing could have been more superficial than these changes. English class divisions survived the sixties to become more deeply entrenched than ever, and the gulf between the two nations of the north and south grew even wider. I suppose most people came to maturity anxiously looking for jobs and took out mortgages without realizing that they were part of a swinging generation which had never had it so good. Only middle-aged men, and headmasters in particular, seemed affected by the myth of swinging London. Perhaps they had an uneasy suspicion that the young people of the day were having a better time than they had ever experienced and the thought made them exceedingly bitter.

The fact that England became thought of as fashionable in America, however, brought money for British movies and we had a film industry, a vital part of any nation's culture. In the early sixties, when Jack Clayton's *Room at the Top* had liberated our cinema in the way that *Look Back in Anger* gave a new life to the theatre, a large number of British films became possible, which would be unthinkable today. Seemingly unlikely subjects were chosen, and Peter Sellers even agreed to make a film of *The Dock Brief*, a project sportingly produced by Anatole de Grunwald's brother, Dimitri.

I found Mr Sellers to be a gentle man who, in his private life, appeared sad and even desperate. He once said that he couldn't play himself because 'to see me in the cinema would be one of the dullest experiences anyone could imagine'. He was a man who couldn't come truly to life until he had found someone to imitate, with an inch or two of moustache perhaps, or a walk, or an odd movement of the shoulders, and always with a voice. He used to say that he was no more than a medium for the character and the writer, and he used his innumerable voices as a shield against, I suppose, the dread of some hollowness within. When he wasn't acting he spent most of his time buying things which might help him to establish an identity: motor cars he quickly tired of, more and more elaborate cameras and, one morning when we were working together, a large electric organ which no one he knew could play. He seemed to have to acquire his innumerable possessions quickly, as he collected houses and companies and even wives, being in daily dread that his world as a successful film actor would vanish and he would be back where he started, doing split weeks in Aldershot or appearing, plump and shock-headed, as the Director of Entertainment at a Jersey holiday camp, putting on a succession of caps and funny accents and topping the evening with a ukelele and an imitation of George Formby. In his way, Peter Sellers was like the late Sir Edward Marshall Hall, a man who stood empty, waiting to be inhabited by other people.

The voices would come to him unexpectedly, out of the most obscure associations and once there they proved extremely difficult to exorcize. We were sitting in the restaurant at Shepperton Studios just before he started to play Morgenhall, the unsuccessful barrister in *The Dock Brief*, and Mr Sellers unfortunately ordered a plate of cockles. He had been desperately uncertain as to how to play the part, but the shellfish came to him with a whiff of the sea and the memory of Morecambe. They brought a faded north-country accent and the suggestion of a scrappy moustache. He felt he had been thrown the lifeline of a voice and work could begin. It took a great deal of patience and tact by the director, James Hill, to undo the effect of the cockles, to find another sort of voice and return poor old Wilfred Morgenhall to what I felt were undoubtedly his southern origins.

Mr Sellers' anxieties (one was that he was being pursued by the Mafia because of his undoubted affection for Sophia Loren), his frequent despair and as frequent love affairs sometimes seemed to me to exist only in his imagination. The real world came to him in the fragments he borrowed, other people's hats and walks and voices, because he was certainly a mimic of genius. I don't think it common for actors to provide such a degree of blankness for others to write on, indeed many actors have huge and extravagant personalities. The Peter Sellers character may be more common, however, in everyday life than it is comfortable to realize. How many people are there who feel they scarcely exist until they can get to their props, the headmaster's gown, the doctor's stethoscope or what Henry Winter once called my 'barrister's set'? Do they as desperately grasp the Sergeant-Major's voice, the Trades Union leader's jargon, the politician's ingratiating fireside manner, as articles of make-up, stripped of which they feel naked and non-existent, liable to be sent back, at any moment, to the bottom of the bill on the pier at Weston-Super-Mare?

An actor who never runs out of his own positive personality and who has no need of a stick of make-up or an inch of false hair is Trevor Howard. I had met him, when he was doing a remake of *Mutiny on the Bounty*, in a bar just outside the teetotal desert of the studio where we were both working. I had made an exceedingly pretentious remark about Hollywood being the 'suburbia of the soul' which he had somehow appreciated and he agreed to be in a play I had written called *Two Stars for Comfort*. He gave a performance which combined great strength with vulnerability, influenced a good deal by the brilliant but wayward actor Wilfred Lawson, whom he greatly admired.

Two Stars for Comfort had its origins in an old, unpublished novel and had to do with Henley, our local town, and in particular with the river. The river at Henley seemed entirely devoted to pleasure, with its fleet of skiffs with wrought-iron seats and slow-moving punts and ancient steamers for day trips from Reading and Oxford. There was the island with a small white folly, a classical temple, and another island on which a long-deserted wooden building with faded numbers on the bedroom doors might once have been a small hotel for illicit weekends, taking the overspill from Maidenhead. The best days of my school holidays were always spent on the river, paddling rocking canoes into secret places under overhanging branches, and tossing bread to the swans until they became uncontrollably greedy and pursued the boat, flapping their strong wings which I had been told could break a leg. Penelope and I had spent an early holiday on an island in the river and we had each written books in the soggy garden and gone to 'Flannel Dances' in the Town Hall for a treat on Saturday nights. At the time of the Regatta old men came out in white trousers, which were yellowing to match their nicotine-stained moustaches, worn with button-bursting blazers, pink socks and schoolboy caps. The rowers flashed past in skiffs as fragile as the insects which skimmed the water for one day and died the next morning. On Saturday there was a fair and, in the evening, a display in which the winner of the Diamond Sculls was picked out in hissing fireworks which were reflected in the water. When I was young we used to swim in the river, feeling the reeds wrap around our legs and the mud ooze between our toes. Most of all we enjoyed going through the locks, hanging on to the slimy green chains as the punts sank into an apparently bottomless cavern, or rising on a swirling tide to jump out and buy chocolate at the lock-keeper's cottage before the sluice-gates opened.

The play I wrote was about a man who always told people what he thought they wanted to hear, an extension of the pleasure principle which only works in the extremely short term. It was about the harsh inequalities caused by beauty. We could, if we had any real intention of doing so, narrow the wage differential, we could make education, spectacles, false teeth and rides on the Underground open to all, regardless of the accident of birth. No power on earth, however, can abolish the merciless class distinction between those who are physically desirable and the lonely, pallid, spotted, silent, unfancied majority. It is this class envy, I suppose, which makes many men behave with particular boorishness to the prettiest girls; it is what causes the sigh of relief when you have been following a back with admiration and then find a face which is unchallengingly plain. It is why the best news that an envious world often hears about a beautiful woman is that she has 'gone off'.

So a play about the river was one that went back a long way into my life, to days when a punt seemed the height of pleasure and the summer was hotter and lasted longer than it ever has since.

20

AFTER MY FATHER DIED I HAD SLEPT FOR TWO DAYS without interruption. I wrote, at the end of a play: 'I'd been told of all the things you're meant to feel. Sudden freedom, growing up, the end of dependence, the step into the sunlight when no one is taller than you and you're in no one's shadow. I know what I felt. Lonely.'

It also seemed to me that I was now the sole custodian of some private language, the single guardian of a secret we had once shared. Later I realized how widely the seeds of his personality had been scattered. My father had left a part of himself to my children and step-children, to everyone who had heard his stories and laughed at his jokes. After a while I took my son for walks and started to tell him the Sherlock Holmes stories. In the end, at first nervously but then with increasing confidence, I should take over his garden and try to make it look something like the place I remembered. That, however, was in the distant future.

My father was gone and I was alone in his room in chambers. In time I began to wonder what on earth I was doing there. I had a play on, a film of another being made and I was working with Jack Clayton on the script of *The Innocents*, the film of Henry James's story *The Turn of the Screw*. A whole chapter seemed closed, the relentless pursuit of the 'undefended' seemed no longer necessary. Why should I continue to lead tormented wives or deceived husbands through the maze of the old divorce law? Other guides could be found who were not forever slipping off to Hollywood. Why should I still be harrowed by cases about the custody of children? These great issues were then tried by the Judge reading unilluminating affidavits drafted by lawyers; he rarely saw the parents and hardly ever met the children. The time had come, I thought, to let others comfort weeping mothers outside the summons room. In any case, I fell out of love with the law after sitting in the Court of Appeal listening to a dispute over an eight-year-old girl. The parents were Welsh and the father wanted custody because he said the mother had allowed the child to become backward in reading. Unusually the presiding Judge had the subject of this litigation brought into Court and handed down to her the huge volume of the Rules of the Supreme Court, known with awe to the legal profession simply as 'The White Book'. The child staggered slightly under the weight of the open book and the Judge, looking down on her from a great height, said, 'All right. Now let's see if you can read Order 58 Rule 3(1).'

There was a terrible moment of silence and suspense. The father looked piously triumphant. The mother stared in terror at the child she seemed about to lose. And then, quite suddenly, a small but perfectly clear Welsh voice rang out. 'An appeal to the Court of Appeal', it piped, 'shall be by way of rehearing and shall be brought by Notice of Motion. . . .' The case was won, but I had begun to grow impatient with a world in which a child's future might depend on whether or not she could read the White Book.

Why did I need all that? For the first time it became quite clear to me what I should do for a living. Of course I would write, at my leisure. Perhaps I could live abroad. I would sit in the sunshine by some Italian lake and never have to think of the White Book again, never choke back my fury at what seemed to me some peculiarly heartless order and bow and say, 'If your Lordship pleases.' Leonard had left to become a Judge's clerk shortly before my father died. We had a new clerk who, breaking with tradition, I actually called by his real name which was 'Charlie'. I told Charlie I was going to leave the bar. I sat in my father's room and made arrangements for selling off his books, his huge dusty volumes of Moore's *Privy Council Cases* and Haggard's *Ecclesiastical Reports* which traced the tortured history of Wills and marriages back to the Middle Ages.

It was sometime during this period of limbo, when I had gradually made up my mind to divorce myself from the law, that I was asked by Amnesty International to go to a criminal trial in Nigeria for the purpose, I suppose, of seeing that no manifest injustice was done. I think I was chosen for the task, ironically, less for my legal expertise than because the man in the dock was a playwright.

I suppose that Jack Clayton, the film director who taught me how to make the end of one scene fit on to the start of the next by the use of similar or contrasting pictures, might have suggested that we cut from my white face in a white wig in London to a black face in a similar white wig in the Court of Ibadan. Perhaps he would have panned down to a spectacle, which one Nigerian lawyer assured me that he had actually seen in some remote criminal trial, of a wigged and gowned barrister with bare feet under the desk at the end of his pin-stripes wiggling his toes at the Judge in the traditional sign of the evil eye. In fact, I found the Nigerian court procedure extremely orderly, well regulated and rather more fair than in some cases at the Old Bailey. This, however, was not exactly what I was led to expect when I was briefed, in the basement of an Italian restaurant near to Holborn Tube Station, by the officers of Amnesty International.

The British, who seem to have carelessly created African countries by simply drawing lines on the map regardless of the warring and disparate tribes ensnared in their arbitrary boundaries (a practice we also adopted in Northern Ireland), had left Nigeria a certain place for tribal conflict. There was a further cause for discontent after an election in the western region when the voters were asked to decide between a notoriously self-seeking government under Chief Akintola and the United Progressive Party led by Awolowa who had been imprisoned for ten years. Although not all dedicated *Guardian* readers, the Progressive Party was, it was explained to me in the Italian restaurant, not only opposed to Akintola, but to the more reactionary Hausa tribe in the north. They claimed the allegiance of the few Ibos who lived in that region, including the brilliant writer, Wole Soyinka, whose play *The Road* had been performed in London. He it was who was to stand trial, charged with robbery with violence in that he entered the local broadcasting station and took two tapes, value two pounds twelve and sixpence.

What had happened might be regarded as a serious political crime or a hilarious practical joke. Nigerians apparently expected their elections to be attended by a moderate degree of cheerful chicanery, but the rigging of this particular democratic exercise was so ridiculous as to be an affront. Extra ballot papers were allegedly smuggled into voting booths in hats, ladies' corsets and loaves of bread, voting lists were manipulated so that Progressive Party supporters had to travel many miles to vote and a curfew was imposed so that their officials couldn't supervise the count. For a month the Returning Officer refused to count the Progressive Party votes. In spite of all this the opposition claimed to have won 68 out of 94 seats in the western region. However Chief Akintola declared that his government had been returned and announced his intention of broadcasting his thanks to the loyal electorate after the 7 p.m. news.

As the eager listeners tuned in they heard, not the victorious Chief Akintola, but a voice which said, 'This is Free Nigeria', and went on, in uncomplimentary terms, to advise him to leave the country with his 'crew of renegades'. The rebel broadcast was then untimely ripped from the air.

The prosecution case was that the Premier had taped the broadcast and at 7.15 the acting head of programmes, a Mr Oshin, together with his engineer, were in the sound cubicle at Ibadan radio station ready to play back the words of the leader. Mr Oshin said that an intruder entered the cubicle, produced a gun and made him remove the Premier's tape and substitute his own rousing message to the nation. There was, however, some friendly chat before the gun was produced, because Mr Oshin had recognized his visitor as Wole Soyinka and had briefly discussed with him such matters as the Commonwealth Arts Festival and the success of *The Road* at Stratford East. So arose the charge of robbery with violence, and the officials of Amnesty feared that there would be a rigged and politically activated trial and that the distinguished dramatist was being kept in solitary confinement and possibly subjected to torture.

I travelled to the continent that had been denied to me when Mr Moxer's film studio vanished. It was all new to me, the dry musty smell of Africa, the extraordinary cheerfulness in the most appalling situations, the politicians whose oratory was as flamboyantly effective as that of Nye Bevan, and the barristers who retired, shining with sweat in their stiff collars and bands, to eat bacon and eggs and drink 7-Up during the midday adjournment. I stayed with an English writer and his wife in Lagos and we drove up the long road to Ibadan. It was the sort of road Wole Soyinka wrote about, a line of life through the dripping rain forest, always thronged with people walking huge distances, loaded bicycles and overflowing trucks. Along the sides of such a road the dramas of life, death and politics, war and witchcraft were endlessly enacted. As we drove we saw burnt-out, riot-wrecked cars. The day before a Judge had been found decapitated in a ditch. Many people had been killed as the police fired on women in open markets. When we got to Ibadan I met a young Nigerian publisher. 'I could have run you up here in my Jag,' he said, 'but some fools have gone and thrown their assegais through the rear window.' In his opinion those responsible were the Muslim Hausa tribesmen from the north.

I found Wole Soyinka entertaining his family and friends in the local

CID office. He was smoking a Gauloise and pouring out Algerian wine. He was surrounded by books for his university degree and was then reading a Penguin edition of P. G. Wodehouse. The Nigerian playwright discussed the political situation with great equanimity and sent his best wishes to Joan Littlewood. When he made jokes the CID officer, who seemed to be wearing a Westminster Bank rowing-club blazer, laughed appreciatively. The next morning, in the modern courtroom, the Prosecuting Counsel applied to have the prisoner more strictly confined, whereupon the young Judge, acting with more humanity than many of his English counterparts, said, 'Perhaps you'd like to take him home with you. You could keep a pretty close eye on him there!'

At the end of the long road through the rain forest, the barristers were greeting their opponents with the soft badinage of the Middle Temple and saying, 'If your Lordship pleases', and 'If your Lordship would bear with me for a moment', in the age-old legal circumlocutions we all use when we mean to say, 'For God's sake shut up and listen'. They were patiently quoting House of Lords decisions to erect elaborate arguments as to the admissibility of evidence and the Judge was outraged when he discovered that the prosecution hadn't served their witnesses' statements on the defence.

'When I saw the gun coming out,' said Mr Oshin, tall, bowing and softly spoken, 'I thought I was in a kind of dream.' The barristers laughed discreetly and one of them, passing the witness-box, gave Wole Soyinka a gentle and reassuring pat on the arm.

That night I drove with my publisher friend out to a village. We could hear the distant cries of rioting gangs through the shattered back window of the car. He whistled into the darkness and some girls with bright cloths wound round their heads joined us and we went back to the hotel, where the girls drank Guinness and shivered in the air-conditioning. One told me that her work lay on the 'Publicity and Exploitation side of Lever Brothers Limited'.

None of the witnesses identified Wole Soyinka satisfactorily and he was acquitted. Eventually there was another political upheaval and he disappeared. But as I drove away from Ibadan I thought of the law as something other than a maze of absurdities from which people had to be rescued. We had been stopped for a long time at a level crossing the night before and seen the flash of knives and machetes in the bush, and heard the cries of the wounded; and yet, wearing their absurd version of English eighteenth-century legal costume, barristers had been arguing reasonably and a Judge had been determined to convict no one unless he was satisfied beyond reasonable doubt. Perhaps you have to go a great distance to appreciate the virtues of our legal system, up the long road into a rain forest, or even to South Africa where, with the politicians daily violating natural justice, a fearless barrister can still set an example by asking all the wrong questions at the inquest on a political prisoner unaccountably dead in the alleged safety of a cell. Since then I have stood in a Far-Eastern country and cross-examined its Prime Minister according to our procedure, before the inscrutable figure of a wigged and gowned Chinese Judge. In the countries which have received our law it often proves a most durable commodity, keeping a flicker of freedom alive when all else has broken down. Driving away from Ibadan I had the unoriginal thought that British law might, together with Shakespeare, Wordsworth, Lord Byron and the herbaceous border, be one of our great contributions to the world. I decided not to abandon the law, but to try and practise it more interestingly in the future.

And then I saw a girl up a high ladder pasting a huge poster, depicting a bar of 'Lifebuoy' soap, on to the side of a building. She smiled and waved her brush at me as I called to her, for I had recognized her as my friend from the 'Publicity and Exploitation department of Lever Brothers'.

We got back to Lagos where I was staying with the English writer and his wife. The house was reassuring as it presented the usual North London scene of drying nappies, plastic knickers, chewed bikkipegs swinging from the sides of cots, crumpled copies of the *Manchester Guardian* and paperback Hemingways ripped from the shelves and stamped on by an apparently intoxicated three-year-old. One night I wanted to go out to the Post Office to wire an article I had written to London. My hostess agreed to drive me. She was a flamboyant driver and we screeched through the curiously deserted streets of Lagos, still subject to rioting and sudden death, until we were stopped by an enormous policeman, a Hausa, perhaps, from the north, hung with every conceivable armament and brandishing a riot stick. He asked for my hostess's driver's licence and, when it was clear it had run out six months previously, he told us both to follow him to the station. I saw my return to England postponed indefinitely whilst I sat in an airless cell deprived even of Algerian wine and P. G. Wodehouse. However, instead of docilely accompanying the huge officer, my hostess leapt from the driving seat and attacked him with her dangerously sharp finger-nails, brilliantly coloured by chipped varnish. After one swift claw from the roused lady *Guardian*-reader, the police-officer turned tail and ran into the darkness, his revolver thudding against his side, wailing with uncontrollable fear as though pursued by evil spirits. We heard no more of the matter and so I left Nigeria with increased respect for our legal system and a new awareness of the almost invincible power of the middle-class housewife.

21

THE CRACKS SPREAD ACROSS THE CEILING IN OUR NORTH London house like ever-widening rivers on a map, and the plaster powdered the stair-carpets. Step-daughters, who had been lurking with lovers in the shadowy upper stories, left home. In spite of the simplicities of the law I used to practise, there is no one cause you can write on the death certificate of a marriage; the patient is at the mercy of a multiplicity of sicknesses, and when two writers in one house are involved resistance may be seriously weakened. I knew how my clients felt at the end of a long and familiar life and their fear at the prospect of unaccustomed freedom. For a long time every effort is made to keep the true facts from the family. Meanwhile there is a constant and increasingly hopeless search for a cure.

At one period of history we might have put our affairs in the hands of priests or vicars. Nowadays the dissolution of marriage seems to be attended by grave and sympathetic chartered accountants. The affluent sixties brought, I'm sure, a great increase in the number of psycho-analysts. Such doctors, a red-faced Scot with a breezy commonsense manner, or a pale and uncommunicative Central European who sat by the gas fire in the house he never left, while his family listened uneasily to the opening of the front door and the tentative footstep on the stair, become the third parties in our lives. They were the rivals, granted the long private hours of self-examination, whose enigmatic advice could be repeated and, perhaps, improved upon. Bred to a scepticism which found the Book of Genesis, the Oedipus Complex and the Collective Unconscious merely myths of varying usefulness, I found my visits to these doctors puzzling. The breezy Scotsman, for instance, suggested that the situation might improve were I to take up golf. It seemed, at a time of advancing despair, an extreme but probably fruitless remedy.

I had, I suppose, reached that moment when well-settled people set out for a second visit to their youth. Mine was a place I had never seen before, having been too involved with children, 'undefendeds', overdrafts and getting on in the law. Gaugin gave up his bourgeois life and set sail for Tahiti. Many men, I imagine, travel the same route, and if their South Sea island is only the adolescence they never enjoyed, it is subject to the same disadvantages, heat, disease, disillusion, loneliness and the slow disintegration of life in the tropics. I suppose it's possible that Gaugin might have painted his pictures of the South Seas while still living with his Danish wife and during his spare time from the bank. Such considerations never dissuade anyone from attempting the journey, however much they may regret arriving at their destination.

These thoughts, confused and hardly understood, were half exhilarating and half paralysing to the will. It became an enormous effort to open letters, still more to do an 'undefended', and much time seemed to be spent in watching the cracks trace their slow way across the ceiling. Some sort of new start was clearly necessary, but I had no idea where to begin.

It seems, looking back on it, to have been a period of doctors' waiting-rooms, of days when men with soft voices wrote down our history and did their best not to show surprise and disbelief at the birth of so many children. I remember climbing up the staircase in a Golders Green house in the wake of a beautiful woman who was wearing a white motor-cycling outfit and carrying a crash-helmet like a huge goldfish bowl. I was not on my way to see her, to my regret, but her small stockily-built husband, a Mr Durst, who was a lapsed Jungian with, so it was said, a deft way of disposing of writers' problems.

It was the Kleenex that ruined my relationship with Mr Durst. As soon as I came into the room he would emerge from behind his desk, carefully abstract one tissue from a cardboard carton and lay it neatly and reverently on the headpiece of his couch. If only I would put my head to the Kleenex, it seemed, a marvellous relaxation would come over me and Mr Durst would be able to dive down into the secret caverns of my soul and release the timid and inhibited impulses there imprisoned. Somehow I couldn't lie down. Did my fear of self-revelation prevent me, or could I not bear the thought of becoming just another transient stain on Mr Durst's pillow. Did I detect something over-cautious in the gesture with the Kleenex which made me deny Mr Durst my full confidence? Whatever it was, my refusal to lie down in his presence made him testy.

'You won't trust me,' he said in his severe accent. 'You are so very, very English and you think I am a bloody foreigner. Is this not so?'

'Not at all,' I said truthfully. 'It's nothing to do with you being German. It's just the Kleenex.'

'The what?'

'It's just that I'd feel ridiculous, with my head on a bit of Kleenex.'

'What are you trying to hide, that you attack me for simply taking reasonable precautions with my sofa?'

'I am trying to hide nothing.'

'You have some strange secrets?'

'None that I can remember.'

'Then why do you waste my time coming here at all, once a week and at considerable expense to yourself?'

I thought of telling him that it was in part due to the pleasure I derived from seeing his wife mount the staircase, but I hesitated, wondering if my relationship with Mr Durst could bear the weight of so much truth.

'I am finding it almost impossible to open envelopes and extremely difficult to do "undefendeds".'

'Undefendeds?' Mr Durst looked puzzled.

'Yes. They are part of my work as a barrister. Rather a dull part, as a matter of fact. I'd rather like a change. I even thought I might take silk.' And then I explained, 'That's what we call applying to become a Queen's Counsel.'

'I know what taking silk is,' Mr Durst almost snarled at me. 'Oh, you have to treat me, don't you, in this terribly English fashion! You think I am the poor bloody foreigner who is so ignorant he doesn't know what it means "taking silk".'

'I was only trying to explain . . .'

'This is your secret that you are keeping from me. That you are within reach of "silk".'

'Well, I've been hacking away at the law for a long time now.'

'Modesty! Modesty!' Mr Durst threw up his hands in disgust. 'That is your English way of showing off.' He was silent for a while and then he picked the Kleenex off the couch, rolled it into a ball and threw it into the waste-paper basket. Then he said, with a sort of reluctant approval, 'Within reach of "silk", eh? No longer a "stuff", is that the expression? The silk gown is almost in your grasp?'

'Well,' I said, feeling that the whole plan was becoming more and more ridiculous. 'You know how it is . . .'

'And you know what you are, don't you?' Mr Durst looked at me triumphantly. 'You are an amiable English Guy Fawkes who seeks to enter the House of Lords *in order to blow it up*!'

Mr Durst's destruction of the Kleenex made me feel that either my cure was complete or that I was too far gone and it was past his power to help me. I never saw him again, but I often think of his description of myself and feel ashamed that it's not more accurate.

Once when Mr Durst asked me what I was writing I told him that I had an idea for a play about a Judge.

'Ah good!' he said with a rare show of pleasure. 'A Judge will be very resonant for you, and entirely archetypal.'

No doubt that was the problem with the play I managed to finish at last, after I had gone to the South Seas around Maida Vale. The central character remained entirely in the resonant and archetypal stage; it was a play that appeared, I noticed to my embarrassment when I saw it, with its symbols showing.

The figure of the Judge was, in fact, resonant enough, pursuing a line which stretched back to the Bloody Assizes and down to the alarming Judges who used to try crime and who, from the safe distance of the Probate, Divorce and Admiralty Division, I only knew by hearsay.

The older type of port-swilling, bawdy, joke-telling, privately foul-mouthed and publicly righteous Judge was in part legend, in part something as dull as an archetype. But there was still some truth in the character. A human and extremely civilized Judge told me that, when at the bar, he had prosecuted one murderer and defended the next two capital cases at a West Country Assize. When he went, after his labours, to a bar dinner he was greeted jovially by the presiding Judge who said, with a large pink gin in his hand, 'I hope to God they're not going to run out of rope in Cornwall!'

In those days Judges, travelling the country on Assize, always went with a Marshal, a young unfledged barrister whose heavy duties were to live in the Judge's lodgings, listen to the Judge's jokes, tee up his golf ball and, when in Court, keep the Judge's papers from getting lost and sharpen his pencils. No doubt in many cases the Marshal's lot could be interesting and even enjoyable, but sometimes it was extremely alarming. When I wrote my play I remembered the horrifying story of the Judge's threepenny bit. It seems that an extremely ferocious and sullen old Judge was sitting with his Marshal during a long evening in the lodgings. They were listening to a Palm Court orchestra on the wireless and the Judge was playing with a handful of small coins which he had taken out of his pocket. As he counted his change for the thirteenth time during a Hungarian Rhapsody he uttered a cry of, 'Marshal! Marshal, I've lost a threepenny bit!' Without a moment's delay a search was instituted. The Marshal was down on his hands and knees. At the Judge's alarmed ring he was joined by the clerk and the butler. The three of them crawled over every inch of carpet whilst the Judge sat glowering at them.

After an hour's fruitless quest the young Marshal's nerves could stand the strain no longer. He crawled behind the sofa, took a threepenny bit from his pocket, dropped it furtively on to the floor and then held it up with a shout of triumph. The clerk and the butler tottered arthritically to their feet, considerably relieved. The contented Judge was escorted up to bed having graciously thanked his Marshal and promised to keep his eye on him during what might well prove, after such an auspicious beginning, to be a brilliant career at the bar.

By the morning, however, the atmosphere had changed. The Marshal came down to breakfast, in a reasonably cheerful mood, to find the Judge frowning at him over the kedgeree and saying, in a voice which called for a black cap, 'Marshal! You will take the next train back to London. You are not to stay one more hour in these lodgings and I hope I shall never be troubled by your presence again. I cannot tolerate a lying Marshal.'

'But, Judge . . .'

'The case is proved, beyond reasonable doubt,' and the Judge held up a small coin. 'I found my threepenny bit last night. It had fallen, Marshal, *into the turn-up of my trousers!*'

Such Judges had, it is fair to say, their advantages. They might turn as savagely on the powers of government and bureaucracy as they did on unhappy murderers. At no time could they be mistaken for civil servants. But our system is a strange one and it means that advocates, who have been trained not to decide cases but to urge others to a decision, are led, late in life, into the strange business of judgment. It's no wonder that such judgments are sometimes reached by Judges who persuade themselves with all their skills of advocacy. Judgment, I was trying to say when I wrote my play, is at best a crude and brutal business because it is always a simplification. We may regard ourselves as too sensitive, or too tolerant to go into the coarse trade of sitting in judgment on our fellow men and women. It's a job we prefer to leave to others, like sweeping out the mortuary or recycling the sewage, and those who undertake it make their own particular sacrifices. A Judge on circuit is almost confined to his lodgings; he can't go for a drink in a pub, he used never to go shopping, if he managed to go to the movies he had to have a police escort. The Judge condemns himself, when he chooses his occupation, as surely as the pickpocket or the embezzler, to long periods of imprisonment.

In those days most British playwrights were well known as German playwrights. Whatever other effects their extraordinary recent history had on the German people it silenced their dramatists who seemed, in that period and greatly to our advantage, at a loss for words. No German town had been without its production of *The Dock Brief* and when *The Judge* opened in Hamburg I arrived there to great acclaim. Indeed a television camera at the airport seemed about to follow me into the 'Gents'. I was lavishly entertained and taken to the strip shows in the Reeperbahn where solid middle-class families sat watching the contortions of naked girls with snakes and hock bottles. When I arrived at the Schauspielhaus the director bowed to me and I was called 'Herr Doktor'. In Europe writers are Herr Doktors or Professori or Chers Maîtres. In England we are treated with an amused contempt which is perhaps healthier and more liberating, although matters go too far in Hollywood where writers are looked on as those anonymous and readily replaceable slaves who built the pyramids. In Hamburg I was assured, as Herr Doktor, that the evening was all set for success and that my play would undoubtedly prove a triumph for Anglo-German relations.

One of the characters in this particular play, referring to the Judge's off-stage arrival, says, 'The Sheriff's at the station. And the Boy Scouts with trumpets.' When the curtain rose in the huge Schauspielhaus I was startled to see the stage filled with rank upon rank of Boy Scouts, stretching out like the chorus from *Lohengrin* and blowing an expert and evocative hunting-call on their trumpets. In the interval a young man in evening dress came up to the Herr Doktor, bowed and asked for an autograph, 'Because I do not like this play one little bit.' As the curtain was about to tremble to the ground for the last time a man in white gloves came to my seat, clicked his heels and whispered, 'You will be expected to make an appearance upon the stage, Herr Doktor. I do not think that they will want to "boo" you tonight.'

No prediction was ever more rash. As I wandered on to the Opera-sized stage, the actors grasped me by the hands and rushed me down towards an auditorium which was resonant with disapproval. 'Typical Hamburg audience.' The leading actor appeared to be enjoying himself hugely. I made a small obeisance and the 'boos' were redoubled. I began to feel strangely elated. I had often bowed my way out after losing a case, but the Judge had never stood up and sent me on my way with a loud 'Yah-Boo!' I left the theatre in a mood of great cheerfulness, spent the whole night at a party and then flew back to England. At the airport I went to the 'Gents' unnoticed by a single television camera.

In England the play was acted by Patrick Wymark and Patience Collier. It was directed by Stuart Burge, who had done *The Dock Brief* in the theatre, and, although it was performed as well as possible, it failed in a more discreet and less sensational way than it had in Germany. Failures are usually instructive and I learnt, from *The Judge*, a freer use of the stage which I was able to develop when I came to write a play about my father. I also learnt to avoid archetypes and stick, in writing, to the people I knew.

A few years later I was doing some part-time, fill-in Judging. I stayed, not in the Judge's lodgings, but in a motel on the by-pass outside the town. I missed out on claret, kippers and lunch with the High Sheriff. I found the proceedings curiously peaceful and free from the almost unendurable strains of advocacy. The Judge is one of the few people in Court who doesn't in the least care who wins. A Judge can also control the speed of a case and when he doesn't know the law he can ask to have it explained to him by all the parties. The judicial duty seemed so unexpectedly relaxing that I couldn't understand why the old Judges of my youth had always been in such an evil temper. Admittedly I was handing out divorce decrees and not death sentences, but I found the work straightforward enough and discovered, as most Judges say they do, that the truth becomes clear at quite an early stage. I did find the life lonely and the regular hours were unsuited to my temperament, and, as I have already written, my mother laughed uncontrollably when I told her that I had been sitting as a Judge.

Becoming a QC, or 'taking silk' as Mr Durst had insisted on calling it, was a proceeding which my father had always thought was attended by a quite unacceptable element of risk. A QC is cut off from the supply of bread and butter work such as drafting pleadings and doing 'undefend-eds', which is the staple diet of the 'Junior' at any age. A QC is only needed for a lengthy or complicated case and such things were not daily events in the Probate, Divorce and Admiralty Division. When a fashion-able divorce called for a modish display of silk, QCs were often brought in from the Common Law or Criminal Courts where it was thought they had learnt to cross-examine with a more deadly elegance. These unfortunate Leaders would often discover that my sexagenarian father was their Junior. He would sit behind them frowning at their best efforts and barking out orders when they were on their feet. Criticized by the Judge from in front and barracked by my father from the rear, such QCs would often remember a pressing matter at Gloucester Assizes and slink timidly away, leaving the field in the hands of their learned Junior. So it was my father's consistently held belief that becoming a QC meant starvation, and he and his contemporaries had before them the example of many divorce practitioners who took silk, became unemployable and ended up as lonely and ill-paid part-time Judges. When, therefore, in search of a more enthralling life in the law, I applied to the Lord Chancellor for permission to wear a silk gown, I was sure my father would have said, 'All very well if you're prepared to draw in your horns, old boy, and live on cheese and Cyprus sherry.'

At the end of my life as a not-so-learned Junior, I was involved in a remarkable Probate action, something my father would have approved of, as it was a good 'money brief' and lasted for almost a year. The testator was a comparatively young German millionaire and the huge cast of alleged beneficiaries of his various Wills included his wife, his mother, his chauffeur, his doctor and a great number of mistresses. We barristers packed the benches and I remember the day that the one sitting next to me unexpectedly passed me his own Will to witness. By the end of the case most of us had suffered a change of life, taken silk, become Judges or merely cashed in the chips after such a surprising run of good luck and left the bar. It was the time of the satire shows on television and Ned Sherrin was producing *Not So Much a Programme More a Way of Life*. Success as a producer of satire had given him an unshakeable urbanity so that he became, as the years went by, more and more like a barrister, a career for which he had had some early training. He always asked me politely, at about 6.30 on Monday mornings, if I had any brilliant ideas. So in the intervals of working out the wider repercussions of German testamentary law I would try my best to be satirical for the sake of a quick sketch on television.

Gerald Gardiner, who had been the undoubted star of the Lady Chatterley case, was a Chancellor who must have found it hard to say no to aspiring QCs. I bought the outfit second-hand from the widow of an old Divorce Court QC and part-time Judge of whom I had once been terrified. In due course I pulled on the used knee-breeches and crammed my feet into the paste-buckled, patent leather shoes. The black silk stockings were a problem, a Judge once told me, best solved by buying a huge elastic suspender belt from a nurses' outfitters. However this was advice I have never taken. I put on the full-bottomed wig which reduces the world to an itchy silence and eventually knelt at prayer in Westminster Abbey beside a more senior QC who insisted on whispering the macabre details of the murder he was doing in Birmingham when he ought to have been intoning the responses. I swore an obscurely-worded oath, apparently designed to assure the Queen that I was ready to advise her, although up to now she has shown no signs of calling on my services.

Then I entered a long gallery of the House of Lords for a strange midday meal known as the 'Lord Chancellor's breakfast'. I was swathed in lace and black silk and wore a tailed coat and knee-breeches. I was carrying white kid gloves. I showed absolutely no sign of blowing the place up as Mr Durst had suggested. Instead I feasted placidly on flabby sausage rolls and bottled Worthington.

22

MY UNEASY AFFAIR WITH THE LAW ENTERED A NEW PHASE
after breakfast with the Lord Chancellor. My legal life changed and I
took, among other things, to crime. After only ever having had one brush
with the criminal law in the long-ago matter of the stolen fish, I found
myself in the front row at a murder trial and with a client who didn't
just have his marriage at stake, but a sizeable chunk of his life depending
on my advocacy.

Crime is regarded as somewhat downmarket by civil lawyers, who
tend to talk about 'Old Bailey hacks' and to see the Commercial Court as
the 'Harrods' and the Central Criminal Court as the 'Tesco' of the legal
profession. For some reason which escapes me, bankers and property
developers are thought to be more desirable customers than indecent
assaulters or petty thieves, or at least create a better impression when
they are sitting round in the waiting-room. The Judges of the House of
Lords, our Supreme Court, who can pick and choose the cases they hear,
appear to relish a cut-throat contest between international cartels, and
only deal with the criminal law rarely and with obvious distaste. And
yet, while civil law is nearly always about money, criminal law is
concerned with more vital matters, such as life, love and the liberty of
the subject.

On the whole lawyers, and in particular defending lawyers in criminal
trials, do not belong, like doctors, nurses and those who read out the
news on the television, to one of the highly-regarded professions. They
are accused of earning huge sums of money out of human misery and of
grave dishonesty in making believe that their patently guilty clients are
innocent. The first suggestion is easily rebutted as the average barrister's
wage is not far above that earned by a really competent secretary, and
even busy Old Bailey hacks may do no better than printers and a great
deal worse than cameramen. They can write off very few expenses and
have no pension to look forward to, so the hard-working defender with
no taste for joining the Civil Service as a Judge must face the possibility

of staggering to his feet in the Old Bailey in his seventies, or coughing his way out of life during his mitigation in yet another long firm fraud.

The charge of intellectual dishonesty is more serious, and the defence to it involves describing a state of mind which comes naturally to defending lawyers and strikes the rest of the world as very peculiar indeed. The defender accepts that he is not a Judge or a Jury. His role is not to make up his mind as to his client's guilt or innocence, it is for him to put forward the case of those who employ him, as strongly as possible. Strangely enough this becomes quite simple when you are actually at work on a case. The final decision, the act of judgment, is often the least interesting moment in life as well as in the law, and the best way to approach many subjects both in and out of Court is with belief and disbelief suspended.

A British criminal trial is not primarily an investigation to discover the truth, although truth may sometimes be disinterred by chance. A criminal trial is a test of the prosecution evidence, a procedure to discover if a case against an accused person can be proved beyond reasonable doubt. There is no point at which a defender has to prove his client's innocence, and so the strength of evidence in support of the accusation can be fairly tested without the advocate being involved in an allegation of innocence. Furthermore it is not always understood, except by barristers who accept it as one of their few articles of faith, that you must not help a client to put forward a story which he has told you is untrue. For this reason Sir Patrick Hastings, a successful and aggressive advocate, would never see a client accused of murder. The risk of a whispered, 'Well, I did do it, squire,' in the cells was far too great.

I suppose some people reading this might feel critical of such a system and suggest an investigative form of trial which would call on the defence to prove its case. Such feelings might persist until we found ourselves being tried, and then I think we should all be grateful that we couldn't be convicted on a theory which *might* fit all the facts, or even on one that *probably* did. We would feel it far more satisfactory to be locked up for a period of years with a couple of violent men and our overflowing chamber-pots, only on the basis of a prosecution which had to make the Jury sure beyond reasonable doubt.

Such golden principles of our law are by no means secure. They are forever under attack, particularly by Chief Constables who seem to feel that all trials should take place in front of the understanding Sarge in the friendly neighbourhood Nick – a Judge that can be relied on to pass a sentence which will encourage police recruitment. Such a tribunal would see that the proceedings weren't unnecessarily held up by money-grubbing old barristers overpaid by the Legal Aid. Our grasp on the principle that no man shall be required to incriminate himself, which is linked to the presumption of innocence, is under constant strain. The Home Office detention of immigrants has undermined the right of Habeas Corpus, once considered an essential ingredient of liberty. It is hard to see who is going to defend these ancient and hard-won rights except for the battered and despised defence barrister who slogs round some pretty mean Courts and makes himself awkward and unpopular, insisting that all guilt must be proved beyond doubt and that the administration of justice is never in the hands of the police.

In the end I achieved a far greater admiration for our criminal law than for the peculiar simplifications and superstitions which governed matters of love and marriage. I also found, to my surprise, that alleged criminals were the most pleasant type of client, often being less malevolent than divorced wives in pursuit of their husbands' property, and a great deal less grasping than beneficiaries in Will cases. It is true that alleged criminals give less trouble than divorce petitioners because they are usually under lock and key and can't ring up in the middle of the night to announce a new enormity about the arrangements for the children's half-term, or the unauthorized sale of the fish-knives. Defendants in criminal cases are strangely uncomplaining; fearing the worst, they are grateful if matters don't turn out quite as badly as they had expected. Even when they're convicted I have never known a customer turn against his defender. It is true, however, that you see a convicted client when he is in a state of shock, unable to look into the future. A week later he may stand in his cell and contemplate a prospect of wasted years, of the perpetual smell of urine and sweet tea and life as a number. Then tears may prick his eyelids; but by then the barrister is out at another Court and hoping, however vainly, for a break in his long line of convictions.

Of all the clients in criminal cases I came to find those accused of murder the easiest to deal with. Murder is not only the most serious crime, but it is often the most understandable. Murder happens, in many cases, in the family. It is the sort of crime that might be committed by ordinary and even decent people who would be quite incapable of taking part in a bank raid or robbing the Co-op.

Contrary to the beliefs of all the great crime writers, murder is hardly ever planned, it almost never involves the search for ingenious methods of killing or the elaborate constructing of false clues. Murder is what happens at the single moment when the long-stifled domestic row, the feeling of rivalry and hatred in the pub or the pang of jealousy and rage in the disco, slither out of control and skid towards an irreversible tragedy. So many scenes between husbands and wives, parents and children, between all people who are passionately involved with each other, contain the seeds of potential murder. Murder trials are not usually about who dunnit, almost always about whether they meant it. What did the accused intend? Was he or she making some kind of a demonstration which ended in the most unlooked-for consequences, with someone once loved, naked on a slab being photographed after the post-mortem, with the testing of blood-stains and stomach contents and pubic hair, and endless questions designed to illuminate that moment which some merciful mental process may have forever obliterated.

I never shared the full Marshall Hall experience of defending in a murder trial in the days of the death penalty. I don't know if I could have done so, or if I could have tolerated a contest where one question too many, one wrong decision about the admissibility of evidence, might bring about your client's death. Certain parts of what was once our Empire still inflict the death penalty, and for offences less than murder. Some of these cases finally find their way to the Judicial Committe of the Privy Council in Downing Street and in that elegant courtroom Judges and barristers still consider a capital case in a detached and disinterested way. At the end of the argument a long-distance telephone call may be made and a scaffold erected in some tropical prison. These clients, of course, have unidentifiable foreign names which are hard to pronounce. The death penalty can easily be discussed when you are half a world away from the hangman.

Those accused of murder have usually, even if they didn't intend it, killed. This act seems, in a curious way, to have drained them of violence. In all but the most rare cases they have killed the one person they are ever likely to kill and are no longer dangerous. Sometimes they speak of what they have done in strange and unforgettable words. I remember one young man who had killed his mother starting his statement with, 'I have either raped a prostitute or killed a peacock in paradise.'

The advocate goes to Brixton Prison and crosses the compound where the Alsatian dogs and the 'trusties' eye each other suspiciously. He is shown into the blue-painted, relatively cheerful interview block. The man who comes to him in the little glass-walled room, who takes a cigarette gratefully from his solicitor's clerk and laughs obediently at his nervous jokes, must live with the fact that he caused a death. The advocate explains the trial to his client, asks him how many of the police statements he challenges and leaves after shaking the hand that killed. The idea that, if the advocate doesn't succeed on the question of what was intended in an isolated moment of emotion, his client will be taken out and ceremonially slaughtered by some part-time pub-keeper in a dark suit seems monstrous and unreal. A judicial killing is always pre-meditated and so, perhaps, more shameful than the crime itself. Ruth Ellis shot her boy-friend outside the Magdela pub in Hampstead in the mid-fifties and I can't say that I felt personally stained or humiliated by the tragedy, nor I'm sure did the public feel so outraged that they could only be satisfied by the blood of that distracted and neurotic girl. However when Ruth Ellis was hanged I remember hiding the newspapers from the children, ashamed of what was being done, so it was said, on our behalf.

When one Home Secretary, I think it was Reggie Maudling, toyed with the idea of a death penalty, an intelligent civil servant said, 'Where would you get the hangmen? Would you advertise in *The Times*?' Hanging is the act of brutality which we commit with the help of some ghastly surrogate. Years ago I remember one husband in a divorce case who was accused of a series of cruel sexual perversions. It was also suggested that he had some secret and undivulged source of income which he was keeping from his wife. When asked about this he said that the answer was an Official Secret. Pressed further he admitted that he was a part-time, assistant hangman. Against all rules of legal etiquette I turned him out and refused to concern myself in his case. It is on such people that those who support the death penalty must depend.

I have said that most murders are spontaneous and not the result of long-term planning. An exception to this rule was the case of my best friend at Oxford, the support and inspiration of the Pacifist Service Unit, Doctor Henry Winter.

Continuing my journey backward I had reached some sort of plateau of adolescence. I had taken a flat in Maida Vale when separated from my wife. I wasted long hours sitting, as I had once sat when I was teaching the models English, in dress shops or waiting in hairdressers. I became, for a while, emotionally attached to the telephone. I was in that exhaust-ing state when every evening has to be planned and the tangled skeins of living kept separate. The crimes I was involved in, the murders I did, were perfectly clear to me. My own life seemed confused and chaotic. I remember getting up in my flat around dawn and thirstily filling the bathroom tumbler. Too late I discovered that I had drunk a pair of mink eyelashes. It was, I suppose, a time of life everyone passes through, although for me it had been postponed because of the pressure of family life.

The children had reacted to our parting with an unexpected calm and lack of surprise. Their lives had started at that grown-up level which I had momentarily abandoned. There is much about that period I remember with great pleasure, including a girl who worked in a tropical-fish shop. She used to drive me to work in her firm's van and I would sit in the front as we crossed the Parks with huge tanks full of angel fish sloshing in the back. I remember the vanished places to dance, 'The Arethusa' and the 'Ad Lib Club' high over Leicester Square and 'Annie's Room'. The tunes of the period of *Help* and *Love Me Do*, which seem so much more remote than the time of *Blue Birds Over the White Cliffs of Dover* or *You Are My Sunshine*, float back into my mind. There is nothing about that time which I particularly regret. It is only important that I should describe accurately how things were when Henry Winter came to see me again after a long time.

My links with the past were growing frail. Oliver Pensotti had vanished, having long ago left the country. I had a postcard from him from Portugal and a pair of cuff-links from Rio, but these communications kept his address a secret and after them I heard no more. My friends seemed to be the actors or directors I worked with. We became involved during a production, saw a lot of each other and then slowly drifted apart. I had begun, once more encouraged by Nesta Pain, to write some radio pieces about my childhood. My mother disliked my doing this. Like her father's suicide and her husband's blindness she felt, understandably, that they were private matters which should not be generally discussed. I went to the country to see her often, but there was always something held back between us, a sort of reserve which didn't melt for a long time. It was as though she were still occupied in caring for my father. We sat together in the garden, but she was suspicious that I would want to break in on her continued solitary pursuit of their joint way of life. My children, who were not going to write anything, met her without inhibition. They often went to stay with her, rescued my old books and model theatre from the attic and seemed grateful that life in my father's house was proceeding as usual. His death, like his blindness, was largely ignored.

At that time I felt conscious of the lack of a guiding light. There seemed to be no one whose instincts were infallibly right, or to whom I could turn at moments of personal or artistic confusion. When I was assailed by these thoughts I remembered Henry Winter, imperturbably pursuing the good life as a doctor in the West Country. I must, I told myself, see Winter soon, but the meeting was, for one reason or another, constantly postponed.

Late one wet afternoon some theatrical occasion, a read through perhaps or part of a rehearsal, was going on in my flat. Actors and actresses were drinking white wine and talking only of the news in their world, which is, in its way, as small and protected as the world of lawyers. There was a ring at the bell and when I opened the front door I discovered Henry Winter, standing in the rain, a sort of plastic mac over his tweed jacket, and he was smiling with his habitual look of modesty and withdrawn wisdom.

I felt as I usually did when I saw him in those days, somehow guilty and corrupt. I got rid of the actors and actresses as quickly as possible. In their presence Winter sat smiling but silent, and I felt that his calm and useful existence compared favourably to the empty excitement of putting on any sort of show. It was not long before we were alone and I said, 'I'm sorry about those people. I'm afraid they're rather boring.'

'Are you? I found them interesting enough. But I wanted to ask your advice.'

'*My* advice?' What could I tell Henry Winter who had surely found, in the village where he practised, the still centre of understanding.

'Yes,' he said and astonished me with, 'I want to know how much I'd have to pay my wife, after a divorce.'

Then he told me the story. It seemed that Winter had fallen hopelessly and obsessively in love with a woman who cleaned at the local hospital. She wasn't young, in fact she was a middle-aged woman with a number of children and she lived with her husband in the Council Houses on the outskirts of the village. The husband was Winter's patient and the good doctor prescribed sleeping-pills which would keep the man drugged while his wife silently left the house and made her way through the sleeping village to the surgery. There, with Winter's children asleep upstairs, they made love on his medical couch.

'It's hopeless,' was the only sort of lawyer's advice I could give him. 'You're bound to get found out.'

'Oh, I know that. In fact I'm quite prepared for it. That's why I want to know how much I'll have to pay my wife after the divorce.'

'So you're treating me like a real lawyer.'

'Real enough to answer my question. It's only the practical things that matter now.'

Like, I thought, the drugs for the husband and the fact of having a couch in a downstairs room. I told him that he'd probably have to give his wife a third of his income and support his children.

'That's all right. We can live on what I'll have left. Annie, that's the woman from the hospital, isn't at all extravagant. She came to the village when she was a child, with the gypsies.'

'They'll strike you off the Medical Register.'

'It doesn't matter. I'm going to work abroad anyway. Probably South America. There'll only be one problem.'

'What's that?' Seeing nothing but insoluble difficulties I was astonished at Winter's calm.

'That'll be if Annie doesn't want to come with me. I mean, if she wants to stay with her husband. There'll only be one answer then, won't there?'

I didn't ask him what the answer was. I didn't feel that I could bear to learn more about Winter's troubles. What had happened? How could it be that life in his placid village was more frenzied than any I had heard of in London? And how had it come about that my friend, the man I depended on most for perpetual and untapped wisdom, had moved away into the shadows of his extraordinary drama and, worst of all, come to see me only because I was a lawyer?

'You know', I said and poured him a glass of white wine, 'I used to think you had the secret of the universe.'

'It's extremely unwise', he warned me, 'to think that anyone has that.'

Not much later he put on his plastic Pakamac and went out into the rain.

What happened then I only read about in the papers, although some further details were given to me by Henry Winter's wife who was, with some reason, bitterly angry. I also learnt a lot from his partner, who now knew that for the last three months of his life my friend was going on his medical rounds, cheering up the elderly and comforting the children, with a sawn-off shotgun worn in a holster under his jacket.

He had asked 'Annie' to leave her family and go with him to South America, but she was never willing to do so. When, at last, he showed her the passports and the money he had for both of them she resolutely refused to go. He killed her with the shotgun and then drove into a wood where he swallowed most of the drugs in his medical case. It was some time before they found his body, but when they did so he was still holding the passports.

I think about these things often, but I cannot explain them. I can only suggest that Henry Winter suffered terribly and unusually from having rejected the violence which was made available to us all at the age when we went to Oxford.

23

IT WAS IN THE MIDDLE OF THE SIXTIES THAT I HAD THE opportunity of learning the true meaning of farce.

Laurence Olivier had started the National Theatre at the Old Vic with its far from luxurious offices in a row of prefabs around Coin Street. Kenneth Tynan played the part of the dramaturge or literary editor of the outfit and formed, with Sir Laurence, a somewhat uneasy partnership. Henry Winter had gone back to study medicine at Oxford after the war and when I visited him I first met Ken Tynan, whom I watched giving a one-man performance of Edgar Allan Poe's *Tell-Tale Heart* on a barge. Later we had met at the Edinburgh Festival at a somewhat disastrous congress of playwrights. Dramatists flew in from all over the world to assemble in the MacEwan Hall, where Ken Tynan organized a most inappropriate happening in the city of John Knox. A naked girl model from a local art school was wheeled round the hall on a camera trolley. After this event the world's distinguished dramatists, together with Mr Tynan, flew away to the South and the unfortunate girl was left to face in the Sheriff's Court a rigorous prosecution for indecent exposure. I remember that at this congress Ken Tynan preached his usual sermon on the virtues of Bertolt Brecht and announced that Beckett's plays were filled with 'privileged despair'.

Tynan was extremely gifted, but the godmothers present at his birth had bestowed on the infant Kenneth irreconcilable gifts. One had brought him the Puritan conscience (essential to the life of the libertine) which led him to overvalue Brecht and pass his unreasonable strictures on Beckett. She gave him his faith in socialism and his urge to be called 'Ken'. This godmother caused him to regard pornography not so much as a diversion but as a duty and led him, in later years, to approach sex, and write of such matters as the history of knickers down the ages, with the sort of apostolic zeal with which the Early Fathers of the Church discussed the Immaculate Conception. She gave him a small bundle of her 'governess' words with which to chastise those who strayed from the paths of righteousness. From then on he was able, in his criticism, to 'chide' Arnold Wesker, to 'grow testy' with Peter Hall and generally to be specially 'irked' by those writers who were his friends, including me.

The second godmother never liked the first and was eager to undo her good work. She came with the well-thumbed essays of Max Beerbohm, *The Unquiet Grave*, most of James Agate's *Ego* and some back numbers of the *New Yorker* stained with genuine drops of the first Dry Martini served to Dorothy Parker in the Algonquin Hotel. 'The stern rebukes', she said, 'which my tedious sister has given you to utter shall be translated into a prose style so remarkably elegant and seductive that many will be deceived. She may have made you a Roundhead, but at least I shall arrange to have you always dressed as a Cavalier.' She then left, leaving the infant Kenneth *Death in the Afternoon*, the *Michelin Guide to the Restaurants of France* and a packet of handmade shirts.

The third fairy godmother entered the room in the shape of a microphone swung from the darkness into a beam of limelight, behind which rolled the cast list of the Mercury Theatre, New York. 'For the confusion of both my sisters,' this godmother boomed eerily, 'I shall make you permanently, enthusiastically besotted with show business', adding, for good measure, 'My name is Orson Welles.'

I owed Ken Tynan a debt of gratitude, read his accounts of acting with great admiration, and followed him through a career which had its eccentricities. I remember an election-night party when his stern Socialist enthusiasm was made less convincing by the fact that he had included, among his guests, a number of life-sized waxwork young ladies dressed as nuns, who were to be found seated on the lavatory or lying, in abandoned attitudes, about the bed. I remember spending a good deal of the evening talking to the lady who hired out these figures. 'Her girls', she made it clear, didn't accept invitations to just any old party, and when they did go out she went along as a chaperone. Ken Tynan also had a device which I believe he had written up for called a 'self-regarder', a sort of mirror which was suspended over his bed. One night it fell unexpectedly, almost putting an end to his distinguished career as a dramatic critic. In due course, and with his usual missionary zeal on the subject of sex, he conceived the idea of *Oh, Calcutta!* and invited me to the dress rehearsal to give the project legal advice. It seemed that a 'dress rehearsal' meant that the cast still wore certain articles of daily use, such as their spectacles, bandages and corn plasters, although otherwise disrobed. It was a show which made me regret the power of his Puritan godmother to wean him away from the sensual delights of writing fine prose.

My debt of gratitude to Ken Tynan was largely due to his asking me if I would like to translate a Feydeau farce called *Puce à l'Oreille* for the National Theatre. He also introduced me to Jacques Charon who was coming over from the Comédie Française to direct the play.

I knew nothing about farce until I read *Puce à l'Orielle*, and had no idea what a deadly serious business it is. Feydeau's plays are really tragedies played at a high speed, and the plot of *Othello* for instance, with its typical Feydeau prop of a lost handkerchief (in *Puce à l'Oreille* it's a pair of braces), would make excellent farce material.

The world of farce is necessarily square, solid, respectable and totally sure of itself, only so can it be exploded. There is nothing comical about a trembling masochist being kicked on the behind, or a sprightly and permissive collection of Swedish teenagers being caught in the wrong bedrooms. These events must occur only to the most dignified and highly moral persons. It is impossible to be funny about funny people and Feydeau's characters are triumphantly serious.

They are also mature, and completely self-satisfied. They have settled, on the whole gratefully, for security, marriage with the director of the Insurance Company, a few nights out at the theatre, and a few safely uncompromising glances at the husband's best friend. It's all sound, predictable and a little dull. The husbands are not quite in their first youth, in bed they have become indolent or worse. The healthy, grown-up, but still somehow schoolgirlish wives 'Breathe', Feydeau said, 'virtue and are forthwith out of breath.' They very much regret that it's hard to take a lover without deceiving your husband. And the husbands still envy their bachelor friends and still cast a wary but interested eye towards the scurrilous hotels they pass on their way home from the office. Feydeau's plays start, like all great drama, at the moment when these small longings become alarming reality.

For then, of course, the world of common sense whirls and dips like a drunkards' bedroom. The first small domestic misunderstanding, the gentlest of white lies, brings down a series of disasters as inevitable and appalling as a Greek tragedy. By then, the husbands and wives and mistresses and lovers have become so inextricably confused that it's hard for them to tell if they're being faithful or not, and there's no time for them to jump into the vaguely longed-for bed as everyone's running far too fast.

Through all this, like hats desperately held on in a high wind, the characters must retain their common sense. Kicked, unexpectedly embraced, shot at, taken for mad, they continue to behave quite rationally: conduct which, of course, greatly increases the lunacy of the situation.

Feydeau created thirty-nine plays, apparently out of extreme indolence. When he was a child his father found him writing and told the governess that he need do no lessons as he'd written a play that morning. From then on Feydeau wrote to avoid sums. He was so lazy that when a friend said to him, 'Turn round. The prettiest woman I've ever seen has just come into the room', he answered, without moving, 'Describe her to me.' He sat in a café in the Rue Vivienne and made wild and ill-calculated investments on the stock exchange. So he had the great traditional stimulant to the industry of an artist, laziness and debt. A friend described him as elegant, gentle and charming, a poet who knew the 'wealth of fantasy and disenchantment that hovers in the smoke rings of a cigar'. It's hard not to see in Feydeau one of his own characters, sensible and detached, choosing a quiet life; but unceremoniously booted into a world of frenetic creation which became, at the drop of a coincidence, gloriously out of control.

All this was taught to me and much else about the theatre and the nature of comedy by Jacques Charon. He was a tall, fat man with slicked-back black hair and a rubbery face lit up with a grin of great amiability. He could be mercilessly honest to himself, and to his actors when he was directing. He said that the most important requirement for a performer was physical fitness, a sound chest and the ability to run at least a mile in the course of an evening. In spite of his comfortable figure he was, as he often boasted, extremely 'sportif' and he could not only dance with extraordinary lightness, as many fat people can, but I have seen him perform with great dexterity on water-skis. He lived in a flat behind the Comédie Française, that Mecca to which he had set his face when, as a small, fat, bourgeois child, he had been taken to the plays of Molière and Racine. When he was in Paris he seemed able to direct a play or a film during the day, as well as act at night and then stay up until dawn with friends in a restaurant. When he arrived at the National he knew hardly any English but demonstrated all the parts, and particularly the women's roles, with such energy and comic flair that the actors learnt a lesson in the truthfulness of comedy that they have never forgotten. And I will always remember what he told me about the solid basis of comic writing.

The construction of a Feydeau play is so wonderful that another playwright can only look at it with the awe with which a junior maths master might approach the work of Einstein. There is a dullish ten minutes in all his plays, and this always occurs at the beginning when he is laying the foundations for the ornate edifice he will build during the course of the evening. Feydeau's concern was with events and he didn't write many verbal jokes, so in translating him I supplied a number of my own. I always noticed that they never got as many laughs as such workman-like Feydeau lines as 'What?', 'Who?' or 'I can't believe it!' said at precisely the right moment. They were very happy days when we sat in the prefabs behind the National and Laurence Olivier lunched off an apple and a bottle of champagne and we read and re-read the play until I hoped it didn't sound like a translation at all, but made the listeners feel that they could understand French. The language of French farce of that period came easily to me, being not far removed from Wodehouse and Jerome K. Jerome and the sort of chat which still lingered in certain areas of the Inns of Court and which I could further explore and develop when I came to write *Rumpole*.

Puce à l'Oreille, which became, inaccurately, *A Flea in Her Ear*, lasted a long time at the National and was remarkable for Geraldine McEwan's acting suspicion like a beautiful Groucho Marx, for Albert Finney's falls and for the Astonishing Revolving Bed. When it went to Canada, Laurence Olivier played the smallest part, that of the butler, and made it memorable. I worked on another Feydeau play with Jacques Charon and some films. We did a film of *A Flea in Her Ear* which was shot in Paris for 20th Century Fox, but as Jacques was acting in the evenings and film was not his medium, he had no real enthusiasm for the day's work with 'Le Fox'. The film was disastrous, but the days spent making it were filled with pleasure, with lunch at the Boulogne studios and staying at the Plaza Athénée and evenings at the 'Elle et Lui' where the boyish waiters in dinner-jackets often turned out to be girls. All those, and many other delights, came to me from the work of translation. The hard fact of the language barrier became clear to me one evening in the presence of an English actress who left her husband for one night when Terence Rattigan was visiting Paris. She was learning French eagerly but slowly by listening to Berlitz records in her hotel bedroom and used to try out her newly-acquired skill whenever possible. After her night of absence, which caused her non-French-speaking husband great anxiety, she reappeared and, although she would give him no adequate explanation, he forgave her and they were reunited.

That evening I went with them to a celebratory dinner at 'Marius et

Janette'. Half-way through the evening the errant wife leant across the table and spoke to me, in ringing tones and with a strong English accent, words which must have taken her a considerable time to prepare. 'Cher John,' she said, 'Hier soir j'ai fucké le chauffeur de Terence Rattigan dans le Bois de Boulogne.' Her husband had the good manners, or good sense, to treat this as a remark couched in such idiomatic French that he was quite unable to understand it. He decided to order the *Sole Meunière* and the dinner proceeded to a peaceful conclusion.

So I shall always feel grateful to Ken Tynan and to Jacques Charon for the opportunity they gave me to learn about the serious side of farce, a form of drama which seems to me often more true to the facts of life as we know them than many great tragedies.

24

THE PUBLISHER JOHN CALDER, WHO WITH HIS THEN partner Marion Boyars was to be immortalized for lawyers in 'R v Calder and Boyars', a notable battle in the long, hard-fought, often serious, sometimes important, frequently farcical, and occasionally trivial, war between the freedom of the written word and our legal system, had been one of the organizers of the playwrights' conference in Edinburgh. He published *Last Exit to Brooklyn* by Herbert Selby Junior, a novel concerned with drug abuse and homosexual prostitution in the slums of New York. It was a powerfully written work, if conspicuously short on the jokes.

At that time I was busy doing murders and less significant crimes and still involved in the occasional divorce. As a 'leading Counsel' I was experiencing the strain of cases in which you are employed because you are expected to work miracles. In the old days at the bar I had been used to rushing from Court to Court, always conscious of the fact that I was about to be called on somewhere else, saying a breathless 'goodbye' to clients before diving down the Underground for a fresh bout of cruelty, adultery or wilful neglect to maintain. Now I was doing selected cases on which I was able to concentrate, and the responsibility seemed far greater and any adverse result far more disastrous. The divorce laws changed and the matrimonial offence was abolished. Having treated women with monstrous unfairness for centuries the law swung heavily in their favour. Wives could expect to strip their husbands of their assets however they had treated them. One insurance executive returned to his home in Wimbledon to find his wife in bed with two members of a pop group, the drummer and the lead guitarist. When he divorced her he was quite puzzled to find that this single act of abandon had earned her a third of his income, a third of his capital and a third of the value of their house which would have to be sold. Confused by the morality of these matters I devoted myself more and more to a life of crime.

John Calder and Marion Boyars, as the publishers of *Last Exit*, were duly prosecuted under the Obscene Publications Act at the Central Criminal Court. The wording of the charge consisted of that immortal phrase coined by Lord Chief Justice Cockburn in the year 1868. His Lordship was faced then with an evangelical Wolverhampton metal broker who had published a disgraceful pamphlet about the alleged methods used by Catholic priests to extract erotic confessions from lady penitents. An article is criminally obscene, Lord Cockburn decided in his great contribution to the law of literature, if it 'tends to deprave and corrupt'. This resonant phrase has been ransacked, in the following century, in the hope that it might yield some sort of intelligible meaning.

Lord Cockburn, of course, didn't consider the question of literary merit and even if the metal broker had written a work to rank with *Abelard and Eloise,* or the love sonnets of John Donne, that fact wouldn't have saved him from the Nick. In 1928 *The Well of Loneliness*, Mrs Radcliffe Hall's novel of lesbian love, was condemned by the Bow Street Magistrate and thirty-nine eminent writers, who had come to testify as to its being as 'sincere, courageous, high-minded and often beautifully expressed', as *The Times Literary Supplement* had said it was, were sent away unheard. (Times change and *The Well of Loneliness* was read out, a few years ago, as the 'Book at Bedtime' on the wireless.) Concerned at this slight to the world of letters, such well-intentioned MPs as Sir Alan Herbert and Mr Roy Jenkins promoted the Obscene Publications Act, 1959. This measure repeated Lord Cockburn's words as the test. A literary work is obscene, says the Statute, if it 'tends to deprave and corrupt those likely to read it'. However, if it is obscene, those who publish it are not to be convicted if its publication can be shown to be for the public good because it has artistic or other merit. The literary conception here enshrined in the tablets of our law is an interesting one. A book is first found to be depraving and corrupting, causing its readers to slaver at the mouth, walk with their knuckles brushing the ground and show a general tendency to breathe heavily down the telephone and rape the lady traffic wardens. However, the same book may then be found to be so exquisitely well written that its effect is ennobling after all. This is the sort of philosophic and aesthetic conception which is, of course, readily understood by your average Brixton Jury. It may not have been totally understood by the masterminds who promoted the Bill itself, men of the undoubted stature and literary repute of Sir Alan Herbert and Mr Roy Jenkins.

On the defence of literary merit expert evidence was made available by the 1959 Act and, in the prosecution of Penguin Books for publishing *Lady Chatterley's Lover*, literary figures entered the witness-box to do battle for the honour of D.H. Lawrence. Natural revulsion at the idea of a book by so highly regarded a writer being attacked in a Criminal Court may have tempted those who gave evidence to exaggerate the value of a somewhat absurd work, but the victory was significant. Lady Chatterley and her gamekeeper were acquitted, much to the irritation of the Judge and the outrage of the Judge's wife. The gentlemanly prosecutor, who suggested that it was not a book which the Jury might wish their wives or their servants to read, was consigned to everlasting ridicule, and Lord Gardiner, who defended Penguin Books, proceeded in a stately fashion to the Woolsack. The tide of progress was flowing and who ever would be able to hold it back? Soon, who doubted it?, the law would have to abandon its ill-judged attempts to censor the written word.

The trial of *Last Exit* took place eight years after the acquittal of *Lady Chatterley*. It was the only obscenity case in which witnesses were produced who said that they had been depraved and corrupted, or in which we were given an opportunity of seeing what a depraved and corrupted person looked like. Sir Basil Blackwell, the Oxford bookseller, said that he had certainly been depraved by the book, but as he was in his eighties at the time the matter didn't seem to be of great practical significance. The Reverend David Sheppard, who had been Captain of the English Cricket Team, also gave evidence to the effect that he had not, metaphorically speaking, held his bat so straight after reading *Last Exit to Brooklyn*, but as he went on to become Bishop of Liverpool the damage, whatever it was, doesn't seem to have been serious. In spite of the industry of a number of literary and clerical witnesses, the book was found to be obscene in its trial at the Old Bailey and the publishers were fined £100. So it came about that John Calder asked me to argue the *Last Exit* case in the Court of Appeal.

We were lucky in our Court. It was presided over by Cyril Salmon, whose casual way with a gold watch and leisurely stroll up to a cross-examination had led me to envious imitation when I was starting at the bar. I found myself standing up at a point where the two great concerns of my life, writing and the law, met and almost failed to recognize each other. Indeed I was trying to explain to three courteous and distinguished Judges the fundamental difference between writers and lawyers, which produces the basic fallacy of all censorship laws. The writer is bound to explore all areas of human experience. The whole of life must be open to his voyage of discovery, he must sail as far as he can and his only duty is to come back with the truth as he sees it. There can't be 'no go' areas in the world of art, and the writer who cuts short a line of work for fear of shocking some people or 'giving offence' is untrue to his calling. But lawyers are trained on 'no go' areas. They are accustomed to find truth concealed behind barriers marked 'inadmissible evidence'. They cannot accept that it's a writer's duty to reveal all truths however unpalatable. I tried my best to explain this to the Court of Appeal in the *Last Exit* case and the Judges listened with great care and attention. The proposition which must be elementary to all students of literature came to their Lordships as an apparent surprise. They looked like three poets who had just been told that you may not call expert evidence on the point the Jury has to decide.

An easier argument in the case was that the descriptions of homosexual prostitution and drug-taking in the book were so revolting that, far from turning anyone on to such practices, they would cause a sharp upswing in the marriage rate and the consumption of unadulterated 'Old Holborn' tobacco. The Judges were impressed by this argument which became known as the 'Aversion Theory' and withstood the test of a good many obscenity cases. The Court also ruled out the more usual meanings of the word 'obscene' which the trial Judge had given them. Publishing a book that was merely disgusting, or immoral, or erotic, or rude was clearly not a crime: it had to be blessed with the mysterious 'tendency to deprave and corrupt'. In the end the Court allowed John Calder's and Marion Boyars' appeal and set aside the conviction. *Last Exit* became a best seller for a short while and I was led into a new department of law which I, in my more elevated moments, called arguments about free speech, but most of the friendly hacks in the robing-room call 'dirty-book cases'.

I became more and more aware of the gulf that is fixed between the law and any sort of literature. One of the most difficult things to explain to Courts is that writers don't necessarily approve of their characters' behaviour. Because Shakespeare wrote *Othello* and *Macbeth* it doesn't mean that he approved of wife murder and the stabbing of house guests. The putting-out of Gloucester's eyes in *King Lear* is a deeply disturbing, shocking and horrific scene; but it tells a terrible truth about man's inhumanity to man. The purpose of a play, Shakespeare said, is to hold a mirror up to nature: censorship laws would ensure that the mirror is a rose-coloured distortion.

Courts are very unclear about the effect of books on readers. Reading is done in a world of the imagination which has, it would appear, little direct result on the reader's behaviour. I suppose the worst crime is murder and murder is nowhere written about more freely than in the works of Agatha Christie. If books had the effect claimed for them by the censors, every English country house would have a bloodstained butler in the library, dead with a knife between his shoulder-blades. James Bond, licensed to kill, is read about and enjoyed by millions of inoffensive people who catch the train to the office every day and have never killed anyone with a karate chop or slept with a Chinese air hostess. It has been said that it is a strange anomaly of the censoring attitude that murder is against the law, but it is no crime to write about it. Sex is not against the law, but to write about it has often been held a criminal offence.

Doing these cases I began to find myself in a dangerous situation as an advocate. I came to believe in the truth of what I was saying. I was no longer entirely what my professional duties demanded. the old taxi on the rank waiting for the client to open the door and give his instruction, prepared to drive off in any direction, with the disbelief suspended. The attempts of the law to control the written word seemed to me dangerous and likely to put our Courts of Justice in a somewhat ridiculous light. I suppose that writers should, in a way, feel flattered by the censorship laws. They show a primitive fear and dread at the fearful magic of print.

One of the difficulties of laws which tried to control books and habits of reading was that they assumed that our society was as one, as it no doubt was in 1868 when Lord Cockburn made his resonant pronouncement, and not a loose federation of groups with their own languages, customs, taboos, freedoms, courting habits and senses of morality. In England the moral values of a group of retired army officers and their wives frequenting a golf-course in Worthing are not the same as those of a crowd of art students in a Kings Cross squat. What appears permissible in the Surrey commuter belt, among bright young advertising men and their wives, would be looked on with horror by the Puritan Pakistanis of Bradford. Of course all these groups must be subject to a basic strongly enforced criminal law; they must not be allowed to assault or pillage or rape or rob one another. But in such a society, tolerance demands that no one group may be allowed to impose its own moral views, however strongly held, upon another; still less should they be able to use the severe sanctions of the criminal law to do so. The law, it has always seemed to me, is at its best when it is enforcing practical remedies for specific crimes; it is at its worst when it tries to enforce the morality of one group in society upon another which may, for quite sincere and logical reasons, refuse to accept it.

And it is significant that the attempted use of force is all one way. I did not wish to compel any member of the Festival of Light to sit through *Oh, Calcutta!* or read *Gay News*, although they do appear, no doubt from the highest motives and in the spirit of martyrdom, quite prepared to submit themselves to such works in the call of duty. No one, in the whole chequered history of censorship, has ever questioned anyone's right not to read a book, to stay away from a play or not to visit a cinema. No one has ever suggested the compulsory sale of television sets without the button necessary to switch them off if you don't like the picture.

The administration of the censorship laws entails dividing society into the sensible and the idiotic, the strong and the weaker brethren, and we all know, of course, where *we* belong. Time and again in obscenity cases Judges and barristers say to Juries, 'Of course, we've all read stuff like this for years and it doesn't affect us [and you can be sure it doesn't or there would be permanent orgies in the Judges' chambers, bondage suits on sale in Chancery Lane and the sound of whips echoing from the Inns of Court], but there *are* people, members of the Jury, whom you may think *would* be affected . . .' The assumption is that there is always a second-class citizen, who, at the glimpse of a doubtful paragraph or dubious magazine, would go uncontrollably mad. The attitude of censorship depends on the assumption that there is a superior type of person qualified to tell the rest of us what it is good for us to read.

The English law which seeks to control what our citizens read or write is ancient, confused and has not, on the whole, shown the Courts that administer it in a particularly favourable light. I came to believe that this is because such a law is unnecessary and inoperable, and its existence is unfortunate not only because it attacks free speech but because its somewhat ridiculous results bring the law into disrepute. I also thought that such a law is undesirable for this reason. If you commit a murder or a robbery, it is perfectly clear to you that you are doing so. If you take part in an illegal publication, you may have no idea that you have committed a crime at all until months later when a Jury decides whether or not the words you have published are 'obscene' or in any way offend against the law. Life is difficult enough for the ordinary citizen without the existence of crimes into which he or she may blunder without any intention of offending or any way of knowing that what has been done is in fact illegal.

The existence of censorship laws, although now admittedly mostly applied to books no one would miss, has been used in the past as a political weapon. The blasphemy laws were used to imprison Chartists who sold the works of Tom Paine. More recently the publisher of a book called *The Little Red Schoolbook* was successfully prosecuted under the obscenity laws. Among some much-needed advice on contraception, the book asked awkward questions about whether a capitalist society does not deliberately keep the majority of its citizens under-educated in order that they may be obedient and content with menial tasks. The question may have been naïve, but the fact that it challenged our brand of democracy may have had something to do with its prosecution.

Slogging round the Criminal Courts in the defence of literary values, I became increasingly aware of the presence of Mrs Mary Whitehouse. At first she appeared as a lonely figure. At a later trial she stood with her adherents outside the Court when the Jury had retired, apparently praying that they might be guided to a conviction. I came to have a great deal of respect for her courage and, indeed, for her cunning as a debater. During the *Oz* trial we took part in a debate in the Cambridge Union with Richard Neville, who was then on bail. The hall was packed to the rafters with somewhat over-excited students and, when Mrs Whitehouse rose to speak, someone lowered a skull over her head which bore the legend 'Alas, poor Muggeridge, I knew him well'. She continued her attack upon the powers of profanity and darkness unperturbed.

I had a friend, a journalist, who went up to Mrs Whitehouse outside a court and told her that a film was to be made of her life starring Dame Anna Neagle. She seemed extremely gratified. Later he told her that the casting had been changed and she was to be played by Jessie Matthews who was better at ballroom dancing. He alleged that Mrs Whitehouse had shown some slight disappointment.

Brought up by a father who questioned everything, raised as an only child who was unable to sink himself loyally into a group or take the moral lectures of headmasters seriously, these cases suited me better than struggles between warring spouses. I found it was occasionally possible, during such trials, to make Juries and even Judges laugh, and laughter is as much an enemy to the laws of censorship as it is to the heavy breathing and appalling humourlessness of most pornography.

However, a practice in obscenity cases is held, by many lawyers, to be a few degrees less respectable than dealing with murder or armed robbery. I remember one day, when I was appearing for a 'gay' magazine, there was a small posse of homosexuals holding up placards outside the Old Bailey. When I went into the robing-room to put on the legal fancy dress, an old silk greeted me disapprovingly from the shadows by growling, 'Well, Mortimer. I see you've got your friends from Rent-a-Bum outside today.'

Among the anomalies of censorship in the sixties was the strange figure of the Lord Chamberlain, a curious official usually concerned with such weighty matters as keeping the co-respondents in divorce cases off the Queen's Lawn at Ascot. The Lord Chamberlain had been given the task of licensing plays by an Act of Parliament passed in 1737, and in 1843 was enjoined to prevent the production of any play in the interest of 'good manners, decorum, or for the public peace'. In the interests of good manners and decorum successive Lord Chamberlains had banned works by Shelley, Ibsen, Wilde, Shaw, Granville-Barker and John Osborne. Marc Connelly's play *Green Pastures* was banned because an actor appeared as God. Many of the playwrights of the sixties treasured letters from the Lord Chamberlain insisting on alterations to their dialogue. This authority wrote to Charles Wood, 'Wherever the word "shit" appears it must be changed to "it"', and to M. Jean Genet, author of *The Balcony*, 'The huge Spanish Crucifixion must not be visible from the brothel room'. The Lord Chamberlain also forbade Mr Wood to use the expressions 'I'll have your cobblers' and 'I'll have your taters' in his play *Meals on Wheels* and was seriously perturbed when the actors substituted the mysterious and sinister phrase, 'I'll have your ollies'.

There were many suggestions afoot to improve on this office, but it did seem to me that a ridiculous censor was easier to remove than a rational one. With Ken Tynan among many others, I did my best, through the Arts Council, to organize the aboliton of the Lords Chamberlain and the passing of the 'Theatres Act' which protected plays from private prosecution. As my own works dealt largely with old men and middle-class failures, they did not contain much material likely to offend the Chamberlain; however he had insisted that one line in *The Wrong Side of the Park* which went, 'With the single exception of your mother I've never had a woman in my life' be changed to, 'I've never been with a woman in my life', which seemed to me a typically enigmatic command. In the course of our campaign I called on the then Lord Chamberlain to enquire if he wished to be abolished. Lord Cobbold, a banker who had been Lord Chamberlain of Her Majesty's Household since 1963, was a charming gentleman who seemed prepared to give up his onerous theatrical duties without too much of a struggle. When I asked him what subject he would be most likely to ban in a play, irrespective of its merits as a work of art, he answered with the single word 'Regicide', which seemed to rule out a good deal of Greek drama as well as many of the works of Shakespeare.

In the course of time, prosecutions of serious works gave way to cases solely concerned with what the more pretentious booksellers would call 'adult reading matter of an exotic nature'. Poorly produced and monotonously written, such books are, on the whole, less sexually stimulating than the omnibus edition of *The Archers* and could, perhaps, best be prosecuted under the Trades Descriptions Act as failing to fulfil their erotic promises. However a new defence was evolved which was roughly to the effect that such works were for the public good in that they relieved complexes, removed inhibitions, and acted as a safe substitute for sex with living people. In that period of the obscenity cases, barristers toured the country with a team of psychiatrists and doctors who were prepared to say, in various provincial centres, that masturbation is good for you. One such doctor had a joke. This concerned a boy who said to his mother, 'If it really makes you blind can I just do it until I become short-sighted?' Sometimes this joke went down well with Juries, sometimes it fell like a lead balloon.

Unhappily, one of these cases was lost and the unwise bookseller appealed to the House of Lords. No one has felt the full glory of a barrister's life who has not, in wig and gown, been called to the podium in the committee room of the House of Lords by an official in full evening dress and, on a wet Monday morning, lectured five elderly Law Lords in lounge suits on the virtues of masturbation. Their Lordships had no difficulty in deciding that the Obscene Publications Act did not permit such evidence to be given, and the 'joke' was heard no more in the land.

25

I HAVE BOASTED, WITH NO PARTICULAR VANITY, OF BEING
the best playwright ever to have defended a murderer at the Central
Criminal Court. I have said this to the murderers I have defended. I
doubt whether they have felt particularly encouraged. For them the Old
Bailey is far removed from any sort of place of entertainment. I once
congratulated a Jury on having sat through what was undoubtedly the
most boring case of the year, and the Judge was perfectly correct in his
summing-up when he said, 'The sole purpose of the criminal law is not
to amuse Mr Mortimer.'

And yet the practice of advocacy can only be a matter of deep interest
to the writer whose daily obsession is with words. Standing to address
a Jury, looking, as some have done, for a friend to support or an enemy
to convert, the advocate tests the immediate effect of language. Like
the actor he must lower or raise his voice to ensure attention. He must
make his listeners feel that he is talking to them alone and yet he
must seek for a combined response. In Court the right argument in
the correct words may have the most obvious results; years of a man's or
woman's life may depend on them. And in the theatre words have to
prove themselves immediately, by solid laughter which unites an audience, or by that attentive silence when even the most bronchial listeners
forget to cough, which is the greatest compliment that can be paid to the
writer.

Oratory is no longer, as it was in classical times, or in the eighteenth
century, considered an art. Most politicians' speeches are merely shrill
assertions of their opponents' errors, and addresses in Court have become dull rehearsals of facts. It is as though we have become scared of
our emotions and, if there are few calls now to the sense of freedom or
natural justice, it may be because it's thought that such ideals would no
longer interest an audience who, it is assumed, only care about wage
differentials, law and order and 2p off the income tax. Alexander Herzen,
who managed to preserve and develop his political beliefs during the

gloomiest days of Czarist tyranny, said, 'You can waken men only by dreaming their dreams more clearly than they can dream them themselves, not by demonstrating their lives as geometrical theorems are demonstrated.' That, it seems to me, is a lesson which needs to be learnt, not only by the writer before his blank sheet of paper, but by everyone who gets up to make a speech.

And yet how many cases are won by advocacy? No doubt the answer is far, far fewer than the advocate cares to think. The facts of the matter are dealt to the barrister, like a hand at cards, or a bundle of inherited or acquired characteristics. At first glance he can tell if it is a rotten case or a winner and, although in the course of the argument he may persuade himself that a different result is possible, most cases turn out exactly as you had thought they would in the first half hour after undoing the tape and opening the brief. Clearly cases and hands at bridge can be lost, just as lives can be thrown away, by carelessness, over-confidence, letting in unnecessary evidence, failing to lead out trumps or not noticing when the queen went. And the consequences of defeat can be mitigated. Skill and persuasion, in the vast majority of cases, can go no further: we are stuck with the cards we are dealt and have to act out, as well as we can, the lives which we have been allotted. 'Everything is in other hands, Lucillius,' wrote Seneca the Stoic. 'Time alone is ours.'

I don't know if the 'marriage ending' cards were dealt when we first stood on the beach in Ireland and Penelope was overcome with thoughts of death. Perhaps the course was set as we grew up far apart, in a faithless lawyer's garden and a sceptical parson's vicarage. At any rate the time had come to do what I had done for so many other people and plan a divorce. I remember a meeting we had, a lunch in the Rose Garden at Regent's Park, to discuss the depressing details, the sorting out of money, the allocation of books and pictures, which go with funerals and the formal ending of a marriage.

I had had a minor dental disaster that morning, a part of the façade of a cap had come adrift and I went to have it stuck on again. My dentist at that time was a cheerful Australian who had a surgery complete with nurses in white mini-skirts, Vivaldi tapes and a pattern of coloured lights to keep you entertained while in the chair. Later my dentist disappeared in a mysterious fashion but that, as they say, is another story. I emerged from the 'Son et Lumière' with my tooth repaired to keep my open-air luncheon appointment with the wife who had once helped me by typing out my divorce petitions. She came to the Rose Garden Restaurant with her dog and put the lead and her packet of cigarettes and her lighter on the table. We sat in the sunshine and Penelope ordered spare-ribs. It was extraordinarily peaceful as we sat surrounded by a silence which was only emphasized by the distant murmur of traffic. We talked, in perfect friendliness, and discussed our plans for the future. I remembered staying with her parents at the vicarage, the huge family meals, the feeling of daring and excitement as I left the scene of my lonely childhood and joined what seemed like a great colony of people whom I had later seen grow up and leave to live their separate lives. I remembered the places we had visited, the houses we had taken, the years we had spent writing and reading each other's words, waiting, in terrible suspense, for each other's smallest sign of approval. As we talked Penelope lifted a spare-rib and bit into it.

Suddenly, and it was like a frozen frame in a movie, my wife sat, spare-rib in hand, immobilized and with a look of horror. Then the film moved on again. She gathered up her dog, her cigarettes and her lighter and, without a word of explanation, she was gone from the Park.

I sat on at the table, half expecting her to return. I had a feeling of being suspended and lost in time. I might sit there, perhaps forever, and that table in that place might be the end of a journey and I would have to go no further. Or I could walk away from Regent's Park into a new life and leave the Law Courts and the rehearsal rooms forever.

Thinking all these things I lifted the half-eaten spare-rib from Penelope's plate and bit into it. I felt a slight pull on a gum and then I realized that something was missing from my mouth. My exotic dentist had been too distracted by the mini-skirts or the subliminal Vivaldi to fix the broken section of the cap on properly.

Before I had time to consider the full implications of the loss, the waitress said there was a telephone call for me. I went, puzzled, into the shadows of the restaurant, lifted the receiver and heard from Penelope who had just reached her house. She said she was sorry she had left so abruptly. I said that I understood perfectly and that it was not an easy thing for anyone to sit at lunch discussing a divorce. It wasn't that exactly, she explained. What had happened was that, as she bit into her spare-rib, a cap came off her tooth and she didn't want to go on sitting with a mouth full of gap. Again I understood entirely and said we'd meet again soon, wouldn't we?

I went out into the sunshine where the plates hadn't yet been cleared away. And there was the spare-rib which had captured fragments of dentistry from each of us and which held them tightly and remorselessly together.

26

AT THE END OF THE SIXTIES I BECAME, WITH WANING
interest, known for appearing in cases which were alleged to be testing
the frontiers of tolerance. One evening I was in my flat minding my own
business when the telephone rang. It was clearly being rung from a
call-box as there was a bleep, bleep, bleep and then the button was
pressed and an unknown, middle-aged, female voice rang out. She asked
me my name and I admitted to it.

'I say, I hope you're not having food?'

No, I reassured her, I wasn't having food.

'I'm on my way home to the country. I'm ringing you from Paddington
Station.'

'Oh, yes.'

'And you see, my children are grown up now and Frank, well, to put
it mildly, Frank's not the most *lively* companion.'

'Who's Frank?'

'Oh, Frank's my husband, of course. Frightfully respectable.' She gave
what I believe is known as a 'light laugh'.

I didn't reply to this and she asked, in a concerned way, 'I say, are you
sure you're not having food?'

'Quite sure.'

'I wouldn't want to pester you when you're having food. But what I
want to ask you is, do you think I ought to join the permissive society?'

Then she was silenced as her money ran out. I stood looking at the
telephone, picturing a woman loaded with Harrods' bags on her way
home to Newbury, and wondered if everything had perhaps gone too far
and the fabric of society, as they say in the House of Lords, was really
coming apart at the seams. Then the telephone rang again. There was a
bleep, bleep, bleep and more money was inserted.

'I say, are you still there?'

'Yes, I am.'

'Thank goodness for that. I ran out of cash.'

'So I heard.'

'Well, what do you think? Shall I go in for the permissive?'

'I really don't know.'

'But you're the expert.'

'Not at all.'

'I thought I ought to give the permissive a try. Now the children are grown-up, you know.'

'It's entirely a matter for you to decide. I mean, it's *your* life and ...'

'And you can't advise me?'

'I'm afraid not. Or only not to do anything you might regret.' I was beginning to feel sorry for Frank.

'Oh dear.' She sounded disappointed, but she was kind enough to give me an excuse for my uselessness. 'I suppose that the fact is, you're having food.' And then she ran out of money again.

Thoughts of my childhood returned to me in inappropriate places.

We lawyers went to see blue movies in the office of the Obscene Publications (The Dirty) Squad at Scotland Yard. The officers of this branch of the Force have a discouraging club tie, on which a book is depicted being cut in half by a large pair of scissors. A Constable works the projector in order to show the lawyers involved the questionable films which are the subject of criminal proceedings.

That day I had visited Scotland Yard with a most charming and courteous Prosecuting Counsel, always elegantly dressed from a wardrobe that ran to double-breasted waistcoats, broadly-striped shirts and a bowler-hat. He arrived at the building with a rolled umbrella and, as I happened to notice, a tin of film.

The official programme that morning was extremely depressing, consisting, as I remember it, of a couple of masterpieces entitled *Toilet Orgies* and *Double Pain Date in the Tower of Terror*. During the showing of these works I had recourse to the usual device of removing my glasses, so the screen was reduced to a comfortable and pinkish blur. While the officer in charge of the projector was changing a reel, my courtroom opponent told us that he and his wife kept a remarkably well-stocked herb garden which had been filmed by a friend. Unhappily they had no means of showing the film and would the Constable be good enough to run it through the projector? The Constable was good enough and for a blissful ten minutes we sat watching a gentle wind stirring the mint and thyme, the tarragon and the rosemary, before we were reluctantly returned to the depressing world of Adult Viewing. I had come a long way, undoubtedly too far, from my father's garden.

In my mother's time some of the kitchen garden had reverted to its natural state and the shrubbery at the top of the orchard had returned to jungle. But, in her eighties, she did all she could to keep the flower-beds as they had been when my father was alive. She was, as she always had been, shy, timid and extremely sceptical. She didn't return to drawing or painting, her loves before she met my father, as I hoped she might have done, but, with no clear idea of leaving England, she started to learn Italian at evening classes.

I told my mother that I had gone to America and helped secure the services of Mr Dustin Hoffman for a film, and she laughed; but more tolerantly than she had done when I had told her about being a part-time Judge. I told her about the four short plays I had written dealing with middle-aged love, which would be done in one evening and called *Come As You Are*, and the difficulties we had casting them. 'It's always been the same with you, hasn't it?' she said. 'One step forward and then one step back.' At least I was able to tell her that Glynis Johns had agreed to act in the plays, and she said that now I had got that settled perhaps I could concentrate on my work at the bar. She had come to Westminster Abbey and the House of Lords when I took silk. She had seen me in the elaborated version of my father's fancy dress, the knee-breeches and lace cuffs and silk stockings and said, 'You do look rather killing.' We never mentioned the radio plays I had written about my childhood and my father, some of which I had turned into a play for television.

In time a new hand would be dealt to me, although many of the cards would be distinctly familiar. There would be other years of unlooked-for happiness, another marriage, another child (the child of middle age so greatly loved because you can see much more clearly the limit set on your time together) who would run through the daffodils or climb among the blossom to have breakfast on a sunny morning on a rickety platform in a cherry tree. I would reclaim the kitchen garden, clear the jungle, and on Sundays my children and stepchildren would come, bringing a new generation to go on the treasure-hunts and hide in the copses. The house would hear sounds and see sights it never dreamed of: the sound of opera which I discovered as a new and magical world when I was past fifty, and of parties and people who had drunk too much falling into the swimming-pool which my mother would never have permitted and would have decided made the place look far too much like a 'Road House', which perhaps it does.

The years of delayed adolescence were over. I was looking for someone with whom I could attempt again, after many hard lessons learnt, the difficult and risky journey of a marriage.

There were false trails and mirages. I met an Israeli model who had been an army sergeant in her own country, but had borrowed a military vehicle to escape across the border and find freedom in the world of high fashion. I was fond of Rachel, but she talked a great deal about battles and the delight she would have in machine-gunning Arabs, and at mealtimes, when she looked at the food her profession forbade her to eat, her large dark eyes would fill with tears. I had also met a very beautiful girl who was an Angel. She rang me up and asked me to take her out to lunch so she could tell me about it.

'I'm an Angel,' she said. 'It came to me when I was sitting on a mountain in France. One of the Angels of the Lord. So far I've only told three people.'

'Really. Who are they?'

'The man who's Head of the Methodist Church, the Cardinal Archbishop of Westminster, and you. I chose you as representing the atheists.'

'And what did the others say?' I asked, as Captain of the Unbelievers.

'The Cardinal said that there might be an opening for me doing good works among young people, and the Methodist asked me if there were a history of insanity in my family. What do *you* think?'

'Oh, I'm absolutely convinced you're an Angel.' It takes, of course, an atheist to show any degree of faith in these sceptical times.

However the Angel, who had been living with a dress designer in the King's Road, went off to join a colony of mystics and Rachel went to New York and married her gynaecologist. At a New Year's Eve party, as the sixties rattled to a halt, I met my future wife. When she told her family about our meeting, her mother protested and asked if I were not an older man. When she heard that I was, in fact, only a year older than she, I doubt if my future mother-in-law was greatly reassured.

I visited the family in the faint hope of being approved of as a suitor. My future wife's mother was an enthusiastic swimmer who left their Kentish farm every day of the year to plunge into the grey and unwelcoming waters of the English Channel. She had won the record for staying in longer than anyone else on Boxing Day. It was in a windy

April that I made my first visit and, when she told me how the 'townees' stood on the beach and laughed at this grim endurance test, I said that 'townees', of course, understood nothing of the splendours and delights of year-round bathing. I should have held my tongue. That afternoon I, who hadn't heard English spoken on a beach for many years, was led tiptoeing across the cruel shingle towards a grey, icy and even more cruel sea. As I groaned and sank into the gritty, marrow-chilling water, I was not only plunging into the future but swimming back, towards a childhood when I stood shivering on the beach near my uncle's beach hut in Sussex, washing myself free, I hoped, in that symbolic and agonizing gesture, of the grimy accumulation of the years.

We took a house in Ravello, near to the Villa Cimbrone with its row of pale statues on the edge of the precipice between the garden and the sea, where I had first met Arthur Jeffries. It was a big house with marble floors and a four-poster, and a view down to the Mediterranean where we could see the white steamer off on its regular, punctual journey to Positano. My mother, almost nine years after my father had died, made her Great Escape from his house and garden. She climbed aboard an aeroplane for the first time in her life and came to stay with us in Italy.

I met my mother, who was blinking in the sun and spurning all assistance, at Naples airport. We embraced then, as if we had met after a long, long separation, and on that happy, all-forgiving coast the reserve, the sort of wariness with which we had always treated each other, melted away entirely. I couldn't remember why I had thought for so long that my mother was a stranger to me, totally involved in the supreme sacrifice of her life with my father. And in the hot sunshine, in the marble shadows of the house, or out on the terrace among the bougainvillaea, drinking cold 'Caruso' wine and looking miles down to the sea, she giggled, made jokes, became a girl again, the large-eyed, shy but also daring girl she had been when, a schoolteacher in South Africa, she galloped bare-back on her pony or stood naked in a waterfall.

In Italy my mother climbed down to the beach, took the long day's boat trip to Capri, sat on a chair put for her in the doorway of the grocer's shop as we did our shopping or tried out, on a grinning Sorrentine butcher, the careful and perfect Italian which she had learnt in Marlow. Each morning we met on the terrace, whilst the others were still asleep, and she was wearing a dressing-gown with her long hair down over her shoulders like a young girl. She would smile and say 'Buon Giorno' and we would kiss and plan another day of our great new-found friendship, at ease in a foreign house and a garden where my father had never been.

Home in England my mother was careful not to watch *Voyage Round My Father* when it came on television. I had the chance of writing a longer version to do on the stage at the Greenwich Theatre, which she would also never see. I went with my son, still at school and always passionate for Greece, to Rhodes. We puttered round the island on hired motor bikes and took donkey rides up to Lindos and boat trips to the Turkish coast and, at night, I sat in the hotel bedroom and wrote new scenes for the play.

Perhaps my mother was right and I should never have started on the work in progress. The writer's gluttony for material, his habit of eating his life as a caterpillar consumes the leaf it sits on, and spinning it out changed and perhaps unrecognizable, may not only be an embarrassment to his immediate family. Writing down events is the writer's great protection, his defence and his safety-valve. Anger and misery, defeat, humiliation and self-disgust can be changed and used to provide a sense of achievement as he fills his pages. And yet the catharsis is often too complete, the life he has led vanishes into his work and leaves him empty. After months of writing dialogue for my father I became confused, unable to distinguish between what he had said and what I had invented for him to say. Gradually he left me and became a character in a play. In giving him to other people I came, after a time, to lose him for myself. I don't think that this means that I should have done as my mother wanted and not written the play. The process is one of the many disadvantages of the writer's life, like the constant guilt at not working. It is, perhaps, what makes writers less interesting to talk to than many other professionals: their lives are no longer there to be discovered privately. They have been thrown open to the public.

The play was to open in Greenwich on 27 November. A set had been designed consisting of large mechanical cubes which would move about the stage suggesting a change of place, and could be opened to disgorge properties. By some happy chance the machinery in these devices (like most stage machinery) failed to work on the opening night and the audience was able to concentrate on the play without the distraction of menacing geometric shapes dancing the *Merry Widow* waltz. Mark Dignam, who played the part of my father so well on television, was to do it on the stage, and we had the same director, Claude Watham. All that November we were working in the cold and fog of a South London rehearsal room, in search of those far distant moments at breakfast when my father had cursed cold plates and runny eggs and expounded Darwin's theory and sung *Pretty Little Polly Perkins of Paddington Green*.

A neighbour, walking along the common, kept an eye on my mother's house. Once she didn't answer to a ring and the police were sent for. They drove out through the snow, climbed a ladder and peered through her bedroom window to see her sitting up in bed reading Italian short stories. Usually quiet and courteous she rebuked them severely. One evening in that November, however, my mother was trying, as she had so often done with my father, to finish the crossword. Her blood pressure had been high in her last years and she had a stroke and fell on to the carpet in front of the dying logs of her modest and economical fire.

When I saw her in hospital my mother smiled. She seemed distressed but, with her immense courage, amused at her helplessness. We held hands but, as it had been so often with us, she couldn't speak.

As I say, the play was to open on 27 November. On the 26th we worked all night, the lighting was difficult, the stage machinery didn't work, the overworked Greenwich technicians were exhausted and no one had any particular faith in a play that had no story and was more about blindness than sex. The next day part of my life, which had been, and perhaps should have stayed, my own private and particular concern, was to be revealed. I sat in the deserted stalls of the theatre, watching an endless lighting rehearsal, drinking cooling instant coffee and became filled with gloom and apprehension. Far away from the theatre she wouldn't visit, in a small country hospital, my mother died without regaining her speech. The next night her part was taken by an actress.

The advocate goes through changing emotions in the course of a case. At first he feels nervous, cast down, perhaps, by the obvious difficulties. His nerves are calmed, as are the actor's, as soon as he opens his mouth and he begins to think he can find answers to most, at least, of the difficult questions. He works out his final speech which is his way of putting his case to the Jury as convincingly as possible. When he rises to speak he is nervous again, his hands may be sweating and his voice uncertain. It's a long slog, two or three hours perhaps, of standing and sweating and trying to persuade, and then comes a moment of intense relief. 'Ladies and gentlemen of the Jury,' the advocate may say, particularly if like me he has more than a touch of the Marshall Hall's, 'my task is done. The defence is now in your hands.'

He sits down and there is always, I think for advocates, an extraordinary lightening of the spirit. The job is done for better or for worse, you have said all you can say. You are free from the burden of responsibility. In a mood of rare relaxation you close your eyes, dimly aware that somewhere, it seems very far away, a Judge is summing up.

Of course there are bad times to come. The Jury are sent out to consider their verdict and there is nothing you can do, you feel too tense to read or even to do the crossword, you fill yourself with 'coffee' in the Old Bailey canteen until you are awash with the greyish, tasteless liquid, and then you go down to the cells to cheer up your waiting client. Such meetings are seldom happy; you think of all the questions you might have asked and the points you might have made in your speech. You work out the most your client is likely to get and, looking gloomily on the bright side, calculate just how long that means by taking off a third plus the months he has been in custody already. You wonder if it's a good sign that the Jury have been out for so long and know, secretly, that it probably isn't. Then, as often as not, a silence falls between you.

In the years that were to come, I was to invent a down-at-heel old barrister with a certain low courtroom cunning who was to become the hero of a television series. I sat in the usual embarrassed silence with an East End totter whom I had been defending on a charge of attempted murder. He had been accused of stabbing the man next door with the knife he used to cut up carrots for the pony that drew his cart. The motive suggested was that the son of the next-door neighbour had stolen my client's Victory Medal. As we sat together, the totter and I, in the cells beneath the Old Bailey, waiting for a word from the Jury, and as I thought, as usual, of all the things I might have said, art took its revenge on life.

'Your Mr Rumpole could've got me out of this,' the totter said, 'so why the hell can't you?'

Life seems to have been full of verdicts. The editors of *Oz* magazine were sent to prison one weekend for publishing their 'Schoolkids' number; a few days later an Appeal Judge set them free. In the end their convictions were set aside. Alec Guinness played *Voyage Round My Father* at the Haymarket. On all these occasions I walked Law Court corridors waiting for verdicts, or stood on Paddington Station to buy the papers and read the notices, with a dry mouth and a certainty of disaster. For that year, the year I sat in Court and discussed the love life of Rupert Bear, the year my mother and father, gone from me as the characters in plays leave and take on another and more remote existence, were acted in the West End, disasters were, temporarily, postponed. There would be other verdicts, other opening nights, and other closing speeches. There is always time for failure.

I walked into the house and felt that I didn't own it and that I had no right to move the books or rearrange the furniture. We lit a fire and the chimney smoked, we opened cupboards and drawers feeling like intruders. I went into the winter garden and thought of how it might be put back in time to the day when I planted a tree and met Penelope, to when Henry Winter came to stay, to when I sat beside my father's hammock and he swung himself gently as I read him the Sherlock Holmes stories which he already knew by heart. So much of the garden had vanished into the icy and tangled undergrowth that I didn't know how it could be managed.

That is how it was, a part of life, seen from one point of view. Much more happened that I cannot tell or remember. To others it would be, I am quite sure, a different story. I have written all I can write about it now, and these are the things that stayed with me for a while, before they left to go into a book.